FOUNDATION COURSE
SPIRITUAL DISCERNMENT, RELIGIOUS FEELING, SACRAMENTAL ACTION

Rudolf Steiner

15 lectures given in Dornach, between
26 September and 10 October 1921.

Translated by Hanna von Maltitz

ANTHROPOSOPHICAL PUBLICATIONS
FREMONT, MICHIGAN, UNITED STATES

THE FOUNDATION COURSE
Copyright © 2022 by
Anthroposophical Publications

All rights reserved. No part of this book may be reproduced in any form or by any electronic or mechanical means including information storage and retrieval systems, without permission in writing from the author. The only exception is by a reviewer, who may quote short excerpts in a review.

Cover designed by James D. Stewart

Rudolf Steiner Portrait by
Peter Gospodinov

Translation by Hanna von Maltitz
Cover painting
"Heaven's Gate"
by Hanna von Maltitz
https://go.elib.com/HeavensGate

Thanks to the Basil Gibaud Charitable Trust for their support in the creation of this translation.

The e.Lib, Inc.
Visit the website at https://www.elib.com/

Printed in the United States of America

First Printing: July 2022
Anthroposophical Publications
https://AnthroposophicalPublications.org/

ISBN-13: 978-1-948302-37-1 paperback
978-1-948302-38-8 eBook

Contents

Foundation Course i
Summaries Of Lectures vii
The Relationship Of Anthroposophy To Religious Life. 1
Essence And Elements Of Sacramentalism. 23
    Open Letter To Dr Rudolf Steiner September 1921 43
Theoretical Thinking And Living In The Spirit. 49
Anthroposophy And Religion. 69
Conceptual Knowledge And Observational Knowledge. 91
Creative Speech And Language. 111
Formation Of Speech. 135
Prayer And Symbolism 157
Religious Feeling And Intellectualism 179
Composition Of The Gospels. 201
Insights Into Mystery Of Golgotha, Priest Ordination 225
Prophecy, Dogma And Paganism 249
The Sacraments, Evolution And Involution 269
Gnostics And Montanists 289
Ordination And Transubstantiation 311
Other Books 337

SUMMARIES OF LECTURES

Spiritual discernment, religious feeling, sacramental action.

1. **Anthroposophy and Religious life.**
   The relationship of Anthroposophy to the religious life. The search for secure foundation of religious awareness with various Protestant and Catholic theologians. Meaning of prayer for the religious life. Incompatible conceptions of the development of humanity in the modern scientific thinking methods and in the Gospels. What is understood in the Catholicism under the original revelation? What is conveyed in ancient mysteries? The mystery of Birth. Theology and imagination of God before Christ. Origins of worship. Understanding spiritual realities in prayer.

2. **The essence and elements of sacramentalism.**
   The discerning and acting person. The sinfulness of modern science. Essence and elements of sacramentalism. The experience of words, speech and hearing. The in-streaming of the divine into the word: Gospels. Objectification of action in the Offering. Conversion of natural processes into spiritual processes. Transubstantiation. Uniting with the transformed substances: communion. The physical-soul-spiritual relationship of people to the universe and their representation through sacraments: recognition through the word and offering, dealt through transubstantiation and communion. Question: Do the Gospel and Offering have an impact in the course of outer events? Is the inner experience of transubstantiation and communion something real outside a congregant? Open letter of Dr Friedrich Rittelmeyer to Rudolf Steiner.

3. **Theory and living spirit**

Discussion resulting from the questions and objections presented by Dr Rittelmeyer. Lack of understanding of the exercises in my book "Knowledge of the higher Worlds." Regarding the meaning of repetition. Theoretical thinking or living in the spirit? The big question at present: How is the realm of morality to be based in the realm of natural necessities? The indifference of theologians regarding "Christ as the sun regent." Unfounded allegations against Anthroposophy.

4. **Anthroposophy and religion.**
Regarding a priest's communication which calls for an answer to the question: How is Anthroposophy contained in religion and how should religion be held by Anthroposophy? — How can a person today get to know the super-sensible world directly? Regarding the difficulties in expressing spiritual scientific knowledge in modern language. Methods of human knowledge in modern psychology and biology in Anthroposophy. Necessary observations of people in their relationship to the physical-mineral, to the earth's etherisation and to the cosmic-astral environment of the earth. The four elements during the Greek times and direct experiences of yearly cycles in ancient times. How can actions of worship be understood? The mood of expectancy in the ancient mysteries. The foundation of true Christianity.

5. **Conceptual knowledge and observation.**
Through the knowledge of observation, the relationship between belief and knowledge changes. Religiousness and egoism: selflessly acquired thoughts. The necessity of reaching a concept of belief which is not only bound to the temporal forces in man. Answers to questions out of the circle of participants: Can we define religion? Don't we have to renounce knowledge to come to religion? When art, science and social life adapt religious forms, will religion then stop being independent? Is there a differentiation of values between religion and Anthroposophy or are they both necessary?

SUMMARIES OF LECTURES

6. **Creative speech and Language.**
Germinating speech forms in Anthroposophy. Differentiated speech and the nature of sound. Earlier and future relationships to sound. Creative power of speech in the Gospels. The Mass as expression of the entire pastoral process. The Sermon. The intellectualistic process or image-rich speech in relation to community building. The meaning of symbols in the sermon. The evangelists in their meaning for alchemists; the Gospels analysed philologically. Various philosophic systems as exercises in thought. Anthroposophical help in arriving at images. Anthroposophy and religion.

7. **Speech formation.**
Answers to questions of the participants: Power of speech formation/moulding: gaining sound understanding, sense of speech and language conscience. Vocals, consonant and rhythm. Connection of speech with the totality of mankind. Eurythmy. A new understanding of the Bible: experiencing language and the start of St John's Gospel. Apostolic succession: meaning of the priestly "Family Tree." Celebrating the Catholic Mass as essential/real action. Outlook towards a new form of sacramental life.

8. **Prayer and symbolism**
The necessity of prayer. The *Our Father* as real dialogue with the Divine. The sound content in prayer. Regarding religious impulses becoming conscious in people. Reading the Gospels. Truth content and vital content in the Gospels. The 13th chapter of the Gospel of St Matthew as training for the preacher. Transformation of natural processes into creative soul images. Sunlight and Moonlight; the symbol of the transubstantiation in communion. Sensitivity for the efficacy of symbols during the first Christian centuries. Symbol, living word and will, divinely imbued.

9. **Religious feeling and intellectualism.**
Obtaining documents of judgement for the decisions of the participants in this course. In new community building everything must be given over to what Christ wants in the world. Catholicism, Protestantism and sacrifice

of sacrament. The mystery of birth and death. Cosmic activity in the embryo. Steps of incarnation and its reverse in the sacrament of mass. The earth since the Mystery of Golgotha. The demons' outcry on recognising Christ on earth. Meaning of the sacrament of mass in life. Loss of religious feeling in the historical development of the last centuries. Intellectualism and sacramentalism. How can we rediscover the sacrament out of freedom? Summary of questions and responses about the sacrifice of mass as a reversal of the incarnating process.

10. **Composition of the Gospels**
Harmony of the four Gospels. The Wise Men from the Orient's stellar wisdom (Mathew Gospel) and shepherds' experience in the fields (Luke's Gospel). Changes in mankind's state of mind through evolution. From heart-felt experience to outer knowledge. Composition of the 13 chapters of the Mathew Gospel. Parables given to people and parables for the disciples only. Ears that hear in error and eyes that sleep (Mat 13,15). Differences between the organisation of hearing and seeing. Breathing, speaking, hearing. Christian community building. Material still to be discussed.

11. **Insights into the Mystery of Golgotha**
Soul constitution of people at the time of the Mystery of Golgotha (formation of mind or consciousness soul). **Mystery of Golgotha** as a cosmic, free divine deed; change in soul conception since Golgotha. Renewal of dying earth existence. Rise of intellectualism, working of spirit in matter ever less understood. Scotus Eriugena, Augustinus. Start of dogma and ritual in Catholic Church. Anthroposophy to help clarify present day understanding regarding Golgotha. Luther and the rise of two time streams. Luther and Faust. Christian symbolism in art. Meaning of priest ordination.

12. **Prophecy, dogma and paganism.**
About predicting future events. Characteristics of literature of church fathers: allegorical interpretation of Old Testament, references to Christ's return, element of law in church. Relationship of Catholic clerics to dogma

and saints. Prophesies in Mark's Gospel: fall of world and rise of God's kingdom. Herman Grimm: the abyss between understanding Roman and Greek history. Heathen sensitivity of the divine in paganism, Judaism and Christianity, the ungodly in Roman Caesarism. Christianity today.

13. **Sacraments, evolution and involution.**
What does it mean, to experience shaping the divine within? Fundamental ideas on the being of the sacramental. Seven sacraments and their relation to life. Rhythmic exchange from evolution to involution processes in nature and life's history. Healing these processes through sacraments. Regarding birth, maturity, incarnation, memory, death and sanctification through baptism, confirmation, act of consecration, penance and last anointment. Human relations to the soul-spiritual, which are no longer of an individual nature and their image of the sacrament: marriage, priest ordination.

14. **Gnostics and Montanists.**
Pastoral care and handling the living word. The opposite poles of Gnosis (Basilides) und Montanism (Montanus). Striving of the Gnostics for knowledge (macrocosmic) and visions of the Montanists (microcosmic surrender). Dangers of straying to both sides. Christ conception of the Gnostics and Montanists. Augustus' exchange with Bishop Faust. Writer of John's Gospel between Gnosticism and Montanism. Inflow of Roman elements into Christianity. "Divine State" of Augustus. Centuries long struggle over the question: How do we save the moral, imbued with God, from the external legal element? Crusader mood.

15. **Ordination and transubstantiation.**
Development of Christian sacrament of ordination out of the old Mysteries. Initiation and state of consciousness. Initiation and transformation of material substances in humans. Regarding the ordination earlier, and today. What means dedication? The soul constitution of the Apostles and experience of apostolic succession. Apostolic succession today? Novalis' and Shelling's knowledge of true Christianity. Inner reasons that led to celibacy.

FOUNDATION COURSE

THE RELATIONSHIP OF ANTHROPOSOPHY TO RELIGIOUS LIFE.

Lecture One by Rudolf Steiner given in Dornach, 26 September 1921.

My dear friends! I sincerely thank Licentiate Bock for his welcoming words, and I promise you that I want to apply everything in my power to contribute at least partly, towards all you are looking for during your stay here.

Today I would like to discuss some orientation details so that we may understand one another in the right way. It will be our particular task — also during the various hours of discussion we are going to have — to express exactly what lies particularly close to your heart for your future work. I hope that what I have to say to you will be said in the correct way, when during the coming discussion hour your wishes and tasks you ask about, will be heard.

Anthroposophy, my dear friends, must certainly remain on the foundation of which I've often spoken, when I say: Anthroposophy as such can't represent religious education; anthroposophy as such must limit its task as a spiritual science to fructify present culture and civilization and it is not its purpose to represent religious education. Actually, it is quite far from such direct involvement in any way, in the evolutionary process of religious life. Nevertheless, it appears to me to be certainly justified in relation to the tasks you have just set yourselves, that for religious activity something can be extracted out of Anthroposophy. Indirectly it can not only be obtained through Anthroposophy, but it must be extracted, and this must be said; your experience is quite correct that religious life as such needs deepening, which can come out of the source of anthroposophical science.

I presume, my dear friends, that you want to actively position yourself in this religious life and that you have looked for this Anthroposophic course because you have felt that religious activity has lead you increasingly towards a dead end, and that through the religious work today — with our traditions, with the historic development and others, which we will still discuss — elements are missing which actually should be within it. We notice how just today even important personalities are searching for a new foundation for religious activity, because they believe this is needed in order to progress in a certain direction. I would like to indicate it as a start, how even the most conscientious personalities ask themselves how one can reach a certain foundation of religious awareness, and how then these personalities actually search more or less for a kind of — one can also call it something else — a kind of philosophy. I remind you only how a home is sought for a kind of philosophic foundation for religious awareness. Obviously, one has to, through the current awareness, recognise something absolutely necessary and one should not ignore that an extraordinarily amount has been accomplished this way. However, one can't comprehend, with unprejudiced observation, what is strived for, and come face to face with this: such an effort, instead of leading into the religious life, actually leads out of the religious life. —

Religious life, you will sense, must be something direct, it must be something elementary, entirely connected to human nature, which lives out of the elementary, most inward foundation of human nature. All philosophic thinking is a reflection and is distanced from this direct, elementary experience. If I might express a personal impression, it would be this: When someone philosophises about the religious life and believes that a philosophical foundation is necessary for a religious life, then it always seems to me to be similar to when one wants to turn to the physiology of nutrition in order to attain nourishment oneself. Isn't it true, one can determine the exact foundations of nutritional science but that means nothing for nutrition itself. Nutritional science elucidates nutrition, but nutrition must surely have a sound foundation, it must grow roots in reality; only then can one philosophise about nutrition. So also, the religious life must have roots in reality. It must come to existence out of reality, only when it is there can one philosophise about it. It is certainly not possible at all to substantiate or justify the religious life with some or other philosophic consideration.

That's the one thing. The other one is something which I can best indicate — I always like referring to realities — through a book which had already came into existed several decades ago in Basle, with the title: "The Christian nature of our theology today." It is a book by Overbeck. In it he refers to evidence that the current theology is a kind of theology but that it is actually not Christian any longer. Now, when one takes Harnack's book "The being of Christianity" and in its arguments everywhere simply exchanges the word "God" in every instance where he has "Christ," then one will not really change anything in the inner content of Harnack's book. This is already expressed in what Adolf Harnack says, that in the Gospels actually only the proclamation of the Father is needed and not those of Christ Jesus, while naturally during the earlier centuries the Christian development of the Gospels was above all regarded according to the proclamations of Christ Jesus. However, if the Gospels are really considered as the actual proclamations of Christ Jesus, then one has to, beside the Father-experience, that means beside the experience of the world in general being permeated by the Godhead, have the Christ-experience as something extra special. One must be able to have both of these experiences. A theology like Adolf Harnack's no longer has both of these experiences, but only a God-experience, and as a result it is necessary for him that what he finds in his imagination of God, he baptises it with the name of Christ; purely out of a historical foundation, because as he is even a representative of Christianity, he calls his God-experience by the name of Christ.

These incisive, important things exist already. Certainly, they are not made properly clear but they are felt, and I presume that currently, where nearly everything is shaken up in people's minds, a young theology in particular needs to show itself, in how these things can't really be completed, as is seen to some extent today with theologians, without being permeated by the actual being of Christ. Out of this experience such a book as Von Overbeck's was created regarding the current Christianity of theology, where basically the answer is given to why modern theology is no longer Christian because it deals with a general philosophising about a world permeated by God, and not in the real sense of the Christ experience creating the foundation for the entire treatment of religious problems. Religious problems are dealt with based only as Father-problems and not actually the Christ experience.

Today we basically all have an education inculcated in us, derived from modern science, this science which actually only started in the middle of the 15th Century but which has entered into all forms of modern people's thinking. One basically can't be different because one has been educated this way from the lowest primary classes, by forming thoughts according to modern science. This has resulted in theology of the 19th Century wanting to orientate itself according to the research of modern science. I'd like to say they feel themselves responsible for the judge's chair of modern science and as a result have become what they are today. One can only find a basis of true religiosity today by, at the same time, considering the entire authorisation and also the complete meaning of the scientific element of life.

To some of you I have possibly already referred to a man who needs to be taken seriously in relation to religious life, *Gideon Spicker*, who for a long time studied philosophy at the Münster university. He proceeded from a strict Christian conception of the world, which he gradually developed into his philosophy which was never considered a philosophy but more an instrument for the understanding of religious problems. Modern thinking didn't offer him the possibility to find a sure foundation. So we find in his booklet, entitled "At the turning point of the Christian world period" the hopelessness of modern man which characterised him so clearly, because he says: 'Today we have metaphysics without transcendental conviction, we have a theory of knowledge without objective meaning, we have psychology without a soul, logic without content, ethics without liability and the result is that we can't find some or other foundation for religious consciousness.' — Gideon Spicker stood very close to the actual crux which lies at the basis of all religious dichotomies in modern mankind. One can take it like a symptom, to indicate where the actual crux, I could call it, lies. If modern man is discerning, if he tries to create an image through his imagination of the world, then at the same time he clearly has the feeling that this discernment doesn't penetrate the depths. Gideon Spicker expressed it like this: 'We have a theory of knowledge without objective meaning', which means we have our insights without being in the position to find the power within us to create something really objective out of our assembled insights. So, the modern discerning man sickens because he fails to find the possibility of a guarantee for his knowledge of objectivity in the world, for existence as such. He finds it in what he experiences subjectively in the knowledge, not really out of the thing itself.

All of this of course, because it is philosophy, has nothing to do with religious experience. Still, one can say that religious life today is certainly under an influence which heads in a similar direction. The kind of humanity which is not in the position to say about knowledge: 'in this realization there exists objective existence for me' — such a type of humanity feels this same insecurity rise up at another point, and that is religious life. The insecurity is situated at the same pivotal point where actual religious life exists today. We will see how other problems will huddle around this pivot point. This pivotal point lies in prayer, in the meaning of prayer. The religious person must feel that prayer has real meaning; some or other reality must be connected to prayer. However, in a time epoch when the discerning person fails to come out of his subjective knowledge and fails to find reality in knowledge, in the same time epoch religious people won't find the possibility, during prayer, of becoming aware that prayer is no mere subjective deed, but that within prayer an objective experience takes place. For a person who is unable to realise that prayer is an objective experience, for him or her it would be impossible to find a real religious hold. Particularly in the nature of current humanity prayer must focus on the religious life. Various other areas must focus on prayer. However, a prayer which only has subjective meaning would make people religiously insecure.

It is the same root which grows out of us on the one side for the insecurity of knowledge, the Ignorabimus, and on the other side in fear; worry, which do not live in prayer in divine objectivity, but which is involved in subjectivity.

You see, the problem of faith and the problem of knowledge, all problems, which involve people from the theological side, are connected to the same characteristics. Everything which depresses people from the side of direct religious experience, which needs confirmation, which must be maintained, this all comes from the same source. You can hardly answer this question if you don't orientate yourself historically where it will quite clearly show how far we have actually become distanced with our sciences from what we can call Christian today, while on the other hand today there is the constant attempt to proceed by pushing anything Christian out with science. Take everything in the Gospels which is Christian tradition. You can't but say: in this, there is another conception of the human being than what modern science claims. In modern science the human being is traced back to some or other primitive archetypal creature — I absolutely don't want to say that mankind had perhaps developed out of an animal origin — we are referred back to a primitive Ur-human, which gradually developed itself and, in whose development, existed a progression, an advance. Modern humanity is satisfied to look back according to scientific foundations, to the primitive archetypal beings, who through some inherent power, it is said, they created an ever greater and bigger cultural accomplishment, and to behold the unexpected future of this perfection.

If one now places within this evolution, the development of the Christ, the Mystery of Golgotha, then one can in an honest way hold on to the Gospels and say nothing other than: into this He doesn't fit, what fits here is a historic conception which goes around the Mystery of Golgotha and leaves it out, but the Christ of the Gospels don't fit into this conception. The Christ of the Gospels can't be considered in any other way than if one somehow believes what happened in the 18th Century especially among the most enlightened, the most spiritual people as a matter of course. Take for instance Saint Martin — I now want to look further from religious development and want to point out someone who was in the most imminent sense a scientist of the 18th Century — and that was Saint Martin. He had a completely clear awareness that the human being at the start of his earthly development came from a certain height downwards, that he had been in another world milieu earlier, in another environment and through a mighty event, through a crisis was thrown down to a sphere which lay below the level of his previous existence, so that the human being is no longer what he once had been.

While our modern natural science points back to a primitive archetypal being out of which we have developed; this observation of Saint Martin must refer back to the fallen mankind, to those human beings which had once been more elevated. This was something, like I said, which to Saint Martin appeared as a matter of course. Saint Martin experienced this fall of mankind as a feeling of shame. You see, if the Christ is placed in such a conception of human evolution, where the human being, by starting his earth existence through a descent and is now more humble than he was before, then the Christ becomes that Being who would save humanity from its previous fall, then the Christ bears mankind again up into those conditions where it had existed before.

We will see in what modification this imagination must appear to our souls. In any case this involves a disproportion between our modern understanding of mankind's evolution and the understanding of the Gospels; there's always dishonesty when one goes hither and thither and does not confess that one is simultaneously a supporter of modern scientific thinking and also the Christ. This must actually be clear for every honest, particularly religiously honest sensitive person. Here is something where a bridge must be formed if the religious life is to be healthy once again. Without this bridging, religious life will never ever be healthy again. Actually, there are people who come along like David Friedrich Strauss, and to the question "Are we still Christians?" reply with a No, indicating that they are still more honest than some of the modern theologians, whoever and again overlook the radical differences between what the modern human being regards as pure science and the Gospel concept of the Christ. This is the characteristic of modern theology. It is basically the impotent attempt to treat the Christ conception of the Gospels in such a way that it can be validated in front of modern science. Here nothing originates which somehow can be held.

Yet, theology still exists. The modern pastor is given very little support for his line of work in the kind of theology presented at his schooling currently, from the foundation which has been indicated already and about which we will still come to in the course of our observations. The modern pastor must of course be a theologian even though theology is not religion. However, in order to work, a theological education is needed, and this educational background suffers from all the defects which I've briefly indicated in our introduction today.

You see, the Catholic church knows quite well what it is doing, because it doesn't allow modern science to come into theology. Not as if the Catholic church doesn't care for modern science, it takes care of it. The greatest scholars can certainly be found within the Catholic ecclesiastics. I'm reminded of Father Secchi, a great astrophysicist, I remember people such as Wasmann, a significant zoologist, and many others, above all one can remind oneself of the extraordinarily important scientific accomplishments, worldly scientific accomplishments of the Benedictine order and so on. But what role did modern science play in the Catholic church? The Catholic church wants to care for modern science, that there are real luminaries in it. However, people want this modern scientific way to be applied in connection with the outer sensory world, it wants to distance itself strongly from the conceptions of anything pertaining to spirituality, no statements should be made about this spirituality. Hence it is therefore forbidden to express something about the spiritual, because scientists must not enter into this mix when something is being said about the legitimacy of the spiritual life. So, Catholicism relegates science to its boundaries, it rejects science from all that is theology. That it, for instance in modernism, gradually came into it, has caused Catholicism to experience it as dispensable; hence the war against modernism. The Catholic church knows precisely that in that moment when science penetrates theology, extraordinary dangers lie ahead, and it is impossible to cope with scientific research in theology.

It is basically quite hopeless if it is expressed in abstract terms: theology we must have but it will be scorched, burnt by modern science. — Where does this come from? That is the next big burning question. Where does this come from?

Yes, my dear friends, theology as we have it now, is rooted in quite different conditions than those of modern mankind. Ultimately the foundation of theology — if it wants to be correctly understood — is precisely the same foundations as that of the Gospels themselves. I have just expressed a sentence and naturally in its being said, it is not immediately understood, but it has extraordinary importance for our discussions here. Theology as inherited tradition doesn't appear in the form in which modern science appears. Theology is mostly in a form of something handed down, as such it goes back to the earlier ways of understanding. Certainly, logic was later applied to modern theology, which changed the form of theology somewhat; theology no longer appeared as it had been once upon a time. On the other hand, it is Catholicism which actually has something in this relationship which works in an extraordinarily enchanting manner on the more intelligent people and which is firmly adhered to in many Catholic clerics upon studying theology, through what has been handed down as knowledge of the so-called Primordial Revelation (Uroffenbahrung).

Primordial Revelation! You have to be aware that Catholicism does not merely have the revelation which we usually call the revelation of the New Testament, nor this being only the revelation spoken about in the Old Testament, but that Catholicism — as far as it is theology — speaks about a *Primordial* Revelation. This Primordial Revelation is usually characterised by saying: that which was revealed by the Christ had been experienced once before by mankind, at that time humanity acquired the revelation through another, a cosmic world milieu. This revelation was lost through the Fall, but an inheritance of this great revelation was still available through the Old Testament and through pagan teachings. — That is Catholic thinking. Once upon a time, before people became sinners, a revelation was made to them; had mankind not fallen into sin, so the entire act of salvation of Christ Jesus would not have become necessary. However, the primordial revelation had been tarnished through humanity falling into the sinful world and in the course of time up to the Mystery of Golgotha the human being increasingly forgot what the primordial revelation had been. To a certain extent in the beginning there still remained glimpses of this primordial revelation, then however, as the generation went further and further away, this primordial revelation darkened, and it had become totally dark in the time of the Mystery of Golgotha which came as a new revelation.

This is what Christianity looks like today — under theological instruction — in Old Testament teaching and above all in the pagan teaching it is seen as a corrupted primordial revelation. Catholicism has an insight into what I've often spoken about in

Anthroposophy, namely the old Mysteries. In my book "Christianity as mystical fact" I pointed these things out, but, not quite, but only as far as possible because these things are as much unknown as possible in today's world and most people are not prepared for these things. Only, here we can speak about it, and about one point.

Everywhere in the pagan-religious mysteries there are certain experiences which allowed people to learn more than those communicated outwardly, exoterically, to a large crowd. These experiences didn't happen under supervision but through asceticism, through practice, they happened by the person going through certain experiences; a kind of drama was experienced leading to a culmination, with a catharsis, until the person came to sense the lightening of the divine laws of the world. This is simply a fact and within esoteric Catholicism it engendered an awareness of what existed in the Mysteries. It is even said that modern times are filled with worldly science and that this worldly science must not enter theology with arguments; as a result, we'd rather protect our knowledge of the Mysteries so that worldly science doesn't come in to explain it, because explaining the Mysteries would be a great danger under any circumstances. Catholicism was afraid that scientific involvement would reveal what one could possibly know about such things.

Now we come to the question: what did the Mysteries actually impart during these olden times? The Mysteries didn't produce a mere theoretical knowledge, it produced an evolution of consciousness, a real transformation of consciousness. A person who had gone through the Mysteries learnt to experience life differently to those people who hadn't gone through them. A person who stands fully awake in the world, experiences outside the sleep state, the outer sense world; he experiences memories, he can through these memories relive his life within himself when after various interruptions he comes to a certain point in his life which lies a couple of years after his birth. With an individual who has gone through hard exercises in the Mysteries, something quite different rises up in his awareness than what he usually can find in his consciousness. In the old Mysteries one expressed this experience as a "rebirth." Why does one call it a rebirth? Because in fact a person goes through a kind of embryonic experience in his consciousness; an awareness comes to the fore in the manner and way the person had lived through during his time as an embryo. During the time of being an embryo, our inner experience is namely of the same kind as are the experiences during thinking, because what is experienced in our senses is only done so through our mother's body. An embryonic experience is woken up, that's why we call it a "rebirth." A person goes back in his embryonic life up to the time of his birth, and so, just like memories rise up, so that what is being experienced also rises up. In this way a person feels himself coming out of a spiritual world, being partially connected to a spiritual world. These were the mysteries of birth, under which time one understood the blossoming of the Mysteries as something which human beings could go through during such an initiation. What he went through during such an initiation was considered a shadowed knowledge of such a state he was in, before he descended into the world of the senses. Thus, through the "rebirth" the human being re-places himself again to a certain extend back into a human form of existence free of sin.

In earlier times, knowledge which was not of this world was called "theology," and this knowledge could be acquired through the return to the wisdom that human beings had had before entering into this world, a wisdom which had been corrupted because people had dragged it into this world.

I'm sketching these things for you and later we will naturally bring today's considerations to our awareness. Theology in olden times was a gift from the gods, which could only be achieved through such exercises which could lift people out of their senses and bring them at least back to the experience of motherly love, enabling them to take up this wisdom again, this uncorrupted wisdom. This cannot be taken up in the form or modern logical concepts. Within the Mysteries people could not be given logical concepts in the modern sense, they received images. All knowledge which is gained in this way is gained in pictures, images. The more a person actually entered into the real world of existence — not only associated himself with existence — the more he lives into this existence, like when he lives within the existence of motherly love, so much more will consciousness stop living in abstract concepts, so much more will he live in images. Thus, what was designated as "theology" in olden times, in pre-Christian times, visual science, was science living in images. For this reason, I could say: this theology certainly had a similar form of expression as the one living in the Gospels, because in the Gospels we find images, and the further we go back, the more we find that the Gospels are still being expressed in the attitude of the old theology; there is certainly no differentiation between religion and theology. Here theology itself is something which has been received from God, here in theology one looks upon a God, and sees how the theology is given through a communication with God. Here is something which is alive, in theology. Then it came about that theology was experienced differently, somewhat like the conditions in which one lives when you grow older. At that time therefore, in olden times, theology was nourished through the religious life. This particular way of living though-oneself in the world of religious experience, this actually was getting lost to humanity at the same time as the Mystery of Golgotha was occurring.

So you see, when we look towards the east as it is connected historically to the source of our religious life, we have, we can say, the Indian religious life. What nourishes the Indian religious life? It is nourished through the observation of nature, but the observation of nature was something quite different then to what it is for modern humanity. Nature observation was for all Indians such that one can say: an Indian observed spiritually when looking at nature, but he only observed the spirit which lay beneath the actual being of humanity. The Indian observed the mineral world spiritually, likewise the plant world, animal world; he was aware of the divine spiritual foundation of these worlds; but when he wanted to attain the human world as well, it didn't reveal itself to him. By wanting to access the actual being of the human being in the world, which he had himself, there he found nothing: Nirvana, the entry in nothingness towards what could be perceived in relation to the human being. Thus, the fervour of the Indian's religious life, which certainly was still present at that time, where theology, religion and science were one, was Nirvana. We have an escape from what is perceived from the natural basis of the image-rich consciousness, an escape into Nirvana, where everything that is given to the senses is obliterated. This self-abandonment to Nirvana must be experienced religiously in order to find a possible form for the religious stream of experience for individuals.

Now, when we consider this religious observation of the world further, with the Persians and later with the Chaldeans, we see how they turn their gaze outward, they don't experience the world like us, they live through a world permeated with spirit, everywhere the spiritual foundation permeates everything, but immobilises it. There is a different disposition with these peoples compared to the Indians. The Indian strived towards mankind and found nothing. The other peoples who lived to the north and west of the Indians didn't strive towards mankind but towards the world, towards the spiritual in the world. They couldn't understand the spiritual world in any other way than to avoid with all their might, what later human evolution could no longer avoid.

It is unbelievably meaningful, my dear friends, to observe how, on the one hand the old Indian striving came from what he saw, while he, when he strived towards human beings, I might call it, fell into unconsciousness, into Nirvana, while the Old Persian remained in what he was looking at. The divine which is the basis of the mineral, the plant and animal worlds, was understood by the Old Persian and from this came his religious striving; but now he was overcome by fear that he might be urged to seek man, and this turned into abstract thoughts which turned into imagery. This is actually the basic feeling of the near-Asian peoples all the way to Africa. They saw the foundation of nature as being a spiritual world; they didn't see people, but they were afraid to search in people because then they would enter an abstract region, a region into which later, the Romans entered with their religion. Before the Roman time, in the second, third Century there was the aspiration everywhere to avoid entering into abstractions, hence the aspiration to capture what is presented in images. There was even the endeavour to express in images, what one understood, in image form. There was an effort to, in relation to the divine, which one perceives, not to search for it through abstract concepts but in actions made visible; this is the origin of ritual, sacramental action. In this religious area which I'm referring to, is the origin of ritual in worship.

Now place yourself into this entire development of the old Hebraic peoples; the Judaism which strongly feels the urge for its people's development to enter into what one possesses in one's consciousness. Today I only want to make indications in my presentation in order for us to orientate ourselves. The members of the Hebrew people wanted above all to feel the God on which human nature is based. The Old Indian only sensed God, or the gods, who lay at the basis of sub human nature, and as he tried to penetrate with his consciousness into the human being, there he wanted to rise up into Nirvana. The other, the Persian, Chaldean and Egyptian peoples searched for the connection to the Divine in images and applied these according to their character dispositions, to get up to the human being. So we can see how this urge, as in Judaism, to draw the divine and the human together, to bring the divine in a relationship with the human being, lead to the divine appearing at the same time the foundation of humanity. There was not predisposition to that in the Indian when they sailed into Nirvana; there was no longer a conception that the human consciousness wanted to be reached. For the Indian this personal route to the human soul was to be avoided. This personal route of the human soul had even lead to gradually slipping out of existence into nonexistence, so to speak. The other, the Prussian route, came to a standstill with imagery, remaining in ritual only.

We see how the Jewish peoples developed, within these strivings, their own special character and this resulted in the impossibility to reach God out of one's own life. One had to wait and see what God himself gave, and it was there that the actual concept of revelation came into being. One had to wait and see what God would give and on the other hand one had to be careful not to search through the route of imagery or symbolism (Bilderweg), which was to be feared. If the route of symbolism was sought, then one arrived at a subhuman God, not at a God who carries humanity. In Judaism the symbolic route was not to be followed, it would not be through ritual an also not through the content of knowledge that one would speak to God. The Olden time Jew wanted to meet their god by Him revealing himself, and human beings would communicate in a human way, while from their side, not make outwardly fulfilled sacrifices, but what arises subjectively: the promise — revelation, promise and the contract between both; a judicial relationship one could call it, between the people and their God.

So the Jewish religion positioned itself and thus the Jewish religion stood in the entire evolution of humanity. therefore, one can say: here already a relationship is the example which is performed in our modern time, where science wants to be beside religion but where science has nothing to say about religion, just like the olden time Jew removed everything which appeared as imagery. This is already performed in Judaism, and precisely in the modern differentiation between knowledge and faith, lies unbelievably much Judaism. In Harnack's "The Being of Christianity" everything is again based on Judaism. You have to see through this that we get sick with these things.

Human evolution is penetrated by more and more things. Something is continuously developing which belongs to the Jews in particular: the awareness of personality, which is urged by ego development. With the Greeks there developed a mighty inner world beside the outer world of observed nature but this inner world could raise doubts, because it was observed merely as a world of mythology. Sensing the religious element rising in Hellenism, which lives in Greek mythology, through mythological fantasy, which people are searching for — because it was not to be found in nature — is what rises up in man. The Greek however didn't grasp the actual important point within the human inner life, resulting from mythological fantasy, which the Romans evolved into abstract thinking, which certainly already started with Aristotle, but which was developed particularly in Rome. This abstract way of thinking which is so powerful as to being people to the point of their I, bringing them to self-consciousness, to I-consciousness, this is something which we today still carry in us today and we carry it heavily in us, in the form of modern agnosticism.

My dear friends, basically there is no spiritual teaching other than modern materialism. This sounds like an extraordinary paradox and yet it is so. What the modern materialistic thinker carries in his head is quite spiritualized, so spiritualised that it is quite abstract and has no connection to reality any more. That's Romanism in full swing. We actually have become unbelievably spiritual in the course of the 19th Century, but we deny this spirituality because we maintain that through this spirituality, we can understand matter. In reality our souls are in a spiritualised content, right into our ideas are we spiritualised, but we maintain that through all of this we can only understand a material world. Thus, human beings have grasped their ego through this spiritualisation, but as a result they have become separated from the world. Today humanity must again look for its connection to the world, the search need to be for inner knowledge, there needs to be the possibility to not only have "knowledge without objective meaning" but knowledge *with* objective meaning, in order for knowledge to reveal the being of the world, and on the other hand to authenticate what is hidden within the human being as objective.

You see, the Greeks had a great advantage compared to the oriental world, they could to draw together their innermost nature so to speak. From within themselves they could draw a content, but this content could first only attach as filled with fantasy, imagination. However, there was something the Greeks didn't know. They had brought the development of humanity to internalisation but didn't attach it to the inner life. The internalisation and the hardening continued in the Roman times and beyond, and man had to learn — today still we need to learn to understand — how one can attach what is within, what permeates this inner being. The Greeks could think about their gods in grandiose fantasy images but what the Greek could not do, was to pray. The prayer only cam about later and for prayer the possibility had to be found of connecting the one praying, to reality. To this we must connect those times in which prayer was not merely spoken, not merely thought or not merely felt, but in which prayer became one with the sacramental ritual. Then again Catholicism knows quite well why they don't separate themselves from ritual, from the sacrificial act, from the central sacrifice of the mass.

We'll talk more about these things.

FOUNDATION COURSE

ESSENCE AND ELEMENTS OF SACRAMENTALISM.

Lecture two by Rudolf Steiner given in Dornach, 27 September 1921.

(Including a letter to Dr Steiner from Friedrich Rittelmeyer.)

My dear friends! Yesterday my stating point was to indicate in a few words how Anthroposophy can certainly not be considered as an education of religion and in no way can it directly enter into the development of religious life, but only, as I indicated, indirectly. Anthroposophy must, according to its nature, live as a free deed in the human spirit, it must depend on the free deeds of the human spirit — like natural science as well, which heads in the opposite direction — while religious life must be based on communication with the godhead with whom one knows one is connected and with whom one knows one is dependant in religious life.

At first a serious abyss could open up between those who can offer Anthroposophy to contemporary civilization, and the blossoming of religious life. Perhaps in the totality of what we will talk about here will show you that this abyss doesn't exist. I would just like to call your attention today to how anthroposophical life intervenes in the academic world in such a way that it lends a religious colouring to it.

It is quite without doubt that the modern world rules the relationship of humanity to the cosmos and its earthly environment with agnosticism, and religious people who do not acknowledge this, will come up against a very serious mistake. They would like to remain, to a certain extent, stuck in the comfortable old form and would not contribute anything to ensure that the essence of the old form can remain intact for the earth's development. This mistake unfortunately applies to many people at present. They shut themselves off from the necessity that the epoch we are entering into, requires that we clarify and move towards a conscious, awakened knowledge with human prudence in every area. If religious life is artificially distanced from this knowledge, so it would — while undoubtedly knowledge of a larger authority is being addressed — cause this knowledge to perish, as it once before had threatened to do in the 19th Century, when the materialistic knowledge wanted to destroy religious life in a certain sense.

What I have said regarding this must simply penetrate our sensitivities, it must be clear, and when it is clear, my dear friends, then our mental picture, as I bring it up in front of you, will not seem like such a paradox, as it might be for those who encounter and hear it for the first time.

The agnosticism, the Ignorabimus, is something which has sprung up out of the scientific way of thinking of modern time. What kind of knowledge is it which professes ignorance or agnosticism? It is based on something which it agrees with completely; it is based on the fact that people have gradually been trying to totally shut out their life of soul from knowledge. It is namely so that the ideal human knowledge according to the modern scientist, also the historian, is to shut out subjectivity and only retain what is objectively valid. As a result, the process of obtaining knowledge — for scientific research as well — is completely bound to the physical body of man. Please understand this, my dear friends, in all earnest. Materialism namely has the right when it takes this knowledge which is available to it, not only in regard to what is totally due to material conditions, but which appear as material processes. What really happens between people, in their search for scientific knowledge and the outer world, moves between the outer material things and the relationship to the sense organs; this means their relationship with the material, physical body. The real process of seeking knowledge in connection to the earthly world is a material process right into the final phases of cognition. What the human being experiences in this cognition, is lived through as an observer; he experiences it with his soul-spiritual "side-stepping," so that *the* human being actually is quite right in the cognitive process as being understood physically and to recognise this as the only decisive conception. The human being as observer, which has no activity within himself — this has already often been mentioned by scientists who have thought about this, recognised it and spoken about it.

You see, for in this process of acquiring knowledge, where the human being is actually a mere observer, everything a person has as inner journeys in his soul life, is discounted by the observed reality. The human being observes the outer things, he thinks about these outer objects, he is reminded by outer things, but he certainly also observes how in his reminiscences, his memories, how his emotions of feelings and willing come into it, only *how* this happens, he doesn't know because he is completely unsure about the origin of these feelings and willing, so that for this knowledge, which can only be acknowledged in the present, the only thing which comes into consideration is what happens between the observation and the memory. This is only a picture; it runs as a parallel occurrence next to the real materialistic process running alongside it. The material process is the reality and the recognition runs alongside the material process.

If one had the means for really absorbing what was approaching in the epoch leading up to the Mystery of Golgotha, in the teachers and pupils of the mysteries, and what in that time, one could say, through three decades during which it happened, the then Gnostic orientated mystery teachers spoke about their most inner heartfelt convictions, then one can do no other than to say: they anticipated that the human being will experience himself as a mere observer in the world, and that even his process of acquiring knowledge will occur without his soul's participation. This experience ruled throughout the prevailing mood of the beings of the mysteries during the times of the Mystery of Golgotha.

How can we come to terms with this knowledge today regarding ignorance and agnosticism? We arrive, as we've said, at something which appears as a paradox. Knowledge is the result of the material process, even tied to the material world, while the human being experiences spiritually, but is a mere observer in his spirit. If we now expand the Christian point of view of this phenomenon, then we finally reach a point of integrating this knowledge into the process itself that the Christian view of the various human processes ever had. We reach a point in a sense, which we characterised yesterday, to regard the recognition of human sinfulness in our time as the final phase of the Fall of mankind from its former conditions. Only then will we understand our current science out of religious foundations, when we can regard science as the final phase of the expression of the sinful human being, when we can place it into the realm of sin. This is what appears as a paradox. Out of sinfulness comes ignorance, out of sinfulness, religiously expressed, comes agnosticism.

Only when we feel this way regarding modern science, can we feel Christian towards science. Then again — and we will actually see this in the following days — quite a necessary path results from the understanding of the sinfulness of today's science, an inner human path which can be understood as grace.

With this I have initially indicated what we will be undertaking in the following days; because sometimes you have to do things a little differently to what is customary with today's science, when one wants to explain things in a proper way. To a certain extent one must first draw the outer circle and go inward from there and not start with a theory and draw conclusions from that.

With this at least something real is indicated in humanity. If we simply remain stuck in the ordinary knowledge of current science, then we remain stuck in images. The moment we sense within these images — and all of science today is an image — the sinfulness within this modern scientific element, we comprehend matter with a reality within ourselves, then we are on the way to take science itself into reality. One must be able to develop a feeling, if one wants to rise to it, to ask questions in such a way that something of reality is felt: how is it possible, in a religious sense that, what the human being initially experiences as an observer, can be brought into something real through which human life here on earth is not merely a nonhuman, material life and that the human being is not a mere observer but that a person with his own true being can express himself by processing material existence? When does inner life reach into outer reality so that something is created out of the inward experience and a person is no longer only a mere observer?

You see, there have been attempts to answer this question from time immemorial with the essence of sacramentalism, and one doesn't arrive at another understanding of the essence of sacramentalism than on the basis of such considerations as I've pointed out. First of all, one thing confronts us in human beings and that is the Word.

The Word is actually for current science something quite mysterious, something secretive; because uttered words are at the same time perceived through the sense of hearing. In man there is a moment which lies in the words, when he utters words and he hears them at the same time. In the eyes, in the ability to see, the process has an active and a passive element completely intertwined; it is also present there but is not yet analysed in physiology today. Actually, it is present in all the senses but in relation to hearing and speaking both the active and passive elements are clearly separated from one another. When we speak, we certainly don't consider ourselves as observers of our lives; when we speak, we participate creatively in our life because speaking is simultaneously connected to our breathing process. What takes place in speaking streams over the breathing process. When we breathe in we bring the pressure of the breathing right into our spinal cord canal and in this way, pressure is translated to the brain and works creatively on the cerebral fluid. In the breathing process the outer world streams into us, moulding ourselves. The air we breathe is firstly outside, it enters into us, works formatively on our cerebral fluid and thus also works formatively in the semi-solid parts of the brain. We only understand the brain correctly if we don't just look at it as something which has grown in humans, but if we look at it as something in progressive interaction with the outer world.

In this in-streaming of breath we weave the words which we express. I want to firstly only indicate these things, as I suggested, I want to draw an outer circle and then move gradually inward. By our interweaving our words with our breath — which is indicated in the Old Testament as giving humans their origins — blowing in the air to breathe — through which our word unifies with what is considered in the breath of air as divine, we experience the Word as the Creator within us. We observe something in the world process where we are not merely observers but feel our soul's life working creatively into our body.

We have reached an understanding which allows us to say: in the original creation of mankind was the Word, and everything in human beings was created through the Word. — Just study what it means that the human being, by learning to speak, slowly disentangles his physical organisation through speech. We haven't yet considered the words of the Gospel of St John, but we have discovered the manifestation of something of the bodily nature of the human being in this Gospel. When we contemplate the human being we first of all have his spiritual soul expression and from here the Word comes, which then draws into his bodily organism and shapes him, and thus we have many of these bodily forms which in the course of our lives develop from words themselves, because this is the way we are, we develop out of our words.

What speech/language means to human beings can only really be studied fully in its depths through spiritual science. Already in the sense of the Testaments we have an interweaving of the words which moves through man as the first divine process, that of breathing. Mere thinking which moves in the sphere of the observer is pushed into the creative sphere. When thinking becomes transformed into words, the Divine empowers these thoughts; it is, one could say, the deification of thoughts occur in the words. When one becomes aware that there is much more to words than speech, then words become something through which a person discovers his first connection, his first communication with the Divine in his own behaviour, a behaviour which is like a condensing; like a thought immersed in feeling. While this is to some extent a route from subjective to objective thought, we have the possibility for something which is spiritually objective, to flow into the word. This can be followed by the idea that much more can exist in words than what is in merely man-made thinking; that to a certain extent something divine can flow into the words and that in the words something divine can be expressed, that a divine message can be contained in the words.

So we have the first element, that people from out of themselves, find their way going out into the environment, permeated with what is divine in the words. This is somewhat the way the Words of the Gospels were experienced, the in-streaming of the divine in the words of the Gospels which we can feel in the creative activity of the words for ourselves; here we have the first element how man can change from his subjectivity to the objective, like in ritual.

Now, one can look at what a person doesn't think regarding the world, but what actions he performs in the world. Simply look at human actions. These human actions are seldom regarded in the right light by modern materialism.

Once again, I can only make indications about what this actually involves; we will later enter into them again.

Just imagine the following contrivance: around a pulley a rope, here a weight, and on the other side a larger weight. The rope is pulled down on the side of the heavier weight and pulled up on the opposite side. The same thing can happen if you now pull on the lighter side and lift the heavier side. You could accomplish something yourself which can also happen as an objective process. In the first place, depending on the heavier weight, it happens without you being there; but when you are there, you can shift the weight. What happens in the outer world can also happen without you.

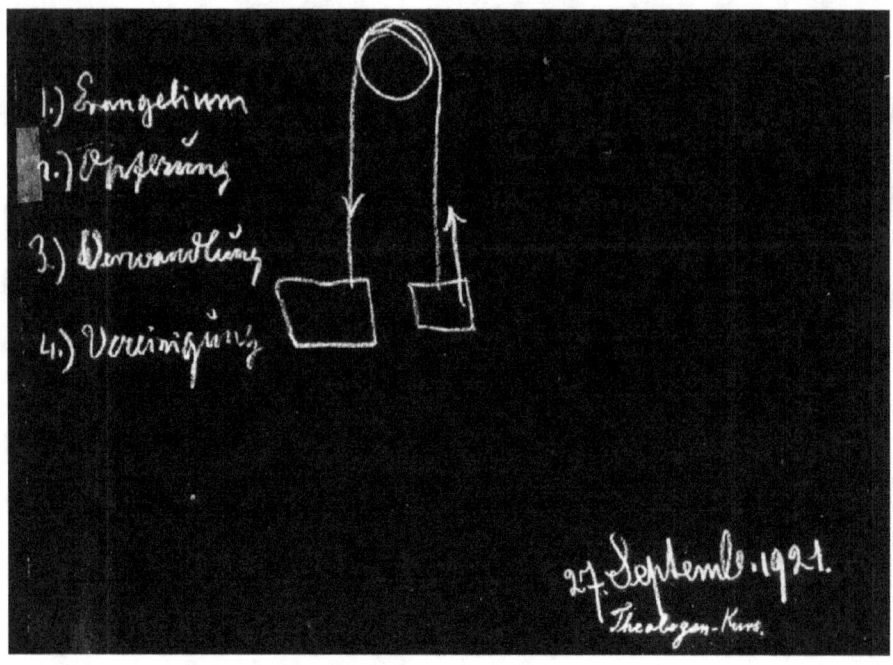

Plate 1   2nd lecture   September 27, 1921, in the morning

This is however a process in inorganic nature. When you study what a person accomplishes in the outer world you realize what is of importance is that it happens in such a way, that it comes from spiritual interrelationships, and that the body of a person only presents the possibility for the action. In our actions we namely — in that we gain knowledge of the world as soul-spiritual observers — only have our body as one ingredient. In our bodies processes take place — processes of movement, of nourishment, of dissolving and so on. What takes place in our bodies is an ingredient, something that is added to what happens objectively. Our body doesn't take part in our actions; we only understand our actions when we consider them when separated from the body. Just as we in the cognitive process, seen materialistically, have something which turns us into observers, so we have in the process of actions for the world, in the process of action, which takes place in the world, something in which the body doesn't participate. Processes which take place in the body remain without cosmic meaning, just like materialistic knowledge has no cosmic meaning. A person remains in materialism in his actions when they only pertain to the earthly, like a hermit standing in the world has no relationship to anything outside of himself. If he searches for this relationship, then he must mix something spiritual into his actions, accomplish actions in such a way that they aren't separated from him, like all earthly actions, then he must allow his thoughts and feelings to enter in a vital way into his actions, so that the actions become signs for what lives in them. Then the actions are a sacrificial act, then they are the sacrifice.

When we look at knowledge in this way, we see knowledge objectified by the validation of the message in words; if we look at the actions, we have the objectification of action, the drawing out of man alone in what is given in the sacrificial act. Here we first have the relationship of a person to the outer world in the sense that it originates out of the human spirit-soul. Out of the spiritual soul now also rises the imagination — in relation to words, which are no longer experienced as a human, but as a divine revelation — and in relation to the sacrificial act, which is no longer being experienced as the manipulation of the human world, in which man is not involved, but as such is involved with his thoughts, his feelings; this he experiences again in his inner life.

The other relationship of the human being to the outer world, we find in human nutrition. We actually have three relationships to the outer world: observation through the senses, breathing and nutrition. Everything else can be referred back to these. Breathing is actually positioned between perception and nutrition because one could say that breathing is half perception and half nutrition. It is undeniable that the breathing process stands between the process of perception and nutrition. You see, it is simultaneously connected to the processes of perception and nourishment. Breathing is the synthesis between observation and nutrition.

Physiology considers nutrition incorrectly. Physiology is of the opinion that we take in nourishment, that we take out of the food what we need and repel the rest. This is not so. That we absorb substance is only a side-effect. The process of life means we are actually constantly opposed and fight back against what is caused by the ingestion of foodstuff into ourselves. We eat, we drink — and the result is something which lies truly very deep in our consciousness, beneath our conscious soul life. What happens there is a constant defensive action. In this physical-physiological process of defence are found the actual processes of life and of nutrition. The life process of nourishment is an averting process. Only when we realize how the organism is organised in this way, to receive the suggestion for a defence — for us to have a defence there naturally has to be suggestion — only when we understand that by the defence against a substance coming from outside as a suggestion in the process of nourishment, will we be able to really understand nourishment. With nourishment a process of aversion is involved, while the absorption of substances is only a side effect through which the finest filaments of the human being the suggestion for resistance is directed from the outside, in order for the aversion to take place in the most outer periphery of the organism. Only at this point of averting does the actual life process of nutrition take place, so that the ordinary earthly process of nourishment is actually a resistance to the earthly. The earthly pushes the nourishing items into us, and we must absorb it, but this is a process of resistance.

This is the reality, but it is not the way science looks at the whole thing. What is actually happening with this repulsion? Something happens which lies completely outside of human consciousness. When we take up nourishment, it is actually a process of the material world. Each substance is actually a concentrated, reduced world process. Processes of the outer world we take into ourselves, we repel them, but by repelling them, a counter process comes about: the process of the outer world becomes something quite different, transformed, and in this transformation, something happens in us. Outer matter is transformed in us. What becomes of it? It becomes spirit within us. This is something which is ordinarily not seen, that the human being in his actual process of digestion, in his transformation of the outer world steers outer material processes to spiritualization.

In the outer world nature goes through world processes, and as a fragment of this world process, we could call it the origin of a seed, from which all other things originated through the seed serving as nourishment. What happens in the outer world becomes firstly transformed within the human being before it goes further on its way to spirituality. It can't be transformed into the spiritual in the outer world, only within the human being can it change into the spiritual. This is simply an objective fact, which I state here, nothing else. However, what I'm presenting here for you happens outside the world of human thoughts. It happens in the deeper regions of human will and partially in the feeling realms. Only certain parts of the feeling life, and will, take part in the process of nourishment, which I've recently indicated. Thought processes don't take part in it; it goes in the opposite direction; through the Word it goes from below into the formation. Here beneath, we have, coming from outside in the opposite direction, like the way the thought process does it, the process of transformation.

If one wants to place this transformative process within the human being so that when one looks at a person according to the manner in which he looks at the outer world, then one must place something in the outside world which actually doesn't happen in the outside world, but only within the human being. With this one had placed a sacramental act in the outside world, something which doesn't take place in natural phenomena, but which takes place within the human being as a human mystery. If one wants to take what belongs to the most inner part of man, which we have just characterised, and place this in front of the human being, then one arrives at the conversion of the bread and the wine as the body and blood (of Christ), which is the transubstantiation. The transubstantiation is not an experience of the outside world; the transubstantiation is revealing to the outside world what is fulfilled within the most inner part of the human being. We see in the transubstantiation what we are unable to see in the outside world, because the outside world is a fragment of existence, not a totality; in the sacraments we add that to the outside world in addition to what the kingdom of nature accomplishes within the human being.

This, my dear friends, is the original idea of the sacrament, that something is added to outer world phenomena, something which inner man doesn't experience consciously but which is within the human being, and because it is not recognised but exists subconsciously, it can through signs be placed into the outside world. To consummate transubstantiation, a person must feel something unconsciously connected with the innermost being of his self to the symbols. He is indeed paving the way for intercommunications with the spirits of the outside world by presenting the transformation, which would otherwise take place behind the veil of memory within him, as a sacrament.

With this we have not yet grasped what the highest achievable thing is by human beings, we have only grasped the spiritualisation process of substance in the human being, the transformation, the transubstantiation. What happens in man as an objective process takes place, I would say, only as separated from our consciousness by a thin veil, behind our consciousness. This happens because from this side, at every moment of our lives, our "I" is stirred up. We dive down below this transformed substance and by our absorbing the matter of the outside world, our process of life exists in this transformation, by our spiritual soul diving under into the transformation of the outside world, our "I" is continually nourished, our "I" is continuously encouraging the union with the substance transformed by this process. The union with the substance after its transformation represents the accessibility of the ego-manifestation to spiritualisation. Let's consider this in a sacramental way.

If we place the sacramental before us then the participation in the sacrament is such that it is materially represented through symbolism; as soon as it is transubstantiated it becomes united with the human being and here we have the fourth link of what in the ritual can be represented as the sacramental signs in the relationship of the human being to the world.

If we look at the human beings in as far as they are involved with the outside world, then we have, what I would call, the realization of the process of knowledge (in spirit) in Words, and in the sacrificial act, which appear outwardly in signs, we have indicated everything which a person can unite with in his soul-spirit and actions. If we look at human beings absorbing the outside world, where we have the proclamation of the message in word and the sacrificial act, if we look at human beings who continuously give birth out of the spiritual, then we have realized this in the sacramental acts of transubstantiation and communion.

With this we have thus the possibility to connect the human being in his relationship to all his actions in the outside world in a real sense. Actions distance themselves from him, his own body walks beside him. In transubstantiation that which does not take place in the world is presented as an event, because the outside world is only a fragment of possible events. In communion a person unites himself with the outside world to which he can't connect through his thinking. Objective processes precede transubstantiation and communion. As a result of this we place a person through a physical-soul-spiritual way in a relationship with the world. We have stopped regarding the human being as in a hermit's existence removed from the world; we've started seeing him as a member of the whole world. We have learnt to regard the world as material, but there, where we see it as a fragment, to look at it as if the spiritual foundation on which matter is based is only a part, spiritualising and perfecting; and we have taken the divine cycle, which is in the outer and inner part of man, and placed it before us ... (Some gaps in stenographer's text made the publisher shorten the text here.)

This is what the people wanted to present to those who said: The human physical-soul-spiritual relationship to the universe can be brought back through the sacraments; recognised through the proclamation, through the sacrificial act, performed through the transubstantiation and communion. You could live together with the entire world by taking what is usually spread over two halves in a person, the soul-spiritual, which just watches, and the physical, which is just an addition to external actions. These can be united by taking what the mere observer wants to remain in relation to the outside world, sacramentalize it in the proclamation of the Word, in the Gospel — which comes out of the "Angelum," out of the realm permeated by the spiritual world — and in the sacrificial act, experienced in his inner life and through which the human being only becomes complete, sacramentalised in the transubstantiation, the transformation, and then by incorporating the human being into this whole in communion, in union. Here you have a real process which is no mere process of knowledge but a process which is connected to your feeling and will, while the process of knowledge takes place in a cold, frozen region of mere abstraction.

What takes place in the coldness of knowledge is warmed somewhat by the proclamation of the Word and in the sacrificial act. That which, however, through overheating can no longer exist consciously, because heat numbs consciousness and thus can't be perceptive, which can happen when the phenomenon is elevated to a noumenon/psyche, means that in place of external processes which are perceived by the senses, the external process of sacramental action is imitated by the human being itself, in which sacramental action is regarded as what lies behind nature, which can't be produced by anything else, with an objective meaning in the world, because it places the events of human life itself in the cosmos.

With this we have given something which our current abstract process for acquiring knowledge actually presents in life. However, a question remains, which is an important question. We can understand that something happens in people through the Word, because the Word works into the corporeality and man forms himself through words. We can also understand that through the sacrificial act something happens in the inner part of man because the sacrificial act is executed in such a way that he is not just holding back what is in his body, but that his feeling and willing takes part in the sacrificial act. As a result, an earthly event in the body is connected to a super-earthly event. This can be comprehended. In fact, quite different feelings are experienced during the sacrificial act than any during any other processes in ordinary outer activities. A dampening of the consciousness which is carried within, is numbed. If we can now say something happens within human beings, then the great question arises which we want to address in future: does this event, which is primarily an independent event, does it not take its course in outer events? Is it not also a world event? If so, then we should ask ourselves, what a person experiences as in an outer action, which is symbolic and thus somehow withdraws from the course of events in natural phenomena — do such actions in their turn somehow weave into the course of events in natural phenomena? Are they something real, outside of the human being? This is the other component of the question. As we said, we will occupy ourselves with this question in the next days.

You will have already noticed in what has come in front of you, that there are four main elements of the sacrifice of mass which rest on the primordial experiences of consciousness, in the mysteries. The four principal constituents of the sacrifice of mass are namely: reading the Gospel, the Offering, the transubstantiation (transformation) and communion (unification).

In everything which I present to you, my dear friends, I have no other goal than to share these things firstly with you. Everything that is to happen now will be based on the fact that, despite our communal confrontations which we know about, the tasks of our time will especially come out of a truly religious consciousness. We will speak about this further, tomorrow.

FOUNDATION COURSE

OPEN LETTER TO DR RUDOLF STEINER SEPTEMBER 1921

Honourable Doctor!

After the devastating impressions of the last years which have gone through the German world, a longing has developed for religious renewal. It is true that on the whole, quite small circles have these longings which are really serious and alive. However, these are circles in which one can hope to find the power for how this can be developed. Some really strong will glows here in the youthful hearts waiting for the aim and leadership. There where one didn't dare to think about it not long ago, lectures are being held regarding the rebirth of the German nation, and one allows certain religious sounds to become agreeable even if one doesn't want to know anything about church life. In newspapers and magazines, and much more so in innumerable dialogues, there is a turn towards higher questions. The feeling that something new and great could come into the inner realm lives in a clear or less clear way in many of the best of us. As hopeful as we at times evoke this mood, at closer inspection we still discover a hopelessness, which is truly a call for mercy. Nearly superstitiously one waits in these circles for religious leaders, but one has no idea in which direction one is steered and vacillates between hope and a deep mistrust in one's own hope. Inspired, one celebrates soon the one and then the other which on the region of the inner life appears strong and safe to talk about, yet to which one has to admit shortly after, that one was disappointed and that the word of fulfilment is not mentioned again. One hopes for intuitions, does not know the at least where it should come from and which are the most believable, and confuses ever more dangerous tendencies of instinctive life with divine revelations. One regards the great personalities of the past, Fichte, Goethe, also Luther, and tries drawing inspiration from their work without really liberating contemporary solutions.

People look for substitutes in community feelings and community experiences and completely forget that each and every great soul had been given by community. There's a demand for a new "ritual" and they don't know that only a new spirit can bring a new ritual/worship, that the right spirit on its own can bring about a satisfactory form of worship from out of himself. People create all kinds of dance and play and enjoy the sure spirit of times gone by, expecting from this to create something which one can't create yourself but should create.

In this general hopelessness, which becomes ever more evident and could bring about a change of heart, Anthroposophy steps in and — multiply this hopelessness! Those who experience Anthroposophy for the first time, express much of the passionate rejection they experience. As one of those who have entered into such a circle where an understanding for your work can be found, I would here like to be the spokesman for these circles. In this way I would like to advise you to make something of the coherence and mood of these people, in order to help them understand Anthroposophic thought and actions better. As vividly as I am empathic on the one hand, how strange, yes, repulsive these people at first encounter Anthroposophy, so sure is my experience on the other hand that a fulfilment of the great, deep longing of our time can be achieved through the correct knowledge of anthroposophic accomplishments.

The people of whom, and for whom, I want to talk about here, long for a great purpose in life. They imagine this purpose of life, consciously or unconsciously, as a unified, powerful thought, as a singular soul-powerful feeing, which carries the whole of life and lift it up. Now the find Anthroposophy and discover an abundance of assertions in all kinds of fields, a mass of individual insights, big and small, which they initially don't know how to approach and towards which they feel helpless. It is as if they want to dangerously push everything away by saying 'One is necessary', which they still experience as a deep human need.

They want a clear, safe way to be indicated up high, which recommends itself to them convincingly and invitingly, a way they can walk forward to with a clear conscience and joyful courage. Now they hear of all kinds of exercises, which could and should be done, through which one laboriously acquires all kinds of abilities which do not seem essential and decisive to them — how one for example focuses your mind on the blossoming and withering of a plant in order to get an impression of the transience of life, the spirituality of a flower and so on. A confusing wealth of advice spreads itself out before them, on the one hand from the moral, known and obvious side and on the other hand, from the 'occult' strange or even questionable side. They would gladly feel free and great, striving at the pinnacle of humanity so to speak, but now they must find that some individuals with deep insights should be far ahead of them, and that they have no prospect in life to even come close to reaching them. As a result, they feel themselves pushed into a lower human class and even robbed of their human kingdom. They feel like an assassination attempt on their human dignity, even if they don't say it out loud.

Many of these people strongly feel that help can only come from a higher world. It is precisely here that Anthroposophy seems to be gradually thrown back on itself. It is for them as if people gradually want to and must push themselves higher, with unending effort and boredom while they long to be seized from above and be filled with new, powerful life forces from above.

Many of them have worked through a large part of knowledge of our time. Just from current science they have received powerfully chilling and paralysing impressions. And now also the realm of belief and the realm of knowledge needs transformation? Must their most precious and highest experiences of their inner soul realm be sacrificed for research and a descriptive 'science'? They fear that this will fall back into a dull intellectualism; they rear a falsification, even desecration of the inner life. It looks to them like a basic, dangerous underestimation of the deep distinction is presented between knowledge which appear through the senses and phenomena, and belief, the inner truth freely acknowledged. Not only a few of these people carried a strong knowledge within, that help must somehow be expected from Christ, not from churchlike Christianity, but from the correctly understood Christ himself. Yes, in individuals you find an instinctive awareness of the "living Christ" as the great helper of mankind. Now they are told that in Anthroposophy, Christ is regarded as the "regent of the sun" or that to begin with the two Jesus children in our time reckon with all kinds of extraordinary details; sincere claims which, as far as they had not found this quite repulsive initially, now in any case mean absolutely nothing and above all doesn't appear to be of help.

Some of them are also influenced by the "culture" of the last decades — the word "culture" itself has become so questionable that it can hardly be heard any more. They all look rather at everything else as a "new culture." Now they experience Anthroposophy penetrating into all outer areas, in architecture, the art of dance, which all want to renew our culture. There it appears that the power of humanity regarding religion as the main focus is pushed aside to a busyness and all kinds of outer work of vain distraction.

Above all, however, we must also remember those by whom the social question has been raised precisely by religious sentiment, becoming the mighty burning question of our time, and who can only through a new spirit, which grasps and truly fulfils humanity with a pure, strong brotherly mood make the salvation possible for the world. To them Anthroposophy seems neither simple nor warm, neither convincing nor contemporary or popular enough to somehow help humanity recover from their current main dilemma.

How much the present theological striving of anthroposophy has remained inadequate, I know all too well. During the last years I've had many hours of embarrassment about it, that this great spiritual movement has been regarded as failed by my theological colleague, in a spiritual and unfortunately also human way. In the abovementioned mood I believe deeper reasons need to be looked for regarding this strong instinctive antipathy which anthroposophy meets in theologians, but also in other religious circles.

Let me at least indicate to ignorant readers — who can say one gets the clear impression that I am again being mistaken through Anthroposophy — that I believe I have the right to know what to expect from all these objections which I have to handle almost daily. I clearly see that the antipathies partly originate out of a false understanding of the tasks which Anthroposophy proposes, which is quite inclusive yet simultaneously humble, when many of its opponents think, partly out of an inadequate insight into the depth and character of the current spiritual crises, and out of a similar inadequate knowledge of the real possibilities for their solution. While you have up to now not according to my knowledge entered explicitly and in detail into this whole circle of concern, I believe that for many there is really a need for you to once and for all answer such questions. Particularly enlightening it could be as well, if you can express yourself regarding how you from your point of view, out of your abilities judge the actual present human being to have "religious impressions" at all. Does one not turn to soul powers which are dwindling relentlessly, when one in some old sense of "pure religious" way want to address current humanity? What exists for the future when people today still speak about a "religious experience" and impressions of God? How can powers, which make people susceptible for the higher worlds, be enlivened and in which way can they be renewed? How do you imagine an active religious proclamation in future? The main issue would be to hear what you have to say, how you see the current religious crisis from your point of view, and how Anthroposophy can and will contribute.

As always with immense gratitude and veneration,
Yours, Friedrich Rittelmeyer.

THEORETICAL THINKING AND LIVING IN THE SPIRIT.

Lecture three by Rudolf Steiner given in Dornach, 27 September 1921, afternoon, in answer to a letter presented in the morning by Friedrich Rittelmeyer.

Emil Bock: I would like to open the hour of our discussion with my immediate task in asking Dr Steiner to give answers regarding the letter of Dr Rittelmeyer. This letter has indeed grown out of various wishes for guidelines regarding possible answers to those who made these objections.

Rudolf Steiner: If we have to start with it, please permit me to make a few points. I ask you however, to link your remarks to those comments I will be making, because obviously some of you here can approach what Dr Rittelmeyer has formulated, from another point of view.

Firstly, I think there is a feeling for many today that some kind of impact is needed in religious life, that religious life needs a kind of renewal in the most diverse areas. Dr Rittelmeyer has formulated the experience which he indicates is present with those familiar with it and I have to admit, something similar has at times confronted me. Already in relation to his first point presented here, one expects unified thoughts, a soul-powerful feeling — and this is summarised in the words "one thing is necessary" — while one finds in Anthroposophy a sum, even perhaps a very large sum of declarations regarding the world content and so for a person, who knows no sure approach, has to say: it appears to me through this experience that in many respects it has already been there for such a long time and has now contributed a lot to the fact that we in our current western civilisation have entered into a dead end.

Just think how vague, how uncertain an experience would be to presume it could perhaps be more succinctly formulated in order to solve the problem. One could even make references to this in our domain. In our domain another kind of domain has arisen out of Anthroposophic foundations where something similar has happened as what is meant with this point, if I understand it correctly. This is in the domain of social thinking. Something like a unified thought has come about, I could say, in the domain of the Threefold social organism. Firstly, I only want to make characteristic comparisons. I must confess this example doesn't show anything significant when it appears publicly in such a short formulation. In life such short formulations don't prove to be really effective; having a decisive importance. I always encounter an objection for instance when someone says: You want to tell me something about the human organism, and instead of giving me a uniform idea, you present an entire physiology. — One must try and understand how the doubt-free comfortable thoughts of modern time have contributed largely to our unhappiness and inner and outer relationships, and what we are suffering from is based on the vague manner of our desire to understand everything in a summary. One has to say to oneself:

precisely because such ideas arise, proves that something must change when things happen, which many expect in a vague way. In particular, when it is then said, instead of such "uniform ideas." instead of "mighty soul feelings," a number of exercises are given, some of them could be of a moral nature — and others — they are called "occult" in the letter, which makes an unusual, thoughtful impression on others — yes, it must even be said: What can one then actually expect? — One can expect that there will simply be a debate about what current humanity is missing. I'm speaking firstly in this way, how in the anthroposophical domain it is by all means necessary; we will soon address the particular religious questions given in the letter itself.

You see, the moral exercises, which are mentioned here as familiar, are such that according to their wording, they certainly would be known if they were moral instructions. Firstly, according to the anthroposophic context, this is not what they are. In an anthroposophic context they are indications for the attainment of higher knowledge. It is certainly presented in such a way that it must be clear: they are indication for the attainment of a higher, supersensible knowledge. One must after all admit: If I would say a person necessarily longs for the attainment of supersensible knowledge, as opposed to if I say, that a kind of tranquillity in relation to "exulting to the skies, grieving to death" provides humanity with a moral stand, there is certainly a more radical difference between them. By me expressing something like the demand for serenity, I'm expressing something which could perhaps be quite well known, and which could initially sound like an obvious moral instruction, but which is not a discussion based on the demand for serenity. Is it said in my book 'Knowledge of the higher Worlds and its attainment' that for the purpose of morality, for the purpose of obtaining moral support it is necessary to develop serenity? No! Something quite different is said. It is said that an exercise needs to be done, it is said that this exercise needs to be repeated, in this way the exercise should be done in a certain rhythm in such a way that one could describe it as done in tranquillity. To repeat a certain exercise is quite different to a moral action. Above all you need to consider what is given in my book 'Knowledge of the higher Worlds and its attainment.'

You see, it is actually the most natural thing that one person can say to another: you need to make an effort to search for the truth. That is a self-evident fact. Here the important thing is that within the rhythmic sequence of thoughts, thoughts are rendered to the truth, in relation of human beings to the truth. This exercise, this making-oneself-conscious-in-the-present within such a content, this repeated rhythmic making-oneself-conscious-in-the-present is what is involved. It is about applying quite a particular mood for spiritual knowledge. I want to explain this attitude to you in more detail. I will deviate from the strict formulation of the letter but maybe this will make some things much clearer.

Let's see, take for example a professor, lecturer or some scholar who gives lectures. Very often it happens that he prepares his lecture, then memorises it and then delivers it. This is indeed not possible if one really allows spiritual science to live within it. If you lived within spiritual science, this would be unworthy of you. Preparation can only be that a certain inner accumulation regarding the subject matter comes about. As a result of this inner assembly you do indeed step — even though you have a been connecting with the subject matter a thousand times — each time again with a new approach regarding the subject matter, so that you gradually grasp it clearly and speak out of the direct observation of it once again. You see, when you learn about something, for example a chapter in geography — good, you learn it, you have it, and then you retain in your thoughts. This doesn't happen in spiritual science at all if it is to be alive. Whoever wants to be a spiritual scientist in reality, must just again and again allow the most elementary things to draw through the soul. What I have written for example in my book "Theosophy" doesn't have a conclusive meaning. What it contains, I had to repeatedly allow to be drawn through my soul for it to have meaning. It can't be said: The book "Theosophy" is there, I know its contents. — It would, on the basis of spiritual science, be the same if one would say: I don't believe that there is a person who could say: I have eaten for 8 days so now I don't need to repeat it. — Every day we sit down to eat and do the same thing. Why? Because it is *Life*, it is not something which can be merely stored in thought form. The life in spiritual science is *Life*, and it declines if it is not ever and again lived through. This is what needs to be considered.

If you have through spiritual science approached life you would have become acquainted with the possibility for instance, that you can help those who have passed through the gate of death, by giving them a kind of meditative content based on the spiritual world which they have entered through the gate of death. This doesn't mean that one, for example, reads something to them once and now recon: now they understand it — no, it involves repeating it ever and again, this living-yourself-into the content, each time, as something new. This is far too seldom respected. People are used to observe everything as theory. Spiritual science is no theory, it is Life; but if one treats it by thinking one can learn it, like you learn about other things, then you make it into a theory. Obviously one can make it into a theory but then if you take it up this way, it is only a theory. Every serious spiritual scientist knows that one must live in it; the exercises are not exhausted by knowing their contents.

These are things which have disappeared from Western consciousness. What this Western consciousness is, shows also in other things. People have come to me who say: There's something awful about the Buddha speeches, they contain mere repetitions; one should surely produce a publication with only the contents of the speeches and leave out the repetitions. — Yet, no one really understands the Buddha-speeches who can make such a statement because the essence of the Buddha speeches depend upon following the rhythmic sequence in very small slots, always repeating the same one. This is an oriental method which does not coincide with our work here and in order to clarify this, I will make some comments.

Continuing with the letter, there is further mentioned about the exercises, that some are strange and questionable. Yes, we must look at the kind of judgement or the basis upon which this assessment is made today. If one speaks about the desire present today for something new, then one must acquaint oneself with why such a desire exists; and what exists must really be characterised. I could, in order to make myself clear, perhaps bring to mind the book of Oswald Spengler "The Decline of the West." Spengler followed up with a small brochure entitled 'Pessimism?' I will quote a sentence from 'Pessimism.' He says:

It is not important to recognise truth, but to make facts matter. — Now a discussion follows regarding this statement, regarding what he understands as 'truth' and as 'facts.' In one place he says: 'Truths are the greats of thought ... what stands in a dissertation is truth, that a candidate fails his dissertation is a fact.' — Now one must imagine that with such a sentence something must somehow be said, but it is complete nonsense. Yet people read over something like this, they take it all in, which says something, and they don't notice anything strange and consider it as something outlandish. One can't possibly have a discussion about such a statement, it is total nonsense. Something like this is not even discussed when it is such nonsense; you don't even notice it. It can't fail that in a time in which such a judgement prevails, many strange and questionable things are found. However, we can imagine where we have actually arrived — in any case in another connection than meant by Spengler. We graduate today, so to say without a fuss, up to the highest levels of our study; here in our knowledge itself there are actually no disasters or turning points. You could say that a disaster happens when a student fails, but not knowledge itself. This involvement of the whole person, so that you are able to live with a problem in such an inner way as you have any other outer experience, is something which is rarely found. When you have written a book or if you are a private tutor you may feel very satisfied, but you don't experience disasters or turning points because of the material. This is something which has, one could say, spread over the entire scientific life.

It is necessary that we come to live within the spirit once again, that the spirit becomes a reality in whose processes we participate. This is no contradiction against tranquillity. Precisely though cultivating tranquillity you acquire the right way to participate more strongly and concretely towards what happens objectively; finally, it is no contradiction against tranquillity when one observes all the horror of a volcanic eruption or some similar events this way.

I would like to say that in our modern time there is hardly any receptivity necessary for the particular way to spiritual science, simply the entire way of thinking, the quite different way of experiencing truth, is first necessary. You see, when someone says: Yes, we don't need thinking, we don't need intellectualism, we need feelings! — it is because he doesn't get the feeling that he's being moved inwardly; what should be given is what is lacking.

You see, is it really enough today, to adhere to ancient religious rules? When one gives a single lecture — and I speak from experience — when one gives a single lecture, let's say, from certain details regarding the social question, then there are many listeners who could say or write: Sure, this is all possible but in this lecture the name of Christ is not mentioned even once. — Yes, my dear friends, there is still a divine commandment which says: You should not pronounce the name of God in vain — and there is the commandment: You should not continuously say, God, God. It can be something very Christian, no not continuously say the name of Christ; perhaps it is even Christian for this reason, because the name of Christ is not misused. It is not through the use of Christ's name in every third line that something becomes Christian.

All these things should stop in the old thinking's comfortable way. Those who don't drop this comfortable thinking — they would also have the vague feeling that something must change — they can't be informed about the demands of the time because everything which exists in the demands of the time is something which they are unable to experience; they can't, because they are merely taught that these demands must be experienced basically as they have always been, and not commit to actually moving to solutions which must be investigated to really meet the demands of the time. Often the enormous difference between theoretical thought and immersed-in-spirit-living, is not considered. However, already during the first step into spiritual science there must be a living-within- the-spirit. I'm not saying you need to be clairvoyant or something of the kind, but that there needs to be a living-in-spirit; there must be another form of experience of truth, of content, than what one is accustomed to these days.

Another objection which Dr Rittelmeyer expressed took me quite by surprise, I must admit, but this is the way it's going to happen. The objection is that people feel insulted when, instead of something being pointed out as within them, they are made aware of what individuals perhaps know, what individuals have seen. People feel, they expressed it as 'their human kingdoms having been stolen', they had felt great and now they must feel small. — Yes, I must admit, this objection surprised me because I don't really understand its content. Isn't it true, what is said consequently in the letter, that people expect something to happen from above, but now they feel thrown back on to themselves, on to exercises they need to do, on to efforts needed to understand something. — I initially feel an extraordinary contradiction between both these allegations. Secondly, I must add this: my whole life I have been — and it has been already quite long — extremely glad if a truth appears somewhere, and I actually find it disturbing when someone rejects the truth, because it has not grown out of their own soil. This is quite an egotistical subjective judgement, but we are stuck in such egotistical subjective judgements, and as a result we need a renewal of thinking in our current time, because it exists.

Here we have a bunch of judgements which indicates how necessary it is that a shift takes place. If these judgemental directions, which have been created by our time, continue to exist, then we will get nowhere. It is already necessary to say, even though it may sound rough, it is above all necessary to mention that the objectors must think about their objections, to what a degree they should not be making them, in order for the entry of the renewal not to be disturbed by the most ancient judgements. This is what has to be said above all things.

Another objection which is of course often made is that Anthroposophy appears in the form of a science and the inference is made that the realm of belief and the realm of knowledge must metamorphose. Actually, the objection depends, when it is made, on the inexact understanding of the context in Anthroposophy. In Anthroposophy the claim is never made that a belief must be transformed into knowledge or something similar, but in Anthroposophy this first positive element appears: it is shown that through knowledge not only can one have something in the sensory world of appearance, but also in the spiritual world. The question can at least be: Are the methods which are applied directed to the real, safe and equivalent? — This can then be examined and re-examined. When the issue is expressed in a way of objecting to imagination, objecting to inspiration and so on, then there is nothing to be discussed. However, no judgement can be made when one says: I feel uncomfortable if something is to be known about it. — It isn't important if something is unpleasant, but it is important that a certain method regarding the super-sensory can be known, just as in the sensory world something can be known. What can be known can't be judged in a way so that one can say the objects of faith were based on the free recognition of inner truths because Anthroposophy is a knowledge forced through "hallucination and proof." — Anthroposophy is just a science and is established as a science, it can't get involved with such an objection because it is a science. One could have the same objection against mathematics; one could say it would be detestable if mathematical truths were actual truths. Such an objection can't actually be made, because it is basically pointless.

An objection which I have heard with the most diverse nuances, is this, that something is expected, which could be something shocking, which you accept and get away with by listening to such things as "Christ is the ruler of the sun" or the issue about the "Two Jesus children." which are equally indifferent to you.

My dear friends, I must admit I don't really understand how these things can be indifferent, when they are understood. The unbelievably important question of the present day is: How can the realm of morality be founded in the realm of natural necessities? We live today on the one side within a scientifically acknowledged realm of natural necessities and one allows that within this realm of necessities, hypotheses are made which are not supported by direct observation. One takes for instance the example of the development of the earth according to geology and so on, spanning only a certain time in history and then according to these impressions arrive at the origin of the earth as coming out of the ancient mists, or like the modified hypotheses in the sense of the Kant-Laplace theories which are no more valid these days; then out of this comes the imagining of the earth's origin and out of the second main statement of the mechanical heat theory, the theory of entropy, the imagining how everything is heading for death through heat (Wärmetod). Who constructs this hypothesis regarding the earth's origin and evolution must say to himself — because according to the scientific point of view on which it is based, it can't be assumed otherwise — that this ancient mist was there as the sovereign entity with laws of aerodynamics and laws of aerostatics, and out of this the laws of hydrodynamics and hydrostatics were created, and then luckily such conditions arose through which connections were created as we find in the simplest cells, the amoebas, and then all that turned into complicated organisms, also humans, and in humans moral ideals rose through which human worth could be felt.

What would we be as humans if we hadn't had our moral ideals, and if through these moral ideals we didn't, through the acceptance of a divine world order in the entire global context, become ennobled? It is useless to just let it go; to say we will separate the realm of the certainty of faith which we have in moral ideals, from what we have as the natural order. Such a separation can only happen with those who aren't really inwardly serious about what they see presented in the natural order.

My dear friends, I once became acquainted with someone who at the time was involved with the great problem of death in the world, explored from Haeckel's point of view. With an earnest attitude, an inner enthusiasm to understand such a point of view, he approached this view which is quite honestly based on the foundation of science. What did he have to say about moral-religious ideals? He said: 'Those are religious foam bubbles rising in human life, it is something people put in front of themselves, it is something on which the human race lives, from which they take their dignity; but one day the great graveyard of the heat death will arrive, and then all outer forms of organisms, everything which appeared as moral-religious foam bubbles will be buried, and in the world's space a sloop will be circling in some curve that can be said to be something which people once created according to mechanistic or dynamic laws, these people allowed bubbles to rise and from this the people derived their worth; and all of that has turned out to be a cosmic cemetery.' —

You see, out of this person's honesty, because he couldn't unhook himself from it, he returned to the blissful womb of the Catholic Church for some years. This is only one example out of many.

This abyss has opened up between the moral-religious world order and the scientific-mechanic world order. There are only a few people capable of enough sensitivity, who doesn't tolerate the entire world view regarding the earth's origin or demise according to science. For example, Herman Grimm said a rotting and decaying carcass bone would be an appetizing piece compared to what the Kant-Laplace theory made of the earth. — What Herman Grimm added is true, future generations of scholars will be able to make astute treatises to explain the nonsense which the Kant-Laplace theory introduced into people's heads, to their detriment.

My dear friends, if with your deepest insight you want to look at what such a point of view has caused for the doom of the human soul, starting in the lowest classes in school, then in order to do what needs to be done today, you must search much deeper than is normally done. You can't get stuck half way and say: We must withdraw religious content from the general view of the world, we must have our own religious certainty and beside it, science may exist. — For then, at most, man's moral-religious view of the world will help him return to the bosom of the blessed Roman Catholic Church to numb himself if he still comes under such an anaesthetic.

In the course of evolution, we have reached the point where we no longer know that the spiritual lives in all-natural laws, that for example what happens within man himself, where there is actually a hearth within him, is accomplished outside in nature. My dear friends, the people from the 19th Century quite correctly were strongly affected by for example what Julius Robert Mayer expressed as a law of conservation of energy and of matter. (Erhaltungssatz der Kraft.) It has really come to the fore that the law of the conservation of power and of matter in the 19th Century dominates our physics today. However, this is valid for outer nature only and there only within certain boundaries which become more limited as time goes by; but in terms of time it doesn't apply to human beings. It is simply true that within man there is a hearth where all material things which he takes into himself, is transformed into nothing, where matter is destroyed, matter is dissolved. By letting our pure thoughts be assimilated by our etheric body and letting these thoughts work on our physical body through the etheric, matter is destroyed in our physical body. (During the next explanation drawings were made on the blackboard. The originals are no longer available.)

I'm sketching diagrammatically, it is intensively spread over the entire human being, I draw it in such a way as if it is only a part. This place in a person where matter becomes destroyed is at the same time the place where matter is created again, when morality, when religious perceptions glows through us. What is created here simply by our perceptions through moral and religious ideals, this is like a seed for future worlds. If the material world perishes, when the material world has been destroyed in the heat death then this earth will be transformed into another world body, and this body of a world will be made from the moral ideals created into material forms. Because our science is not capable of penetrating deeply enough into matter, it is not capable of grasping the thought that matter itself is an abstraction. We may speak about the thermal death of the earth, but at the same time we have to speak of what is cast off from plants, in wilting and drying out, and about the seed surviving into the next year; even as we can speak in relation to the heat death, we can speak about the seed which remains to us and survives the world death.

There is a sphere where scientific truths end; mere scientific truths in the sense of today, where moral ideals end being bubbles of foam, when the earth will expire in the heat death. There is an accessible region for man, where moral ideals are received when physical matter is destroyed, a sphere where the Word becomes a natural scientific truth: "Heaven and Earth will pass away but My words will not pass away!" — There is a sphere where the Bible becomes science; and before this — it needs to be acknowledged in the background of today's aspirations — no healing can occur, before we have the opportunity to advance to a science, not a one-sided science like today, nor one which is a one-sided abstract spiritual science.

Today the term 'spiritual science' is applied only to the science of ideas. For Anthroposophy spiritual science is not only what can be grasped on the other side of materiality, but it is something whose processes penetrate matter.

With results of this research it is then possible, certainly by applying diligent spiritual scientific methods, to consider everything regarding the relationship between the sun and Christ. These things must be considered in the right light. With a certain authority we have during the course of the last three centuries come to see something regarding the stars, sun and moon, which can be calculated. What has brought us misfortune is that we only calculate. We need to once again observe that by looking at the arithmetic of the world's structure, we are in fact investigating a corpse. We need to learn to investigate the spirit of the cosmic whole. Everything depends on this. We won't find the spirit, if we allow matter to violate us in such a way that it presents itself in the universe as something which can only be calculated, or at most be judged according to basic mechanical laws. For this reason, it can already be said that it depends entirely on the individual human being who says: 'For me it is not important that the Christ is the ruler of the sun.' — This sentence must be understood in the correct way: 'For me it is a matter of indifference.'

My dear friends, I've heard a few people say they are indifferent to what the Christ has to do with the sun, but they were not indifferent when their taxes increase by fifty percent.

Yet it is more necessary for the overall salvation of mankind that Christ and the sun are seen to be related than the rising tax of fifty percent is.

How we think in detail about the two Jesus children may be discussed again. However, what would one say to an objection which claims we should practice something that, yes, I don't know what it is, and then the issue about the two Jesus children is put on the table, which leaves us indifferent. I open the Gospel and read a great deal which is presented there, similar to the issue about the two Jesus children mentioned in Anthroposophy. Then again, you don't say: We want religion, but we are quite indifferent whether Jesus was the son of Joseph and Mary or something similar, every single Gospel truth leaves us completely indifferent. — I don't know to what else you don't care about. One doesn't want to enter into something which is of no interest to you, but an objection is not the same, it is definitely not.

Now I would still like to enter into point eight which I've written down for myself, because time is marching on. It is said that a certain progress is expected in people's internalizing; yet through the way culture has been created, people have come to hate culture, they don't want to hear anything more about culture, and now (with Anthroposophy) something arrives which doesn't only speak about internalization, but even what strives to have an effect on architecture and the art of movement.

Yes, my dear friends, if you take life seriously you won't want anything other than what appears in Anthroposophy, what appears to you as spiritual foundations penetrating everything in outer life. I'm still talking about Anthroposophy; we will still touch on what religion has to say about it. That's just the trouble, we are no longer in the position to bring what we experience in the spiritual into our outer life, and finally this happens just in those areas where it is the most noticeable. Just imagine you had said to a Greek that he couldn't express his spiritual experiences in outer life. Just as the Greek thought about his Apollo, as he thought about Zeus, he created his Zeus temple accordingly, his colonnaded temple. We no longer create, we imitate what is old; we don't have the possibility of taking those areas relating to the spirit and also create an external physiognomy of life. The only thing we can create is a department store. The department store is the grandiose creation of the materialistic spirit of the present day. However, if we wanted a home for the spirit and turn to a builder, then he would build it in a romantic, gothic or some or other style, and we would have no feeling, when we stand there within the walls, of anything being expressed of what we had inwardly lived through spiritually.

You see, when the thought was created — not through me but through others — to build a house for Anthroposophy, not for an instant would an idea exist to approach a builder and let him erect a Renaissance or Baroque building and then to move in there, but the idea could come about in the following way. In this building this and that would be spoken about and the forms which would be visible all around should say exactly the same as what is being spoken within it. If this is not only theoretical but life, if the forms are creative, then they are presented — as living — in the world. It is impossible to measure what is created here as a matter of course in comparison with the dishonest cultural activity of the times which has brought us into all this trouble.

This is what I wanted to present primarily, my dear friends. There are too many questions to deal with in one stroke; I will continue with them tomorrow. I've limited myself today by entering into what has been raised against Anthroposophy in general. I will however expand on what in particular will be raised against the service which Anthroposophy will bring towards religious renewal. I would like to stress the following: if somehow an idea develops that it equally represents an existing religious confession, or a creed, which one thinks to justify only through Anthroposophy as its basis, then you do Anthroposophy a wrong because it has never claimed to be a religious education nor is it a religion or wants to establish a religion. This Anthroposophy will not do. Anthroposophy follows impulses to knowledge, goals to knowledge; and whoever says that Anthroposophy is not a religion because it doesn't have the characteristics of religion — say something which Anthroposophy must say about itself from the outset. You can't accuse someone of being something he doesn't even want to be! The objections which are actually made from a religious side, appear to me as if, let's say, someone is active in a field and is accused of not doing what he could in another field.

The objections raised by Dr Rittelmeyer, as far as I have taken into account, certainly involve the relationship people have to Anthroposophy. For this reason, I approached it from this side and will enter into it from the religious side, tomorrow.

FOUNDATION COURSE

ANTHROPOSOPHY AND RELIGION.

Lecture four by Rudolf Steiner given in Dornach, 28 September 1921, morning.

My dear friends! Last night I received a letter from Reverend Dr Schairer in Nagold which contains a number of theses regarding how Anthroposophy can conduct itself regarding religion, and religion conduct itself regarding Anthroposophy, and how a way must be found to initiate this behaviour. Dr Schairer thinks a discussion could be based on this. That also seems to be quite right following on from the first part of the letter — I couldn't read the whole thing, I haven't yet read the last pages — because a lot will be clarified in an exceedingly exact manner. Perhaps this could in some respects provide a good basis for a discussion because it will be a priority in our future work, if I may say so, to bring these fundamental issues in order.

In addition to what I want to say to you today — everything is for the time being still introductory — depends from one side on the main issue of this question, certainly from one specific side. We have to be perfectly clear that Anthroposophy as such must arrive in a positive way at the Mystery of Golgotha so that the manner and way in which this happens regarding this event, can really be ascribed to a concept of knowledge, a knowledge which, if the term is taken seriously, this concept of "knowledge" is also applicable in the modern scientific sense. It is on the other hand right that this special way, first of all — I stress first of all — Anthroposophy needs to get to the Mystery of Golgotha, that at first the Protestant sense of religion from certain foundations need to be brought to consciousness, which can take offence. Only complete clarity about these things can lead to some healing goal.

I must therefore, even if it appears somewhat remote, enter into what I want to say to you today. Anthroposophy or spiritual science actually creates out of supersensible knowledge, and rejects — in principle rejects — anything from older traditions, let's say, the oriental wisdom or historic Gnosticism, through somehow assembling a content, or expanding the content. Anthroposophy quite decisively rejects this because it focuses above all in its comprehensive task of practically answering the question: How much can a person today, who has in his soul, latent, or in ordinary life, not conscious forces in his awareness, how can he now in full consciousness and with full human discretion, recognise the supersensible world instantly? — Spiritual science would like to proceed with this cognition similarly to a mathematician who wants to prove the theory of Pythagoras. He proves it out of something which one can recognise today, and he doesn't reject purely from historical writers what he had encountered before, when he obviously later, in his historic studies, entered into the way the theorem had been found. If you research spiritual science in this way you will certainly conclude that an abyss lies between the way and manner in which current spiritual science arrives at its results through fully conscious research, and what still remains in

Gnosticism or oriental wisdom, which has a more instinctive character on the other hand. Precisely what people want as unmixed knowledge brought to realization, even this, as I've said, needs to be researched. In the course of this research it becomes apparent that something is needed which makes an appearance as if one had reverted back to the old. In the course of research spiritual experiences take place namely for which modern people — the entire modern civilization — the concise words are missing. Our modern language has definitely connected to material thinking patterns; our modern speech has been learnt as linked either to mere outer material or intellectual matters — both these belong together.

Inner intellectualism is nothing other than correlations to the materialistic methods of observation of the external world. What can be recognised about matter is that when one uses the materialistic method, it reflects inwardly as intellectualism. It is like this, that any philosophy which wants to prove its spirit through mere intellect or a spirit comprised from the intellect, will be wafting around in the wind; these would hardly be able to acknowledge that the intellectual is quite rightly spiritual, but that the content of what is intellectual can be nothing other than that of the material world. One must always speak clearly about these things. By expressing a sentence like: "The content of the intellectual can be nothing other than that of the material world," I'm only saying it can be nothing other than *the* content of the world, which can be *viewed* as the sum of material beings and phenomena; whether this is what it *is*, is not yet agreed upon. The intellectual material world could be through and through spiritual and what comprises intellectualism could be an illusion. Therefore, it is important for spiritual scientific discussions there should already be an unusually powerful conscientiousness existing towards knowledge otherwise there will be no progress in spiritual science. This conscientiousness is also noticed by people of the present; they find it necessary to hackle through their sentences in all directions in order to be concise, and people of the present day who are used to the journalistic handling of a style, call this wrestling for conciseness a bad style.

Such things we certainly must understand out of the peculiarities of the time. So, while current materialism and intellectualism have hassled speech/language to such a degree that language only operates in terms of the material, one can hardly find the right words needed to describe one's experiences and then one grasps for the old words which come from instinctive observation, to express that which needs expression. This results in the misunderstanding: people who cling only to words now believe that in the word one borrows what is contained in the translation of the word. This is not the case.

The words "lotus flower" is a borrowed expression from oriental wisdom but what I have indicated (in my book 'Knowledge of the Higher Worlds and its Attainment') is certainly not borrowed from oriental wisdom. This is what I'm asking, for you to always take this into consideration, when on occasion I need through necessity to borrow expressions from history, as I have to do today.

You see, spiritual science first and foremost wants to gain human knowledge through Anthroposophy, modern physiology and biology need to some extent be considered as the most unsuitable instrument for acquiring real human knowledge. Modern physiology and biology unfortunately base their knowledge on what can be seen in man's corpse. Also, when living people are studied, they are unfortunately only studying the corpse. At most they indulge in a certain deception, which extraordinarily characteristically was revealed when Du Bois-Reymond held his famous lecture on the Ignorabimus. He is quite clear that nothing — because he was besides a scientific researcher also a thinker — of this modern manner of research of the soul — he called it consciousness — can be gained; so that one actually through natural science, according to Du Bois-Reymond, can't find out anything about the actual being of man. He is submitting himself to an ever-greater deception; he says that with outer scientific beings we will never be able to recognise conscious people, at most only those who are asleep. When a person lies sleeping in bed, according to Du Bois-Reymond, the sum of all processes is within the person, but at the moment of waking, when the spark of consciousness jumps in, the possibility of observation ends. It would be correct if one was able today, to scientifically understand the life and development of the plant world. The life and development of the plant world is still not comprehensible through science today because the method is not recognised through which this would be understood. So that too, is an illusion, what current science explains about sleeping people; it can only be in their domain to explain sleeping people, the corpse; further than this they don't go. They can only explain those who are sleeping; the ones who are lively they can't explain.

Anthroposophy doesn't follow philosophic speculation about people, but the way which I outline in my book "Knowledge of the Higher Worlds and its Attainment," in the withdrawal of the soul into observation, and then the attainment towards not remaining stuck in the mineral element in man, which is perpetually dead and is incorporated as a dead mineral element in the being of man, but that one gets to, through what could be called the ether body or creative force, observe what the real foundation of the sleeping human being is.

Now people come along out of the current philosophic consciousness; I can refer to one case. When my "Occult Science" was published, there was talk about a Polish Philosopher, Lutoslawski, in an old German monthly publication. In this discussion it was said, among other things, that it is only an abstraction to divide a human being into members of the physical body, the ether body, the astral body and the I, one can certainly as an abstraction divide man into these, but it goes no further. — As far as Lutoslawski at that time regarded it, he was correct in his assertion, but he remained in the field of abstraction, and this depends on the following: As soon as a one moves up to contemplate the ether body one can't remain in the physical body of the human being; as long as one only contemplates the physical body then one doesn't need anything but to investigate within the human skin and at most go as far as to examine the interaction with the outside world through breathing and so on; but nothing further is examined, basically nothing more than by beginning with the boundary of the human skin.

This characteristic I'm offering, you will quite rightly find if you only think about it. One can, if one remains confined in examining the physical body only by what is enclosed by the skin, but one can no longer remain in what is contained by the physical skin when one thoroughly looks at the ether body. Obviously, the basic outlines need to be drawn first, as I have done in my "Occult Science," so attention can be drawn to man's physical body, ether body, astral body and so on. However, Anthroposophy doesn't remain stuck here; Anthroposophy must now expand these things. As soon as knowledge of the ether body is extended one can no longer remain within the human being, but one needs to observe the human being as a single being in connection with everything earthy. One must examine the human being in connection with the earthly. This means as long as the human being is enclosed in his physical body, he leads a relatively independent life, a *relatively* independent life. To a high degree man is dependent on everything possible, air, light and so on, for the physical body; man is dependent on these to a high degree. You can see this in the following example.

When materialism was at the height of its blossoming, Wolff, Büchner and Czolbe very often referred to the dependency of man on the physical environment and one of these writers once listed everything, from gravity, light, the climate and so on and concluded that the human being was the result of every breath of air he breathes. He meant by this — the person concerned was a materialist — the physical organism is dependent on every breath of air. Yes, my dear friends, if one considers the depiction of materialism in this reference in all earnest and contemplate how the human being was as depicted by materialism, then one will become aware that the human being at its highest potency could be a hysteric or a cripple.

The materialists have already described the material human being but not what happens in the world, a being who at its highest potency would be an hysteric. The hysteric at his highest power would be as dependent on his environment as the materialist has described him. — The actual human being in his highest power is independent on what the physical earth environment offers. One can't say this about the etheric man. As soon as one rises to the etheric in man, one can't observe the etheric body as isolated from the entire earth's etheric which needs to be examined, and here man lives in a far higher — naturally not in the physical sense higher — level as his physical body. When one comes to the realm of the etheric while observing the earth, then one can no longer hold on to concepts of chemistry, or mineralogy and so on, but one must now search for completely different conceptions; now one will be confronted with the necessity of wanting to say what one wants to say, at least prove it with expressions which the Greeks had, because it is not possible to do so in today's language.

The (ancient) Greek would, if you demonstrated current chemistry to him, express himself in the following way. Just imagine we have on the one hand a really modern chemist and on the other hand a Greek, an educated ancient Greek, who would like to talk to the chemist, and the modern scientist would say something like the following: 'You Greeks come from far back, you took the four elements of fire, earth, water and air. Those are for us at most, aggregate conditions: fire as all penetrating warmth, air as aeriform, the water as liquid and the earth in a solid physical state. We acknowledge that from you. However, we have placed some seventy elements in place of your four.' If the Greek would study what has been presented as some seventy elements, he would say: 'What we understand under the four elements will not touch many of your seventy elements. We have for what you have in your seventy elements, the collective name of "earth": we call all of that "earth." With our four elements we are referring to something else, we indicate through it how some things express themselves from out of their inner being. What you are pouring out regarding your elements, that is for us aeriform and such further conditions of the earth. Something far more internal than what you acknowledge with your elements, describe for us the expressions of earth, water, fire or heat.'

Exactly to these four elements one is guided when one considers everything surging and weaving which has been spun into the earthy etheric and human etheric. Only when you follow this etheric, which lives in the four elements, as an experience within the circling of the earth's weaving existence, will you understand spring, summer, autumn and winter. In spring, summer, autumn and winter which exist as the foundation of the etheric processes of the earth — not merely as the physical processes of the earth — in this etheric weaving of the earth the human ether body is woven so that one, when one in a sense advances to the etheric body, one must find the etheric body rooted in the earthly-etheric.

What we rediscover again — I have explained this whole relationship in detail in the Hague — sounds like instinctive wisdom of the ancients, which continued right into Greek times. We don't understand the continuity in humanity if we don't, in our way, discover what the content of these instincts were.

Now we will go further and come to the astral body of the human being. The terminology doesn't mean anything to me; the astral body had been spoken about much later, right into the middle ages and even up to present time, but it must have some formulation. When one rises up into the astral body, the actual carrier of thinking, feeling and will in man, then you again come to realise that man cannot be regarded in isolation. Just as one makes the etheric a member of the etheric weaving of the earth, so one needs to make the astral — in quite a spiritual manner — as basically incorporated in what is expressed in the movement and positioning of the stars. The astral in man is simply the expression of the cosmic, the astral relationships; how the stars move and are positioned to one another, this is expressed in the human astral body. Just like the human being through his etheric body is interrelated to the earthly etheric, so man through his astral body is associated through his astral to the earth's surroundings; it lives further in the earthly surrounding, they continue to live in the events, in the processes of his astral body.

You see, it is not an abstraction to structure the human being; we are required to structure the human being because in this structuring we rise from human knowledge to cosmic knowledge, quite naturally. Now we can go back in human evolution to more ancient times which had not actually reached into the Greek times any more. Here we find an instinctive awareness of people's relationship to the starry worlds. Not as if Astronomy was carried on in these ancient times, and if it was, that it could be considered serious, but the connection happened as a direct experience. Human beings experienced themselves in certain times of their earth evolution far less as earthlings than as heavenly beings. In our research we easily reach a time where people, certainly inwardly, lived into the growing and flourishing of the plant world, also in the animal world where everything offered in air and in water were experienced, but as being independent. Similar to how the human being in current times experiences inner processes of nutrition and digestion, processes taking place independently, so the human being once took in all that he experienced in the physical world, as independent, but he didn't take what he lived through in his astral body as independent from the influences of the heavenly worlds. That was something that differentiated itself, imposed itself too strongly upon him, to be taken as independently. When winter shifted closer, when nights lengthened and a person found frost had arrived all around him, he sensed in a certain way how he simply depended on his placement in the world, he felt something within him, like a memory of heaven. During winter he felt himself separated from heaven in a way, he sensed something within him which was like a mere memory of heaven. When by contrast spring approached and the warmth of the earth was interwoven with man, then he felt something dissolve within him as when he shares in the experience, I would call it, of a spreading out breath, the events of the heavens. Now he had heavenly reality, not just a memory of heaven which he had in winter. In this differentiated way he experienced the other seasons also; he actually participated in the seasons.

Today in our inner reflections we have a weak memory of what at that time had been lived through instinctively. We celebrate Christmas and a historic glance reveals to us the connection of the inner memory life of individuals who, during winter, had felt abandoned by heaven, and so nursed their memories in solitude. We still have echoes of experiences, not at one time through astronomical speculation or astronomy, but direct experiences in the determination of the Easter spring celebration according to the relationship of the sun to the moon. What is revealed in our abstract minds and calculations to determine the Easter festival, this was a direct experience for earlier man; it was observed in the heavens after the completion of winter and the time of St John in the soulful feeling of the divine weaving in the heavens, to unite in divine blessedness with the truly Spiritual-Divine which had been only a memory at Christmas time and into which they lived at springtime. The old summer solstice was primarily celebrated as the inner search for the union with the Divine in which man could empathise with how, if the earth would not be enclosed, the earth would be an active being working in the cosmos together with the entire being of humanity towards this cosmic experience.

In other words, what we refer to in spiritual science as an objective experience when we refer to the astral body, this would have been a direct experience for ancient mankind, but such that it didn't only occur in a moment but that it spanned time; from which one knew the stars worked here in their laws, in their movement. Not that man took much notice of sun and moon eclipses; that only happened when religion was transferred to science. In olden times people looked up to the heavens with religious simplicity, but also sensed the heavens within them, for a certain time.

You see, my dear friends, consider what one can think when theology comes forward today and says: What human beings primarily experience through the senses can hardly lead over to the super-sensible; what we have in science, can hardly lead over into the super-sensible; something quite extraordinary must happen in a person if he wants to become accessible to the spiritual worlds. — Such an examination of current theology shows that people are advised to justify religion while life, because we participate in life in the outer world, has no religious character; in a sense it needs to be removed out of ordinary life and placed in a special life in order to feel religious. There once was a time on earth where religious feelings were direct, in the present, and independent, and where one had turned life on earth out of religion. Just as we sense materialistically when we look at the plant world, the animal world and the stars and then need to turn within if we want to have religious experiences, just so once upon a time religious life was the given and if one wanted to turn away from what was given, one would go primarily out from the religious life.

As long as these things are not fully examined, there would be no clarity about the relationship of science, daily life and religious experience. At least once in life one should look at how human evolution is linked to these things, that at one stage in old world imagery there came the appearance of the outer sun, moon and stars which were relatively indifferent, these appearances coming from outside only addressed feeling; but was inwardly experienced. What took place in heaven was an inner experience for man which he could settle with himself, the effect still came from the heavenly realm and that was given to him as a matter of course.

Of course, there was a time where what lived and weaved in the astral body as the result of star activity was to some extent interlinked with an experience that takes place inwardly, in relation to the earth, which we can penetrate recognizably when we move forward to the ether body today. Human beings felt themselves more in the soul-spiritual when, through their astrality, they experienced celestial processes. Then one sees the human being indeed in the earthly, but he wasn't penetrating it as we do today; he penetrated the etheric, into what ruled in fire, water, air and earth. Here he maintains a relationship of which he is deprived according to today's viewpoint and particularly the view of science. Right in the experiences the human being has in these relationships, refer back to the ritual acts which of course for our confessions are actually only inherited traditions.

Yesterday I introduced you to how the Ritual Acts can be grasped out of human understanding. It can also be understood through insight into every interplay between possible experiences through the astral body and those through the etheric body; they go back to the sense which one can have when one follows the celestial vitality and weaving in the earthly etheric. What is revealed as a result is that man is placed in a cosmic process, in a cosmic movement which I can express in the following way. You see, when we turn to the tone which rings out of words, when we thus approach them, for example in the Greek Logos, what lies in the words of the Logos — this what I'm saying right now was certainly still experienced in (ancient) Greece and certainly felt in the composing of the St John's Gospel — when one approaches what lives as tone, what rings out as tone and then turn it to the outside, then one is involved in processes which are about to happen, which are revealed in the air. When we hear a tone or the words and the process is created which I indicated yesterday as it entering into the human being, then we are considering the movement of air being breathed in, which then hits the spinal cord and the brain fluid and continues as a movement; we also have this continuation in the air penetrating into the human being here. When we do further research, we don't only have to deal with this, but, because words manifest an effect in the human being, it acts on the human being's state of warmth. The human being becomes inwardly imbued with warmth, he contains the element of warmth differentiated by the sound entering him, of the word entering inward. This means on the outside warmth or cold is at most a by-product of sound, when the tone is too high or too low; remaining with one tone has no meaning. In the human being actually every differentiation in the word and in the tone is differentiated within, through engendering warmth or cooling, so that we can now say: In our understanding of the *Word*, we find it manifests outwardly in air and we find it manifest inwardly in warmth.

If we now go from what we learnt yesterday, we now approach the Sacrificial Act. These things, like many others, we later will clarify more, but this will be able to give you an indication. In olden times the actual characteristic could be found in the Sacrificial Act, of people experiencing the Sacrificial Act as a total reality. Actually for the more ancient presentation, the Sacrificial Act obviously connected to the smoke-like, to the airy; it was because, while the Sacrificial Act flows from within the human beings people knew — as one can also today really experience this in a Sacrificial Act — that just in this way, how the word sounds inwardly and lives itself out in warmth, the Sacrificial Act realises itself in air. Inwardly it lives itself out in the air. Towards the outside the true Sacrificial Act can't manifest without it somehow or other appearing through light. However, we will speak about these things again later.

When we now go to what we called the Transformation yesterday, we find that with the Transformation we refer to something which already penetrates matter, which already strongly approaches substantiality, but which has not yet been configured, which has not yet taken in an outline; this is experienced in the transformation as characteristic and one refers, in the same sense, to how the Word refers to the warmth, the Offering to the air, the Transformation, the transubstantiation to the water.

What is experienced as living in Communion, in the union, is felt now as through the connection with the etheric and its connection with the earth; one experiences oneself as an earthling, as a true earthling only because one feels so connected to the earthly, that one feels this union as related to the earth.

In the Old Mysteries this was the result: they had seen how the Word outwardly manifested in the air, and inwardly as warmth. (*This was written on the blackboard.*)

Word — Air — Warmth
Offering/Sacrifice (*Opfer*) — Water — Air
Transformation — Earth — Water
Union — earth

ANTHROPOSOPHY AND RELIGION

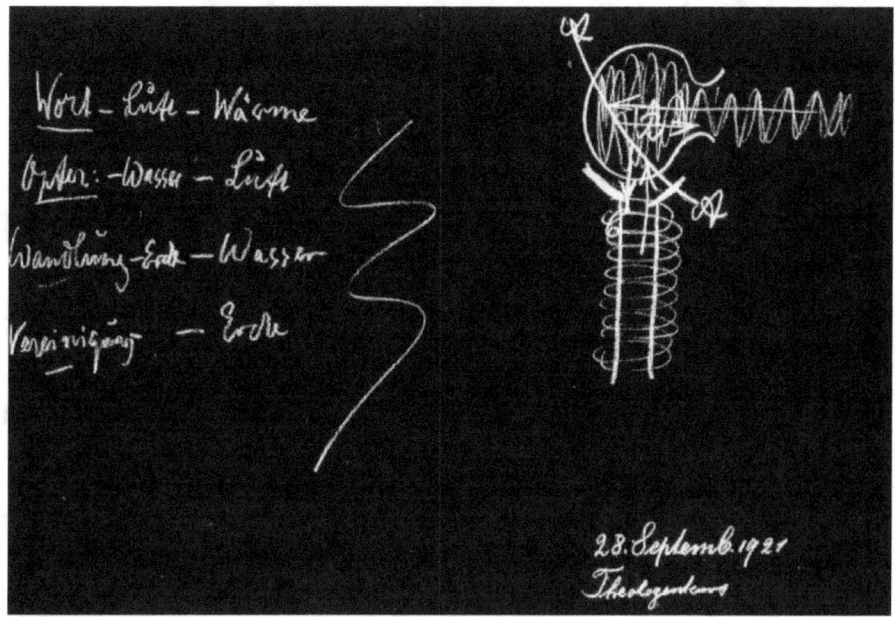

Plate 2   4th Lecture   28. September 1921, in the morning

The Offering manifests itself inwardly, as we've seen, as air. When you come to examine the following things, you could later say: I'm taking notice of these things so that I can say that what referred to water in the Sacrificial Mass of the old Mysteries, has now been retained as a residue in the Baptism. How the spoken word referred outwardly to the air and inwardly to warmth, so the Transformation could accordingly refer to the earth, to what is firm, and only inwardly to water; and what had corresponded to unification, one had nothing. In the human being, one could say to oneself, the connection with the elements shifts. However, already in the Transformation to the extra-terrestrial, the earth is available, which man experiences by turning to be united with it. How can he then experience being united with the earthly? — This was the great question of the Old Mysteries. How can one somehow feel anything at all about the truly earthly?

85

I've even spoke about it from another point of view. One looks around and it becomes obvious that people take their inner processes for granted, but they don't find anything which they want to take up into their consciousness. Symbolic action took on unification, but on the outside the place remained empty, something was necessary, so people said to themselves, for this place to be filled, if one wanted to turn to something within the earthly element itself it could correspond to the uniting taking place in communion. People felt they could look down on the earth. What presented itself within the earth, this could be fulfilled in the communion, but something outwardly was not possible. This is how people basically felt in the Old Mysteries, when they spoke of communion. They spoke about it this way, but they felt it could not be a concluded event. We basically feel this way when are instructed according to the outer statements of the Old Mysteries, how in images the event of Golgotha was foreseen, how it was symbolically carried out, which current research always refer to when they want to show that the Mystery of Golgotha was only something which can be compared to later developments when various sacrificial acts took place in temples, by presenting a sensory image of the representative of man having died, buried and resurrected three days later.

You know how the real crux of the Christ conception resulted from people noticing some similarities between the symbolic religious practices and the event of Golgotha, that they believed, even theologians believed they must speak about Christ as a myth or as something which had developed and reached fulfilment in the temples. The whole thing has now reached a point where this same way of thinking is appearing in other areas: the Our Father prayer has been examined in the same way and now nearly every sentence can be shown to have existed in pre-Christian times. This is regarded as a special catch for religious research. For someone who admits, truly admits to this way of closed thinking, it would be the same as to draw conclusions about people from their clothes. When a father allows his child to inherit his clothes, one can't say the son has become the father, because the son is someone quite different from the father even when he wears the same clothing. Just so the *wording* of the Our Father has passed over on to Christianity, but the *content* has essentially become something new. In order to examine these things, one must first look even deeper into all the connections: one needs to know the foundations from which the Old Mystery priests retained something like an expectation, which resembled something which could not yet have been accomplished on earth.

So there we will, I'd like to say, be led, in the first element, even through quite careful considerations, to a mood of expectation in the Old Mysteries, certainly out of an instinctive science which was completely permeated by religion, how in all Old Mysteries a Christ-expectation mood was there, and then it was fulfilled though the Mystery of Golgotha.

Tomorrow we will look at the entire problem from another side, when we will enter into it more profoundly. However, you see how Anthroposophy approaches the Christ-problem in what could be called a certain scientific manner, by making a lively observation of the ether and astral bodes and also what results from their cooperation. You see, by discovering, so to speak the Christ-experience in the boundary between the astral and etheric bodies, you must arrive in a positive way to the Christ-experience. I must say to you, my dear friends, this is largely the biggest difficulty of Anthroposophy and its task in the present. You see, the somewhat washed out Theosophy which you find for instance in the Theosophical Society, finds this reference far easier. It doesn't enter into the Christ-experience but stops just before it. Therefore, it's easier. To some extent they laid down all religions as equally valid and seek within it the common human element which of course every science must be based on.

Anthroposophy is determined in its own evolution, through the nerve of its entire being, to approach the Mystery of Golgotha in a positive way, and because it wants to remain scientific, to make the task of the events of Golgotha clear to humanity, as clearly as mathematics states the theory of Pythagoras. All religious confessions are in line with this rejection of the event of Golgotha as such. As a result, the world task of Anthroposophy necessary for our time is not easy. How difficult it is, I ask you to read the in words of a poet from Prague, Max Brod, who writes — he has also written some other things — in "Paganism, Christianity, Judaism" about how these things need to be handled; how out of the re-enlivened Jewish consciousness everything that makes Jesus into Christ must be removed, and only to keep Jesus as what does not make him into Christ. What is at the foundation of this tendency? It is the tendency to make it possible for modern Jews to have a relationship with Jesus, in which Jesus can be admitted but in which it is not necessary to see Him as the bearer of the Christ.

Anthroposophy is compelled — and we will still talk about this a great deal — to recognise Jesus as Christ. For Jesus to be taken as valid is what the Jews also strive, as well as the Indians;

the entire East is striving for this, but they only strive to accept Him as he is, and not for being Christ.

Now my dear friends, Harnack's book about the Essentials of Christianity and the Weinel's research about Jesus you can take all in a way in which they could be accepted by all non-Christians to a certain degree. I know there can be some objections, so for this reason I say you could take it in this way — of course they are not like this. However, what we have as a task is this: To fully understand Christianity — not to keep Jesus at the expense of the fact that He is the bearer of the Christ.

Here lies the complete other side of a basis for the true, earnest Christianity through Anthroposophy, because one has to admit, that a communal world task has to be dealt with which encounters the most frightening prejudices. This world task is connected to what we today experience as dissatisfactory in religious experiences. For this reason, this can't be understood in the narrowest sense, but one must allow oneself to enter into what penetrates our religious life as unsatisfactory and look at this from a higher perspective. We will speak further about this tomorrow.

CONCEPTUAL KNOWLEDGE AND OBSERVATIONAL KNOWLEDGE.

Lecture four by Rudolf Steiner given in Dornach, 28 September 1921; afternoon.

At the start of the hour, various participatory questions and objections were presented. The stenographer didn't add to these words, but Rudolf Steiner had jotted down the following key words in one of his notebooks (See the fax page 38-40 NB 127 in the documentary supplements):

Discussion –

?can we define religion?

Impossibilities –

Luther as an answer –

- Do without knowledge to reach religion! –
- Spine of the world – and turn to the divine –
- Gulf – world = God
    ?- another: Contrast between God and World isn't found
    Rel. Connection with God – 3 ways

	Thinking Feeling Willing
Anthrop	due to transformation of world through science
unclear:	or not making religion dependent on knowledge- so that people who have no knowledge, come short –

FOUNDATION COURSE

Good faith =

Dr Geyer:	It is said: Paradox
	Anthrop in the world
	Religion belongs to God
Another:	Can religion become independent?
	or Art – science?
	will religion stop being independent
Another:	if it repulses someone
	faith – endangered
	Secret – deepest being. Despite all unravelable difficulties on hand ... submit/go through to* the soul-like
and another:	religion – relation between one soul and God – but the effects change towards others – this is increased by Anthroposophy
and another:	? leads us to God today?
and another:	Is a value judgement of Anthrop to religion both *necessary*?
	(Ist ein Wertunterschied z. A. u. Rel. beide *nötig?)*
and another:	Living relationship to concepts – are concepts in contrast with corrupted form -
Main concept	*Pledge faith*
	Faith has knowledge content -

>   gradually got lost
>   awareness, which gives knowledge content -
>   the results of today -

(*- words are abbreviated which can create various interpretations- Translator)

To what extent does the Pauline contrast with the Pistis and Gnosis. -

Rudolf Steiner: I would prefer at best to answer you more concretely than in abstractions. First, I would like to approach a difficult question by saying the following.

In Anthroposophy we currently have very few people who are engaged in spiritual activity. Anthroposophy is in the beginning of her work and one can admit that in a relatively short time it may work differently into the human soul, compared with today. One thing is quite remarkable today, and perhaps you'll find that reprehensible, but it is perhaps much better to side with what appears currently than to express it with an abstract reprimand.

Anthroposophy is taught, recited, written in books and I have the basic conviction that the way those questioners here, at least some of them, require Anthroposophy to be a knowledge — and that such a knowledge which is understood by most, at least a good many, for the majority who interest themselves intensively in Anthroposophy, this is not yet the case. Many people today accept something which they have heard about in Anthroposophy, on good faith. Why do they do this? Why are there already such a large number of people who accept Anthroposophy on good faith? You see, among those the majority have acquired religious natures in a specified direction and without them actually claiming to understand things in depth, they follow Anthroposophy because they have become aware of a certain religious style throughout the leadership of Anthroposophical matters. It is just a kind of religious feeling, a religious experience, which brings numerous people to Anthroposophy, who are not in the position of examining Anthroposophy, like botanists who examine botany; this is what is promoted here.

One doesn't usually intensely observe that in relation to what I mean here, Anthroposophy is quite different to the other, the outer, more scientific sciences. Scientific knowledge is in fact quite so that one can say about it: take the human being into consideration and it will in fact be quite dangerous for faith, you'll impair faith. It is not just about science making you uncomfortable, but it is about having the experience of the mystery of faith being disturbed. In the practical handling of this question one finds, as far as it goes beyond where it is another kind of science, as is the case with Anthroposophy, that numerous people experience a consistent religious stance in the way Anthroposophy is presented. Despite it not wanting, as I often repeat, to be a religious education, it is nevertheless felt that it is moving in the direction where a religious feeling can go along with it. Actually, this idea that knowledge kills faith — I have much understanding for this — must be revised regarding Anthroposophy. One must first ask if it is not because Anthroposophy is a not conceptual knowledge, but a knowledge based on observation, that the relationship between faith and knowledge becomes something quite different. Let us not forget that this observation of knowledge killing faith has only been created on the hand of a science which is completely conceptual, completely intellectual. Intellectualism is for Anthroposophy only a starting point, it is only regarded as the basis and foundation, then one rises to observation quite indifferently whether it is one's own or a shared observation.

My view is that it is not necessary at all, to place a wall in front of Anthroposophy, that things should be accepted in good faith. This is not quite so. A certain shyness remains today, to shine a very thorough light into what is said by single anthroposophical researchers. When this shyness is overcome then one doesn't need some of other perception or clairvoyance. Just like one can take a dream as an error or a truth, even if one only experiences the dream for what it is, which is a perception; in the same way one can recognise the truth or error in a painted image. Basically, it's the same for life. This is not easily understood — those involved with spiritual research know. One gets much more out of life when one looks at things yourself rather than being told about them, because observation of life demands a great deal. Yet, these things need to be researched so they can enter into life.

Now, something like the viewpoints of conceptual knowledge which we are already familiar with, is what I noticed in the inquiries of our questioners, whose first point was: How can we define religion? One could — this is how it can be said in the course of the discussion — renounce knowledge, leave the world lying on its back and turn to the Divine because there is an abyss between the world and God, and so on. This is said about it.

Now if you are familiar with my arguments you will have found that I do not give definitions anywhere; in fact, I am sharply against giving definitions in Anthroposophy.

Sometimes, since I speak about popular things, I conceptualise them. Even though I know quite well that definitions can certainly be a help in the more scientific or historic sense of today's kind of knowledge, even though I'm aware of the limited right of definitions, I remind myself how, within Greek philosophy, defining a human being was recommended. The definition is such that a human being is alive, that it has two legs and no feathers. So the next day someone brought along a plucked chicken and said, this is a human being. — You see how far a person is from the immediate observation, even with practical definitions. These things need to be examined.

That is the peculiarity of intellectualistic knowledge, and in it, is to be found many such things which have led to the judgement which sharpens the boundary between belief and knowledge even more. One needs to enter into the intricacies a bit more. You see, already in our simplest sciences are definitions which actually have no authority at all. Open some or other book on physics. You find a definition like the following: What is impenetrability? Impenetrability is the property of objects, that in the place where an object is present, another body cannot be at the same time. — That is the definition of impenetrability. In the entire scope of knowledge and cognition, however, not everything can be defined in this way; the definition of impenetrability is merely a masked postulate. In reality it must be said: One calls an object impenetrable when the place where it is in, can't at the same time be occupied by another object. — It is namely merely to determine an object, to postulate its individual character; and only under the influence of materialistic thinking, postulates masked as definitions are given.

CONCEPTUAL KNOWLEDGE AND OBSERVATIONAL KNOWLEDGE

All of this creates an entire sea of difficulties which current mankind is not aware of at all because people have really been absorbing it from the lowest grade of elementary school; mankind really doesn't know on what fragile ground, on what slippery ice he gets involved with, in reality, when educated through the current system of concepts. This conceptual system which is in fact more corrupt than theological concepts — a physicist often has no inkling that their concepts are corrupt — this is something which not only kills belief, but in many ways, it also kills what relates to life. These corrupt scientific concepts are not only damaging to the soul, but even harmful to physical life. If you are a teacher, you know this.

Therefore, it is no longer important that the spiritual scientist, the Anthroposophist has to say: Precisely this scientific concept must be transformed into the healing of mankind. — Here is where the Anthroposophist becomes misled, when the religious side insists that an abyss be created under all circumstances between belief and knowledge, because, between what one observes with the senses, and Anthroposophy, there is really a great abyss. This is what even from the anthroposophical side needs to be clarified.

Now I would like to consider this question from the religious side and perhaps as a result of me approaching it from the religious side, it will be better understood religiously. You see I can completely understand that the following may be said — that one must turn away from the world to find the way to God. The basic experience that exists, the paths that will have to be taken, those I know. I can also certainly understand when someone talks about how it would be necessary, in a certain sense, that the dew of mystery should cover anything with religious content. I would like to express myself succinctly only; it has already surfaced in the questions. Briefly, I can fully understand if someone strives in a certain way to place everything that can be known on the one side and on the other side, look for a religious path according to such fundamentals as are searched for by a whole row of modern evangelists. This search should take place not through events but in a far more direct way. In the elaboration of Dr Schairer, it was again correctly described: also in the questioning of Bruno Meyer which was given to me yesterday, it is expressed clearly. So, I can understand it well. But I see something else.

You see, what people take from Anthroposophy, quite indifferently now, how far their research comes or in how far they have insight — and as we said, it can be seen without being a researcher or an observer through what you get from Anthroposophy — means they must relinquish quite a few things from their "I," I mean from their egotism. In a certain sense selflessness belongs to this point of departure from one's self, when entering the world. One could say a person needs to radically tear out inborn egoism in order to really find a human relationship to the simplest Anthroposophical knowledge. A feeling for the world as opposed to an ego feeling for oneself must be developed to a high degree, and gradually grow just by following this apparent path of knowledge, which is not only similar to fervent love but equal to it; everything grows from here. Basically, one learns about true submission to objectivity by following anthroposophic content.

In opposition to this, I propose something else. One can relinquish all such involvement in the world, all such conceptual submission of oneself and then try, out of oneself, I don't want to call it "in feelings" but for instance how Dr Schairer expressed it, through "connecting to God" make one's way. One can try to stretch the entire sum of inner life, one could call it, electrically, to find what the direct communication with God is. Also there, I must say, I know what can be achieved by that strong relationship of trust in God, without entering into some kind of unclear mysticism, up to certain mystics who have remained with clear experiences. I've seen it before. Yet I find despite everything that is attempted in devotion to the world, in connecting to the world, in connecting to divine world forces and so on, a large part of egoism, even soul-filled egoism, remains. Someone can be extraordinarily religious out of the most terrible egoism. Prove it for yourself by looking with the eyes of a good psychologist at the religiosity of some monks or nuns. Certainly, you could say, that is not evangelistic belief. It may differ qualitatively, but in relation to what I mean now, it still differs qualitatively. If you prove this, you perhaps find the performing of a devotion to the utmost mortification, yet it sometimes harbours — the true observation of psychologists reveals this — the most terrible egoism. This is something questionable which can give up even a superficial view of an important problem. You see, to find an exchange with God in this way is basically nothing extraordinary because God is there and whoever looks for Him, will find Him. He will obviously be found. Only those who don't find Him are not looking for Him. One can find him, sure, but in many cases, one asks oneself what it is one has found. I may say out of my own experience: What *is* it?

In many cases it is the discovery the forces of the inner life, which only exists between birth and death. One is able to, with these forces which exist between birth and death, to be a very pious person. However, these forces are laid down with us in our graves, we have no possibility of taking these forces with us through the gate of death. Should we acquire thoughts of eternity, acquire thoughts of the supersensible, these we will take with us through the gate of death and while we do so, we must already have become selfless, as I have indicated. You see, this is something which is always questionable to me, when I discover it — what I can quite rightly understand — like Schleiermacher's philosophy of religion. Licentiate Bock has recently told me that with Schleiermacher one could discover something quite different. It would be lovely if something could happen, but according to the usual way Schleiermacher is interpreted, I find in the Schleiermacher way the reference and exchange with the Divine as only created through the forces which are lost when we die. What is this then, that is lost though death, my dear friends? Even if it's religious, if it is lost with death it is nothing more than a refined lust of the soul, an intensification of temporal life. One feels oneself better for it, when one feels secure with God.

You see, I want to speak religiously about the necessity to achieve a concept of belief which lives within the danger of connecting temporal forces to people. This of course has a relationship to the Divine. Here something terrible always appears to me in the great illusion within the numerous people's current lives which consist of people being unable to see how the rejection of a certain content, which must always have a content of knowledge — you could call this observational content, but finally this is only terminology — how the judgement of such content severely endangers religious life. Old religions didn't exist without content and their content of Christian teaching was once full of life, and it only turned into what we call dogma today, at the end of the fourth century after Christ. So one could say this distaste for content, this selfish fear of so-called wisdom

CONCEPTUAL KNOWLEDGE AND OBSERVATIONAL KNOWLEDGE

— I'm fully aware of calling it "so-called wisdom" — that, my dear friends, always reminds me of people living in this illusion, that this fear of knowledge of the supersensible actually is also produced by materialism. Within this concept of faith, I see a materialistic following, I can't help myself; this following of materialism is no conscious following but something which exists in subconscious foundations of the soul as a materialistic following.

I really believe that it will be through religious foundations, particularly for the priest, if he could bring himself to it, to overcome the shyness of the so-called gulf between belief and knowledge. The world and God, and the gulf between them — yes my dear friends, this is indeed the deepest conviction of Anthroposophy itself; what Anthroposophy seeks, is to create a bridge between the two. When this gulf has been bridged, then only will the higher unity of God and world be possible. At first, from the outside, this abyss appears, and only when man has gone through everything which makes this bridging necessary, can the abyss be overcome, and only then does man discover what can be called the unity of God with the world.

Let's consider the religious connection with God. Would a religion — this question was asked in three ways and called thinking feeling and willing — would a religion still be approachable through Anthroposophy, which is dependent on knowledge, to people who do not have knowledge, or will they get a raw deal? — Anthroposophy certainly doesn't make religiousness dependent on knowledge. I must confess in the deepest religious sense I actually can't understand why a dependent religious life should exists beside Anthroposophy because the course of an anthroposophic life becomes such that firstly, of course, single personalities become researchers, who to some extend break through to the observation; then others will apply their healthy human minds to it — yes, this is what it is about. Just recently in Berlin this word was taken as evil from a philosophic view, and opposed on the grounds of the human mind being unable to understand anything super-sensory, and that the human mind which is able to understand something super-sensory, would surely not be healthy. —

A healthy human mind can simply look through the communications of spiritual researchers when he only wants to, if he doesn't put a spoke in his own wheel because of today's scattered prejudices. Certainly, there will be numerous other people who take it on good faith. Now, we can't compare something small with something big, but if this is only about using comparisons, one could perhaps do it. You see, I assume that the Being, Who we call the Christ, possesses an immeasurable higher content within, than human beings who call themselves Christians, and you have but trust in Him. Why should that be unjustified? That knowledge appears through this, knowledge which is not immediately clear, but which arrives in an earnest manner, that is to say as it comes out of personal research, clarifies what is discovered with no need to somehow try to understand why that would let people be given a raw deal. In this I actually find something which ultimately amounts to the fact that one can't acknowledge anything which one has not discovered oneself.

We won't get far in life at all if we are not also presented with something through other means than only direct observation. You see, it is obvious for a spiritual researcher to say: You, living in the present, haven't seen the deeds of Alexander the Great, but there is a connection between the life at present and the regarded-as-truth unseen deeds of Alexander the Great. Here a theologian objected: Yes, Alexander the Great don't interest me any longer, but that which is claimed in Anthroposophy I must see for myself, otherwise it doesn't interest me. — One can't say that everything of interest must always come from something observed. Just imagine if someone could only believe in his father and mother after he has looked at the truth of his belief in them. So, as I've said, I can't quite grasp something by applying precise terms to what is really meant; I would like to rather say, that I find a certain contradiction between, on the one hand, it is said that Anthroposophy wants to be wisdom and therefore appears dubious, and on the other hand, one could accept it, if you knew about things. This doesn't seem like quite a good match.

A particularly important question to me is the following. Perhaps its difficulty has resulted from what I've said myself: A person experiences through the anthroposophic life at the same time something which can meet the religious need. The next question then comes: When art assumes religious form, when science and social life take on religious form, will religion stop being independent and gradually only become something which exists with everything else in the world? — Well, that seems to me or at least seemed to me to be a complete misjudgement of the religious when it is indicated that art will develop in future in such a way, in the anthroposophic sense, and that it will develop social life in such a way according to the anthroposophic sense, that religion as something independent will vanish. Religion has indeed other living conditions, quite other needs than Anthroposophy.

It was so that the old religious foundations always had wisdom in the background. One can say there is no old religion which doesn't have wisdom in its background, and because knowledge existed there, it is not involved in religion. Religion is only created through the relationship of man to what is known. When so much anthroposophic art produced in future is not looked at with a religious mood, it will never make a religious impression. One would never be able to cultivate religion, no matter how hard one tried, in order to say about the social life what can be said out of spiritual science, out of Anthroposophy, when in reality people don't experience in all earnest the meaning of the words: "What you do to the least of my brothers, you also do to me." — The most beautiful anthroposophical impulses could never become a reality in life, if so much should be done, it would remain an empty science if religious life wasn't cultivated.

However, something has to be taken into account. In Shairer's defences there are three images: The first image is that man can approach water in a dual manner, either as a chemist and analyst in H2O, or one can drink water. The supersensible world analyses a person whether he comes as an Anthroposophist, or when he takes possession of a direct experience, then he is a religious person. The religious person equals someone who drinks the water, the Anthroposophist is someone who analyses water and finds H_2O. Dr Shairer's second image is the following: Let's assume I've deposited a large amount of bank notes or gold on the table and I count, divide it and so on, so I calculate the money; but I may also possess this money, that is another relationship. The person who calculates the money is an Anthroposophist; the one who possesses it all, is a religious person. Shairer's third image is particularly characteristic. A person could have studied every possibility of human health and illness; he could know every branch of medicine. The other person can be healthy. So the one who is healthy, is the religious person, and the one who studies everything about illness and health, is the Anthroposophist.

The three examples are, considered abstractly, are extraordinarily accurate but still, only thought about abstractly. They are actually only valid for today's common knowledge. You see, with the water analysis, something can be done. For someone who doesn't study Anthroposophy, it is useless. Because one has to, if one wants to approach it, begin by "drinking" it. Water in Anthroposophy is not there for mere outer analysis; it must be drunk at the same time. The activity of drinking and the activity of the analysing or synthesizing are the same. That one believes something else about it, results from the fact that recently an otherwise excellent man has written in "Tat" that he would have no interest in my statements regarding the Akasha-Chronicle unless I honour him with them in a splendid illustrated edition. — Yes, my dear friends, to use such an image at all, one must acknowledge that the Akasha-Chronicle can only exist for those who allow themselves to experience it spiritually. It can't be allowed to be compared in this way. Already upon this basis I'm quite sure that the modern bad habit of the cinema will not be applied to Anthroposophy — hopefully not.

Therefore, the comparison between drinking water and water analysis is relevant for ordinary science but has no relevance to Anthroposophy. The second image was about counting money and possessing money. This also is not quite so; it is tempting, but it doesn't work this way. I can namely possess money but when I'm too foolish to be unable to count it, then its possession doesn't matter much. Under some circumstances I could possess the whole world but if I can't enter into it, then under the circumstances the world can mean very little.

Now; the thing about medicine. Materialistic medicine can certainly be studied on the one hand while on the other hand one could be healthy. One could certainly, if it's your destiny, be sick despite anthroposophical medicine. However, the comparison on this basis is not entirely true for the reason that materialistic medicine, what one knows about it, actually has nothing to do with being healthy in earthly life, but it is a knowledge and from this knowledge action can result. With Anthroposophy it is namely so, that anthroposophical medicine has to certainly also be a deducted knowledge, but the human being is approached much more closely. Here is something which can be proven with great difficulty, and it is because of the following. Take for example, this is necessary, someone aged forty and recommend, for a start, that he should stop smoking and drinking wine or something, and say to him, it would in fact improve his health, he would live longer than he would otherwise. Now he dies aged 48; and people say he already died at 48, it didn't help him. — I can't prove that if he hadn't avoided wine, he could perhaps have died at 44 already. When one encounters such things, there are small stumbling blocks. It is extraordinarily difficult to deliver proof when that which is to be accomplished, must be created as proof out of the world.

People certainly sometimes think curiously about things. I knew an anatomist, Hyrtl, who was an extraordinary big man who equally had a stimulating influence on his students and had a long life after he retired. He became over 80 years old then he died in a small place into which he had withdrawn. Just after Hyrtl's death, a widow who was a farmer encountered a man and she said to him: "Yes, now Hyrtl has died, we liked him so much, but he studied so much, and that's why he had to die; it doesn't bode well if one studies so much." — To this the man asked: "But you husband, how old was he when he died?" She said: "45 years." — Now the man asked if her husband has studied more than old Hyrtl? — You see, similar things actually happen on closer examination.

Now I don't want to deviate from serious things and would like to say the following. For Anthroposophists it is not important that there should be a distinction between drinking water and water analysis, but there is in fact something where in place of abstract knowledge, of discursive knowledge, an experience occurs within the knowledge of analysis; yet it remains above all knowledge. Only the Leese licentiate has resented calling an experience knowledge while he claimed — not out of a Christian but out of another scientific dogma — he may never take what he has experienced as an object of knowledge. Well, I mean, the thing is, if you really understand what Anthroposophy is as a human experience, this alien-to-life of the scientific no longer applies.

In relation to the secret, the Mystery, I may here insert what I said yesterday. I said it is not so that Anthroposophic knowledge can be obtained and then through thoughts, change into ordinary knowledge. In order to have the correct relationship to it, one must repeatedly return to it. It exists in quite another kind of inner relationship to people than does scientific knowledge. There still exists something of a sacred shyness in the relationship people have to anthroposophical knowledge and it is certainly not the case that clarity is thus undermined according to what is attained through Anthroposophy. You see, basically it's like this: when we go through the Portal of Death and before we enter the Portal of Birth into this earthly world, we live in that world which Anthroposophy speaks about. That is in fact the reality. Through Anthroposophy we take part in the riddle of creation and in the riddle of death, to a certain degree. That one doesn't understand these things in the same way in which one understands ordinary intellectual knowledge, something else must make this possible. You are not going to be guided into such a world as some people suppose. I have heard among thousands of objections, also heard that it is said Anthroposophy wants to solve all world riddles, and when the time comes where there are no more riddles in the world, what will people do with this knowledge? Then the earth will not be interesting anymore; everything which one can know about the earth, exists in them being riddles. —

Certainly, in an abstract sense, this can be an objection. However, even understood abstractly, the riddles do not become smaller, but they become ever bigger. Life has not been made easier by entering into the spiritual world, but at first the immeasurability of the world and the immeasurability of knowledge becomes apparent. That is why, in the case of the Mystery there is no reduction or degradation of the Mystery, but there is actually an elevation of the Mystery. This at least is apparent in experience.

Regarding the question whether there's a difference in value between Anthroposophy and religion or if both are necessary, I would like to say the following. Value differences lead into a subjective area and one has no sure foundations if one wants to assert differences in value. In any case you may from the scant anthroposophic explanations which I've given today and before, actually say that Anthroposophy and religion are both necessary in the future and that Anthroposophy is only necessary for the foundation of the work, which you need towards the renewal of religious life. Anthroposophy itself doesn't want to appear as endowed with religion but it wants to offer every possible help when religious life wants to find renewal.

Now my dear friends, I could, as I see, not answer everything exhaustively, I still want to put some things on hold. I have certainly had feelings through experiences with which I now want to give an answer to the question, which perhaps has not already appeared in the question, for instance this: I also have my religious objections to the faith which serves only those human forces which actually die with us, and that one — according to my experience I can say this — also through religious instruction, say something in a sense of: avoid the world and develop something completely different — and precisely in this way, strongly refer to man's egoism.

I have experienced the following phenomenon. For example, a good Anthroposophist who tried to work with all his might in order to find a path in Anthroposophy, but without a necessary measure of selflessness and without enough self-confidence, when courage failed him, became a Roman monk. I'm not speaking hypothetically but from experience. Yes, this person has experienced nothing other than having failed due to a lack of selflessness which he would have needed and the lack of confidence which he would have needed. This is the strongest appeal to those forces which dissipate with death; it doesn't serve these forces to go through the gate of death with the soul, to penetrate to reality. People just want to go down to where they don't have to be so strong, so there arises a sinking courage, this attach-oneself-on-to-something which through its submission into activity brings a certain inner satisfaction — which is only a kind of inner desire or lust — to become a Roman monk.

It is indeed from a religious basis needed to say that the priest should give a person something which doesn't only work for his communications with God up to death, but beyond death. In this connection Anthroposophy must be honest throughout with its knowledge. If one could know more — which is possible — about what goes beyond the gate of death and what doesn't remain, where for instance one has a mystic like saint Theresa, with an involvement only with the transient, so one could, even if you weren't a mystic, prepare yourself for life after death, where one enters atrophied for being a mystic with desires in life. One does enter, but in such a way of course as one would enter into life without hands or feet.

Through Anthroposophical knowledge a religious impulse can be discovered. To all of this the shyness must be overcome to unite belief and knowledge, which is what Anthroposophy strives for.

CREATIVE SPEECH AND LANGUAGE.

Lecture six by Rudolf Steiner given in Dornach, 29 September 1921, morning.

My dear friends! Up to now I've been introducing my lectures by indicating what the Anthroposophic path is like, implementing my lectures out of Anthroposophy in order to lead towards the initiation of the renewal of religious life, out of the wishes present in the souls of contemporaries.

Naturally first of all it is necessary to look more closely at what would be needed for the actual renewal of religious life. I would like to, in order to bring this into a clearer light, still today refer to the relationship, not of religion to Anthroposophy but the reverse, that of Anthroposophy to religion; but I have to say in advance, my dear friends, it is necessary, if we want to understand one another here, for a clear awareness of the seriousness of the relevant question in relation to its meaning in world history. If someone in a small circle sees some or other deficiency, finds this or that imperfection and is not able to perceive its relationship in our world's entire evolution, they will not quite rightly develop in their heart, or have a sense to develop, what is actually needed at present.

We live in a time where humanity has been deeply shaken and with all the means at its disposal to do something, with all these means humanity has actually failed to move forward. As a result I particularly want to be clear that I believe, even if it perhaps doesn't appear as pertinently — let me quite sincerely and honestly express my opinion on this matter — that I believe the rift between those who have lived for a longer time in pastoral work and those younger ones who stand before this need today, and only enter it today, is far greater. Even though it might not yet be felt so strongly, yet it is still there, and it will appear ever more clearly; I believe that for many the question between older and younger people, if I might express it this way, is to experience its formulation very differently. It seems to me that for the younger ones the formulation as we saw it yesterday, appears no longer to carry the same weight; it has already been dismissed. Let's be quite honest with ourselves, and clear, that there is a difference whether we can, in a sense defend a cause in which we are, or whether it takes strength to get into it. We don't want to have any illusions about that. Of course, when one is older one could say one has the same earnest interest as a youngster. — Yet, we need to take into account all possible subconscious impulses, and for this reason I ask you already, because we are dealing with things of a serious nature, to accept what I want to say today.

You see, Anthroposophy is quite at the start of its work, and anyone who uses Anthroposophy to develop some or other area, certainly has the experience that all he can still experience for himself in anthroposophical knowledge, the biggest difficulty arrives when he wants to share this with the world. This is just a fact, this is the biggest difficulty. Why? Because today we simply don't have the instrument of speech which is fully suited to concisely express what is seen through Anthroposophy. The Anthroposophist has the expectation that through Anthroposophy not merely such knowledge should come which live within the inner life, which they see as an inner observation, because it is unattainable for the human race in its entirety. For us this must be of foremost importance: What is possible in the human community? — and not: What can the individual demand? — Let us be clear, my dear friends, whoever is an Anthroposophist speaks out of reality, and in me speaking to him I don't feel as if I'm merely speaking in general, but when I speak to such a person it seems that either he is a priest or he should become someone who cares for the soul. Theoretically one can thus in the same manner shape one's endeavours in the most varied human areas. As soon as one enters into such a specialised field, one has to always state the most concrete of opinions which one can only take in. Please observe this. I'm making you aware that Anthroposophy certainly knows it stands at the start of its willing, a will which has to develop quite differently than the way in which it has already stepped in front of the world today. On the other hand, one can see that the world longs very, very strongly for what lies as a seed in Anthroposophy

Something exists as a seed in Anthroposophy, which is rarely noticed today. This is the speech formation element itself. If you read Saint Martin's words, who was still a guardian of a religious belief katexochen in the 18th Century — Matthias Claudius has translated the work of Saint Martin entitled "Errors and Truth" which should be republished — if you read Saint Martin, you find him speaking from a certain implicitness that humanity possessed an ancient speech which has been lost, and that one can't actually express in current differentiated languages what could be said about the supersensible worlds, and which should be expressed about the supersensible. So the Anthroposophist often has the feeling he would like to say something or other, but when he tries to formulate it, it leaves him speechless and doesn't come about. Yet Anthroposophy is creative speech. No one is able to meet something in such a way as Anthroposophy — what once was encountered in this way was in olden times and always occurred at the same time as religious formation — no one can encounter anything without a certain theological approach to final things in life like death, immortality, resurrection, judgement, without a certain anticipation of the future, therefore Anthroposophy must in her inward convictions look, at least for a short span of time, into the future and it must to some extent predict what must necessarily happen in the future and for the future of humanity. That is, that mankind is able to strip off all such connections with single individual languages which still exist today, and which more than anything have drawn nations into war and hardship. Ever again one must address the comparison of the Tower of Babylon construction and understand it today when one sees how the world is divided. Anthroposophy already has the power to sense something expressed between the differentiated spoken languages by looking from the original being of the sounds themselves; and Anthroposophy will, and not in the course of many centuries but in a relatively short time — even at is was initially suppressed, it soon rejuvenated — Anthroposophy will, through the most varied languages, not create a type of Yiddish language unit which is an abstraction from another, but it will out of itself creatively enter into the language and become reconciled with what is already in the human language.

Therefore, I want to tell you that Anthroposophy not only provides formal tasks of knowledge but that Anthroposophy has to face historical creative tasks. You can see what is in the hearts of people today who can create such things. I've been wanting for years to take the most important components in anthroposophical terminology, as paradoxical as this may appear, to try and give words formed out of sound. The time has not been ripe yet to accept this. But it is quite possible.

For this reason, I must call your attention to the real tasks of Anthroposophy. Why do I feel myself compelled to call your attention to it? Simply from the basis that as soon as mankind is ripe for the perception of the sound, for the word creative power itself, then everything which has up to now been in other spheres, in a more instinctive-animal way taking its course, must in future take place in the spiritual-human sphere. If humanity has come this far then it can sense the truth in a deed, sense what lives in the proclamation, in the message, in the Gospel, because the truth can't be sensed in the Gospel if one doesn't live in the creative power of a language. To really experience the Gospels, my dear friends, means to experience the details of the Gospels in every moment in which one lives, from having really recreated them within oneself.

Today's tendency is to only basically criticize the Gospels, one can't recreate them; but the possibility for their creation must be reworked. Where are the obstacles? The obstacles lie in already referring to the very first elements which were available for the creation of the Gospels. In fact, Gospel examination is placed on another foundation when the Gospel is thought about this way, than how it needs to happen from the character of the words. You see, under the objections which Dr Rittelmeyer mentioned, not as his but those of others, it is also one which is mentioned besides. It's the objection that it does not interest the religious today whether there are two Jesus children. I can completely understand how, in the religious mood of today, little value is placed in such things. Now there is something else. During the coming days we see, published in the "Kommenden Tag-Verlag," how unbelievable the Gospel understanding is regarding the promotion of this "trivial matter" — it is however no small matter — how the power which created the Gospels is promoted by simply referring to a proof of what stands in the Gospels, regarding the two Jesus children. People don't understand the Gospels, they don't know what is written in them. However, the creative power of speech must be drawn out of further sources, and as a result, develop the heart and mind for these sources so that from the heart and mind the first of the four sections which I've given you in the description of the Mass can be given. You see, it doesn't mean the Mass is only being presented symbolically, but that the Mass symbolism becomes an expression for the totality of the pastoral process. If the totality of the pastoral work does not flow together into the Mass as its central focus, then the Mass has no meaning; the coming together of the pastoral ministry in the Mass or the modern symbolism that can be found — we will speak about this more — only then, in the full measure of the four main sections of the Mass, which I have mentioned, can it be fully experienced.

The reading of the Gospel to the congregation is only a part; the other part is expressed in the sermon. The sermon today is not what it should be, it can't be as it is intellectual because as a rule the preparation for the sermon is only intellectual and arising out of today's education, out of today's theology, can't be anything else. The sermon is only a real sermon when the power of creative speech ensouls the sermon, in other words when it doesn't only come out of its substance but speaks out of the substance of the genius of the language. This is something which must first be acquired. The genius of language is not needed for religiosity which is in one's heart, but one needs the genius of language for the religious process in the human community. Community building must be obligatory for the priest, as a result, elements must be looked for which are supportive of community building. Community building can never be intellectual, because it is precisely the element which creates the possibility of isolation. Intellectualism is just agreed upon by the individual as an individual human being and to the same degree, as a person falls back on his singularity, to that degree does he become intellectual. He can understandably save his intellectualism through faith because faith is a subjective thing of individuals, in the most imminent sense one calls it a thing of the individual. However, for the community we don't just need the subjective, but for the community we need super-sensory content.

Now, just think deeply enough about how it would be possible for you to effectively bring the mere power of faith to the community, without words. You wouldn't be able to do this, it is impossible. Likewise, you couldn't sustain the community by addressing it through mere intellectualism. Intellectual sermons will from the outset form the tendency to atomise the faithful community. Through an intellectual sermon the human being is thrown back onto himself; every single listener will be rejected by himself. This shakes up in him those forces which above all do not agree but are contradictory. This is a simple psychological fact. As soon as one looks deeper into the soul, every listener becomes at the same time a critic and an opponent. Indeed, my dear friends, regarding the secrets of the soul so little has been clarified today. All kinds of contradictions arise in objection to what the other person is saying when the only method of expression he uses is intellectual.

This is precisely the element which split people up today, because they are permeated thoroughly with mere intellectualism. You are therefore unable, through the sermon, to work against atomising, if you remain in intellectualism. Neither in the preparation of the sermon, nor in the delivery of the sermon must you, if you want to build community today, remain in intellectualism. Here is where one can become stuck through our present-day education and above all in the present theological education, because in many ways it has become quite intellectual. In the Catholic Church it has become purely intellectual, and all that which is not intellectual, which should be alive, is not given to individuals but has become the teaching material of the church and must be accepted as the teaching material of the church. A result of this is, because everything which the Catholic Church gives freely as intellectual, the priest is the most free individual one can imagine. The Catholic Church doesn't expect people to somehow submit to their intellect, inasmuch as it releases them from what is not referred to as the supernatural. All they demand is that people submit to the teaching material of the church. Regarding this I can cite an actual example.

I once spoke to a theologian of a university, where at that time it paid general homage to liberal principles, not from the church but from liberal foundations. Of course, the theological faculty was purely for the Catholic priesthood. This person I spoke to had just been given a bad rebuke by Rome. I asked him: How is this actually possible that it is precisely you who received this rebuke, who is relatively pious in comparison to the teacher at the Innsbruck University — who I won't name — who teaches more freely and is watched patiently from Rome? — Well, you see, this man answered, he is actually a Jesuit and I'm a Cistercian. Rome is always sure that a man like him, who studies at the Innsbruck University never drops out, no matter how freely he uses the Word, but that the Word should always be in the service of the church. With us Cistercians Rome believes that we follow our intellect because we can't stand as deeply in our church life as the Jesuit who has had his retreat which has shown him a different way to the one we Cistercians take. — You see how Rome treats intellectualism psychologically. As a rule, Rome knows very clearly what it wants because Rome acts out through human psychology, even though we reject it.

Now, what is important is that above all, the sermon should not remain in intellectualism. All our languages are intellectual, we don't have the possibility at all, when we use common languages, to come away from the intellect. But we must do it. The next thing you come to, with which you need work as purely formative in the power of creative speech, is symbolism, but now formed in the right way, not by remaining within intellectualism but by really experiencing the symbols. To experience symbols indicates much more than one ordinarily means.

You see, as soon as the Anthroposophist comes to imaginative observation or penetrates the imaginative observation of someone else, he actually knows: The human being who stands in front of him is not the same person he had been before he had seen the light of Anthroposophy. You see, this person, who stands in front of us, is considered by current science to be a more highly developed animal; generally speaking. Everything which science offers to corroborate these views and generally justifies it is by saying a person has exactly as many bones and muscles as the higher animals, which is all true, but science comes to a dead end when one really presents the difference between people and animals. The differences between people and animals are not at all to be referred to through comparative anatomy, whether the whole human being or a single part of it, and an entire animal or part of an animal is similar, but to grasp what is human is to understand what results when human organs are situated vertically while the animal organs lie parallel with the surface of the earth. That one can also observe this in the animal kingdom as far as it proves the rule, is quite right, but that doesn't belong here, I must point out the limitations.

Because the human being is organised according to the vertical plane with his spine, he relates in quite a different way to the cosmos than does the animal. The animal arranges itself in the currents circulating the earth, the human being arranges itself in currents which stream from the centre point of the earth in the direction of the radius. One needs to study the human being's situation in relation to space in order to understand him. When one has completed one's study of the human being's relationship to space, and make it alive once again, as regards to what it means that the human being is the image of God. The human being is not at all what comparative anatomy sees, he is no such reality as anatomy describes him to be, but he is, in as far as he is formed, a realization of an image (Bildwirklichkeit). He represents. He is sent out of higher worlds into conception and birth so that he represents what he brings from before his birth. Out of the divine substance we have our spiritual life before birth. This spiritual life dissolves through conception and birth and achieves a representation in the physical person on earth, an imagination. Imagination, drawn out of the world all, becomes the form of man, but what is drawn out of the world all needs to be understood according to its position in the world all. Every single human organ takes place in the verticalization. The human being is placed into the world by God.

This happens directly as an inner experience as the human being is grasped by the imagination. One can no longer intellectually say and believe that when I say the words "Man is the image of God" that we are only talking about a comparison. No, the truth is expressed; super-sensibly derived similarities from the Old and New Testaments can be found not as allegorical similarities, but as truths. We need to reach a stage when our words are again permeated by such experiences, that we learn to speak vividly in this way. In the measure to which we in a lively way enter into vivid characterisation, not through contriving something intellectually, we come to the possibility of the sermon, which should be an instruction.

I have often pointed out that when a teacher stands in front of a child and wants to teach him in a popular form about the immortality of the soul, he should do so through an image. He will need to refer to the insect pupa, how the butterfly flies out of it, and then from there go over to the human soul leaving the human body like a pupa shell; permeating this image with a super-sensible truth. I have always, when I deal with this alleged parable, said: there is a big difference whether a teacher said to himself: I am clever and the child is stupid, therefore I must create a parable for the child so that he can understand what I can understand with my mind. — Whoever speaks in this way has no experience of life, no experience of the imponderables which work in instructions. Because the convincing power with which the child grasps it, what I want to teach with this pupa parable, means very little if I think: I am clever and the child is stupid, I must create a parable for him which works. — What should be working firstly comes about within me, when I work with all the phases and power of belief in my parable. As an Anthroposophist I can create this parable by observing nature. Through my looking at the butterfly, how it curls out of the pupa, I am convinced through it that this is an image of the immortality of the soul, which only appears as a lower manifestation. I believe in my parable with my entire life.

This facing of others in life is what can become a power of community building. Before intellectualism has not been overcome to allow people to live in images once again, before then it will be impossible that a real community building power can occur.

I have experienced the power of community building, but in an unjust field. I would like to tell you about that as well. Once I was impelled to study such things as to listen to an Easter sermon given by a famous Jesuit father. It was completely formulated according to Jesuit training. I want to give you a brief outline of this sermon. It dealt with the theme: How does the Christian face up to the assertion that the Pope would set the Easter proclamation according to dogma, it wouldn't be determined as God's creation but through human creation? — The Jesuit father didn't speak particularly deeply, but Jesuit schooled, he said: Yes my dear Christians, imagine a cannon, and on the cannon an operator or gunner, and the officer in command. Now imagine this quite clearly. What happens? The cannon is loaded, the gunner holds the fuse in his hand, the gunner pulls on the fuse when the command is sounded. You see, this is how it is with the Pope in Rome. He stands as the gunner beside the cannon, holds the fuse and from supernatural worlds the command comes. The Pope in Rome pulls on the fuse and thus gives the command of the Easter proclamation. It is a law from heaven, just like the command does not come from the gunner but from the officer. Yet, something deeper lies behind this, my dear Christians — the father says — something far deeper lies beneath it, when one now looks at the whole process of the Easter proclamation. Can one say the gunner who hears the command and pulls on the fuse, is the inventor of the powder? No. Just as little can one say that the Catholic Pope has instituted the Easter proclamation. —

The faithful are drawn by a feeling into the congregation through the use of this image, this representation but obviously in an unjust a field as possible.

The symbol can be a way for the human heart to actually find the supersensible, but we, like I've indicated with the comparison to the insect pupa, need to learn to live within the symbol; to be able to faithfully take the symbol itself from the outside world. I clearly understand when someone wants to appeal to mere faith as opposed to knowledge. I take this so seriously, that this faith must also manifest and be active in the living of oneself in the face of outer nature, so that the entire outer nature becomes a symbolum in the true sense of the word, an experienced symbolum. My dear friends, before the human being again realizes that in the light not mere comparisons of wisdom live and weave, but that in the light wisdom really live and weave ... (gap in notes) ... light penetrates into our eyes, what is light is then no longer light — with "light" one originally referred to everything which lay at the foundation of human beings as their inner wisdom — because by the light's penetration it becomes inwardly changed, transubstantiated, and each thought which rises within, my dear friends, is changed light in reality, not in a parable. Don't be surprised therefore that the one who has got to know through appropriate exercises that to some extent outer phenomena describe inner human thoughts, by describing them in light imagery. Do not be surprised because that corresponds to reality.

Things were far more concretely taken in the ancient knowledge of mankind than one usually thinks. You must also become knowledgeable with the fact that the power which then still lived in the Gospels, have in the last centuries also got lost, like the original revelation of man has really been lost as has the original language been lost. Now I want to pose the question: do we grasp the Gospels today? We only grasp them when we can really live within them and presently, out of our intellectualized time epoch, we can't experience them thus. I know very well about the opposition expressed against my interpretations presented in my various Gospel lectures, from some or other side, and I'm quite familiar that these are my initial attempts, that they need to become more complete; but attempts to enliven the Gospels, these they are indeed.

I would like to refer back to times, my dear friends, when there were individuals who we today, when you imagine the world order at that time there also existed, those we call chemists. Alchemists they were called in the 12th and 13th centuries, and they were active with the material world which we usually can observe in chemists. What do we do today in order to create a real chemist? Today our preparations for the creation of a chemist is his intellectual conceptions of how matter is analysed and synthesized, how he works with a retort, with a heating apparatus, with electricity and so on. This was not enough, if I may express it this way, for a real chemist, up to the 13th and 14th century — perhaps not to take it word for word — but then the chemist had opened the Bible in front of him and was permeated in a way by what he did, in what he did, by what flowed out of the Bible in a corresponding force. Current humanity will obviously regard this as a paradox. For humanity, only a few centuries ago, this seemed obvious. The awareness which the chemist had at that time, in other words the alchemist, in the accomplishment of his actions, was only slightly different to standing at the altar and reading the mass. Only slightly different, because the reading of the mass already was the supreme alchemical act. We will speak about this more precisely in future.

Should one not be creating knowledge out of these facts that the Gospels have lost their actual power? What have we done in the 19th century? We have analysed the Gospels of Mark, John, Luke and Matthew, we have treated them philologically, we have concluded that John's Gospel can be nothing, but a hymn and that one can hardly believe it corresponds to reality. We have compared the various synoptists with one another and we have reached the stage which ties to the famous blacksmith where distillation takes place: what is said iniquitously about the Christ is the truth because you won't find that with mere hymns of praise. — This is the last consequence of this path. On this path nothing else can happen than what has already happened: the destruction of the Gospels will inevitably arise in this way. While we are still so much into discussing the division between knowledge and faith, it will not be sustained if science destroys the Gospels. One must certainly stand within reality and need to understand how to live out of reality, and therefore it is important that the pastor must come to a living meaning of the perceptible representations, the perceptible-in-image representations. The living image must enter into the sermon. That it should be an acceptable, a good image, it obviously must have a purity of mood, of which we will speak about. It's all in the image; the image is what we need to find.

Now my dear friends, for the discovery of the image you will be most successful with the help of Anthroposophy. Anthroposophy is mocked because of its pictoriality. If you read how the intellectuals — if I may use the word — apply their opposition to my depiction of evolution, you will soon see how easy it is from the intellectual point of view to mock the images which I have to use in my depiction of the Old Saturn-, Sun- and Moon existence. I have to use images otherwise things would fall out of my hands, because only though images I can grasp the reality which has to be searched for. I would like to say, Anthroposophy has in each of its parts definitely a search for images and is for this reason the helper for those who use images. Here lies the real field, where the pastor can firstly benefit much from Anthroposophy. Not as if he has to undertake to believe in

Anthroposophy, not as if he has to say: Well now, let's study anthroposophical images and books, then we can use them. — This is no argument. It needs to come, so to speak, to the opposite of what had to develop in philosophy, into an age that lived contrary to Anthroposophy.

To his I would like to say the following. Philosophers today who are students of a content or a system, or of the belief that a system needs to be established, such philosophers are antiquated; such philosophers have remained behind. Such system-philosophies are no longer possible in the intellectual time epoch. When Hegel presented his purely intellectualism in his last thoughts of the human conception and placed this in his overall system, he had created what I would like to call the corpse of philosophy. Exactly like science studies the human corpse, so can one in Hegel's philosophy in a corpse-like way study what is philosophy — as only that, it is very good. That is why the Hegelian philosophy is so great, because nothing disturbs the flow of intellectualism to really study it. The amazing thing I admire for example, is to develop something pure which is purely intellectualistic. However, *after* Hegel there can no longer be such endeavours which take thought content to create a philosophic system. That is why people create such awful somersaults. Yes, one can't think of worse somersaults than the philosophy of Hans Vaihinger, called the "As-if" (Als Ob). As if one can have something like a philosophy called: "As if." It is created from experience in the mind, this philosophy of "As if." It is not even a philosophy out of what humanity was, but the last imaginative remnants in humanity, which are translated into thoughts. What philosophers are obliged to study today should be a practice in pure thinking. To study philosophy today is meditative thinking and should not be practiced in any other way. I believe that if one looks at these things in an unprejudiced way, one will soon see that what I have offered in my "Riddles of Philosophy" as the development of philosophy, that it constantly proposes one can work through the most diverse philosophic systems as an exercise in thinking. One can learn unbelievably much out of the latest systems, in the Hartmann system and the American system linked to the name of James. One can learn unbelievably much in as far as one lets it work on one to such a degree that one asks: How is thinking trained; what does one gain from thought training? — Please forgive the hard words. Nietzsche had already made an effort to introduce such thought training in philosophy.

This will draw your attention, regarding philosophy, to today's need that man must direct thought content into direct living content, not by positioning oneself as a subject against the truth from outside, but in such a way that truth becomes an experience. Only one who has understood current philosophising in this way will actually be able to understand the contrary; for readers of anthroposophical writing and hearing anthroposophical lectures it does not mean things are to be taken up as dogma. That would be the most incorrect attitude to have. Just think, what is given in Anthroposophy has actually been brought down out of the supersensible, it may have been awkwardly put into words, but when one allows oneself to reach deeper, it will be as if the true philosopher in his thoughts reaches deeper into other philosophies. He would not take anything from other systems, he takes the blame. The image capability for the pictorial, for the sake of clarity, is the first step to educate students in Anthroposophy. When words are encountered which have flowed out of imaginative thinking, when such thoughts are taken up, then it is necessary, in order to really understand them, to raise the pictorial power out of them from soul foundations. Above all, that's what we can do to help Anthroposophy.

One therefore appeals less by saying: Well, I must first for my own sake become clairvoyant, then I can make some decisions about Anthroposophy. — One appeals in such a way that one firstly, quite indifferently, get to know the content of truth in Anthroposophy; one simply takes the sum of all the images which shows how one or other soul paints it. That is at least a fact which they paint for themselves. One takes this and first allows the inherent truth to remain undecided, but then one tries to find within it, how the person speaks who has such supersensible images, and one will see that this is the best way to enter in to seeing for oneself. With many people who encounter Anthroposophy today it is as if they set the wagon straight but then incorrectly spans the horse to it. (A stenographer's note indicates that a horse was drawn on the blackboard with the wagon positioned in one way, while the horse is drawn with its head towards the wagon and its tail pointing to the road ahead. The original drawing was not preserved.) There is no need for this; that one must first learn to be a seer. It could, in fact happen due to a certain arrogance and then the thing as a whole is passed by. If one has the humility to want to experience the seeing adequately, then one can come to the perception without the fear of receiving a suggestion. The fear of receiving a suggestion can only be had by philosophers alien to reality; which we have for instance with Wund, the latecomer of system philosophers who of course from his point of view, argued: Yes, how would I know if what I've first perceived of the supersensible world and look at it, that it was not suggested to me? — One should reply the Wund: How do you actually know the different between a piece of iron with a temperature of 100 degrees or higher which you can only imagine, or another one which is lying in front of you? You can discuss this for a long time but by looking at it you will never discover whether the iron is really lying in front of you or whether it is suggested; but when you grab hold of it and look at your fingers, then you will find the difference — through life. There is no other criterion.

It is however an unmistakable criterion, if one places oneself into life in such a way to come into Anthroposophy. One may however not take on the point of view that one knows everything already. In my life I have found that people learn the least when they believe they already know what they should learn.

It is for instance only possible to be a real teacher when you are a teacher of attitude. How often is it said to teachers in the Waldorf schools — and you have understood, in the course of years it has happened that teaching is characterised by this attitude; it is clearly noticeable — how often is it not said: When one stands in front of a child, then it is best to say to oneself that there is far more wisdom in the child than in oneself, much, much more because it had just arrived from the spiritual world and brings much more wisdom with it. One can learn an unbelievable amount from children. From nothing in the world does one basically learn so much in an outer physical way, as when one wants to learn from a child. The child is the teacher, and the Waldorf teacher knows how little it is true that with teaching, one is the teacher and the child the scholar. One is actually — but this one keeps as an inner mystery for oneself — more of a scholar than a teacher and the child is more teacher than scholar. It seems like a paradox, but it is so.

You see, Anthroposophy directs us to new knowledge about the world, in many special areas in life, so it is worthy of questions which are thought through ... (Gap in notes). Yes, Anthroposophy appears consistently in this mood, with this attitude. Anthroposophy just can't appear without a religious character as part of it. This must also be stressed about Anthroposophy: Anthroposophy does not strive to appear as creating religious instruction, as building a sect; it strives to give humanity a content to their inner experiences which lets them strive to what comes quite out of themselves, which is expressed with religious characteristics. Anthroposophy is not a religion but what it gives is something which works religiously.

Very recently I had to speak to a person whose earlier life situation was not quite over confident, but of a joyful nature, and who descended into a deep depression, a depression which had various, even organic, causes. This man is an Anthroposophist, he wanted to speak about his mood to me. I pointed out that a mood comes out of the totality of a person, and one gets a mood out of what one absorbs from the world in that one confronts the world as a human being.

Anthroposophy itself is a person (Mensch). If it wasn't a person, it wouldn't transform us. Out of us it makes us into someone different. It is a person itself, I say it in the greatest earnestness. Anthroposophy is not a teaching, Anthroposophy has an element of being, it is a person. Only when a person is quite permeated by it and Anthroposophy is like a person who thinks, but also feels, senses and has emotions of will, when

Anthroposophy thinks, feels and wills in us, when it is really like a complete person, then one can grasp it, then you have it. Anthroposophy acts like a being and it enters present culture and civilization like a kind of being. One experiences this entering as by a kind of being. With this at the same time one can say: Religion — spoken from the anthroposophic stand point — religion is a relationship of human beings to God. However, Anthroposophy is a person, and because it is a person, it has a relationship with God; and like a person has a relationship to God, so it has a relationship to God. Thus, it has the direct characteristic of the religious in itself.

I will now summarise this finally in some abstract sentences which do however have life in them. What I have said before and what I say now are interrelated and I don't say it without purpose, my dear friends. The first one which is experienced in this way is that one leans to recognise how godly wisdom acts in the child, where it is creative, where it not only comes to revelation in a brain, but where it still shapes the brain. Yes, "if you would not become like little children, you shall never enter into the kingdom of the heavens ..." That is the way to penetrate into what you notice in the deep humility of the child, that which lies before becoming a child, that which even Goethe experienced so lovingly, that he used the word "growing young" (Jungwerden) for entering into the world, like one can say "growing old" (Altwerden). Growing young means stepping out of the spiritual state, into earthly existence. One goes in a certain sense really through childhood and back to such a state where one still had a direct relationship with the divine. The old Biblical questions become quite real: Can one return into the mother's body, to experience a rebirth? — In spirit one can do this.

However, in the old way where the Bible lay in front of the alchemists, and the new way which prepares us for handling the world, lies an abyss. The abyss must be bridged over. We will however not find the old ways, because we need to find a new way.

I have often spoken out among Anthroposophists what we might find when we are willing to do some kind of manipulation of nature. The "Encheiresis naturae" (an intervention by the hand of nature — Google) we must accomplish again, but we mustn't say "don't cut your nose to spite your face"; we must be able to take it in the greatest earnest then we will have an ideal , in any case only as an ideal, but an ideal which becomes reality. The laboratory workbench will in a certain sense become an altar, and the outer action in the world will become a service of divine worship and all of life be drenched by the light of acts of worship.

Now for the second thing: Anthroposophy as speech formation. Anthroposophy needs to strive to have such a grasp in the world, that I can apply the reality which I've presented today as an apparent contradictory image: the laboratory bench of the chemist, the physics-chemistry of clinical work must in human experience take on the form of an altar. Work on humanity, also the purely technical work — must be able to become a service of divine worship. That one will only be able to find when one has the good will to cross over the abyss which separates our world from the other side where the Gospels lay before the alchemists.

FOUNDATION COURSE

FORMATION OF SPEECH.

*(Please note the German word "Sprache" can mean both **language** or **speech**, and in this context the English difference is not always obvious. Translator)*

Lecture seven by Rudolf Steiner given in Dornach, 29 September 1921, afternoon.

Emil Bock opened the discussion hour and formulated the following questions:

1. Out of the previous lecture this morning, how can we take the power of formative speech to which we still need to gain access, and accomplish a new speech technique, perhaps new forms and a new gestural technique?

2. How do we actually now really speak of a new understanding of the Bible, of a new Bible text? Furthermore, we ask Dr Steiner on occasion to discuss in more detail the two chapters from the synoptic Gospels, Matthew 13 and Mark 13.

3. What is the reality behind the Apostolic succession, the tradition and the ordination of priests in the technical sense, and how can such a reality be made more accessible again in the future?

Rudolf Steiner: With regards to the first question: You would already have seen, my dear friends, that out of what I said this morning, that in the illustration, the soul contents related to the supersensible and also what leads to the power of formative speech, must be searched for. Regarding the power of speech formation: we actually have no direct understanding of sound anymore today; we basically have no more understanding for words, so our words remain signs. Naturally our starting point needs to be out of the spiritual milieu of our time. Man must be responsible for these intimate things out of what currently is available. Precisely such a question brings us naturally into the area of the purely technical. First of all one has to make the understanding for the sound active again, within oneself. One doesn't easily manage the free use of speech when one isn't able to allow the sound as such, to stir within oneself. I would like to continue in such a way that I first draw your attention to certain examples.

You see, when we say "head" (Kopf) in German, we hardly have anything else in mind than the total perception of what reaches us through the ear, which indicates the head. When we say "foot" (Fuss) it is hardly any different to what we experience in the tonality and sound content in relation to some foot. Now we only need, for instance, to refer to the Romance languages where head is testa, tête, foot is pedum, pied, and we get the feeling at the same time that the term is taken from something completely different. When we say the word Kopf in German, the term has come out of the form, from looking at the form. We are not aware of this any longer, yet it is so. When we say Fuss, it is taken from walking where furrows are drawn in the ground. Thus, it has come into existence out of a certain soul content and coined in a word. When we take a word formation like, let's say, "testament" and all other word formations which refer in Romance language terms to head, testa, then we will feel that the term Kopf in the Romantic languages originate through the substantiation and thus not out of the form, but through the human soul with the help of the head, and particularly activating the mouth organs. "Pied" didn't originate from walking or drawing furrows but from standing, pressing down while standing. Today we no longer question the motives which have come out of the soul and into speech formation. We can only discover what can be called, in the real sense, a feeling for the language when we follow the route of making language far more representational than it is currently, abstraction at most. When someone uses a Latin expression in terminology, some Latin expressions are even more representational, but some people use them to denote even more. For example, today one can hardly find the connection between "substance" and "subsist" while the concept of "subsist" has basically been lost. Someone who still has the original feeling for substance and subsistence would say of the Father-God, not that He "exists" but that he "subsists."

Researching language in this way and in another way which I want to mention right now, in order to develop a lively feeling for language again, leads then to something I would like to call a linguistic conscience (Sprachgewissen). We need a linguistic conscience. We speak really so directly these days because as human beings we act more as automatons towards language than we do as living beings. Until we are capable of connecting language in a living way to ourselves, like our skin is connected to us, we will not come to the right symbolization. The skin experiences pain when it is pricked. Language even tolerates being maltreated. One must develop a feeling regarding language that it can be maltreated because it is a closed organism, just like our skin. We can gain much in this area, when we have a lively experience in some or other dialect.

Consider how often we have performed the Christmas Plays, and in these plays there is a sentence spoken by one or more of the innkeepers. When Joseph and Mary come to Bethlehem in search of lodging, they are refused by three innkeepers. Each one of the three innkeepers says: "Ich als a wirt von meiner gstalt, hab in mein haus und ligament gwalt." — Just imagine what this means to a person today. He could hear: "I as a host of my stature ..." — and think that what the host is saying means he is an attractive man, or something like that, or a strong man who has stature within his hostel, in his house. This is certainly not meant. If we want to translate that into High German we'll have to say: "I as a host, who is placed in such a way as to have abundant comfort, I am not dependent on such poor people finding lodgings within, with me." This means: "I as a host in my social position, in my disposition." This shows them it is necessary not only to listen to him — words one often enough hears in speech — but to enter into the spirit of the language. We say "Blitz" (lightening) in High German. In Styria a certain form of lightening is called 'heaven's lashers' (Himmlatzer). In the word "Blitz" there is quite another meaning than in the word "Himmlatzer."

So we start becoming aware of different things when we approach the sense of speech. You see, such an acquisition of the sense of language sometimes leads to something extraordinarily important. Goethe once uttered a sentence, when already in his late life, to the Chancellor von Müller, a statement which has often been quoted and is often used, to understand the entire way in which "Faust," written by Goethe, originated. Goethe said that for him the conception of "Faust" had for 60 years been clear "from the beginning" (von vornherein); the other parts less extensively. Now commentary upon commentary have been written and this sentence was nearly always recalled, because it is psychologically extraordinarily important, and the commentators have it always understood like this: Goethe had a plan from the beginning for his "Faust" and in the 60 years of his life — since he was twenty or about eighteen — he used this plan, he had "from the start," to work from.

In Weimar I met August Fresenius who bemoaned the fact that it was a great misfortune, if I could use such an expression, which had entered into the entire Goethe research, and at the time I had urged an unusually thoughtful and slow philologist to publish this thing as soon as possible in order that it doesn't continue, otherwise one would have a few dozen more such Goethe commentaries. It is important to note that Goethe used the expression "from the start" in no other way than in a descriptive way, not in the sense of "a priori" but "from the beginning" in a very descriptive manner so that in the strictest sense one could refer to Goethe not having an overall plan, but that "at the *beginning*" he only wrote down the first pages (i.e. to begin with) and of the further sections, only single sentences. There can be no argument of an overall plan. It very much depends on how one really experiences words. Many people have, when they hear the word "vornherein" totally have no conscience that it has a "vorn" (in front) and a "herein" (in) and that one sees something spiritual when one pronounces it. This simple dismissal of a word without contemplation is something upon which a tremendous amount depends, if one wants to attain a symbolic manner of speech. Precisely about this direction there would be extraordinarily much to say.

You see, we have the remarkable appearance of the Fritz Mauthner speaking technique where all knowledge and all wisdom is questioned, because all knowledge and wisdom is expressed though speech, and so Fritz Mauthner finds nothing expressed in speech because it does not point to some or other reality. How harsh my little publication "The spiritual guidance of man and of mankind" has been judged in which I mention that in earlier times, all vowel formation expressed people's inner experiences, and all consonant unfolding comes from outer observed or seen events. All that man perceives is expressed in consonants, while vowels are formed by inner experiences, feelings, emotions and so on. With this is connected the peculiar manner in which the consonants are written differently to the vowels in Hebrew. This is also connected to areas where more primitive people used to dwell, where they have not strongly developed their inner life, so predominantly consonant languages occur, not languages based on vowels. This extends very far, this kind of in-consonant-action of language. Only think what African languages have from consonants to click sounds.

So you see, in this way we gain an understanding for what sounds within language. One would be brought beyond the mere sign, which the word is today. Only with today's feeling for language which Fritz Mauthner believes in, can you believe that all knowledge actually depends on language and that language has no connection to some or other reality. A great deal can be accomplished when one enters into one's mother tongue and try to go back into the vernacular. In the vernacular one finds much, very much if you really behave like a human being, that is, respond to what you feel connected to the language. In the vernacular one has the rich opportunity to feel in speech and experience in sound, but also the tendency towards the descriptive, and you have to push it so far that you really, one could say, get into a kind of state of renunciation in regard to expressions that are supposed to phrase something completely separate from human experiences.

Something which thoroughly ruins our sense of language is physics, and in physics, as it is today, it only aspires to study objective processes and refrains from all subjective experience, there it should no longer be spoken at all. According to physics, when one body presses (stoßen) against another, for example in the theory of elasticity, then you are anthropomorphising, because the experience of pressure as soon as you sense sound, means you're only affected by the same kind of pressure as the pressure your own hand makes. Above all, one gets the feeling with the S-sound that nothing other can be described as something like this (a waved line is drawn on the blackboard). The word "Stoß" (push/impacts — ß is the symbol for ss — translator) has two s's, at the end and beginning; it gives the entire word its colouring; so when the word "Stoß" or "stoßen" (to push/thrust) is pronounced one actually can feel how, when your ether body would move, it would not only move but be shoved forwards and continuously be kept up.

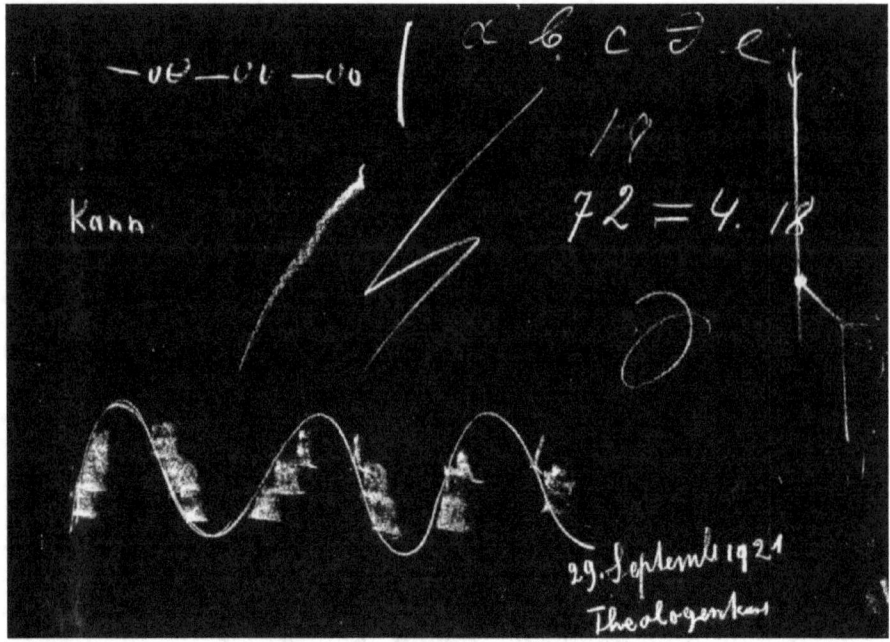

Tafel 3   7. Vortrag   29. September 1921, afternoon

Thus, there are already methods through which one comes to the power of speech formation, which is then no longer far from symbolizing, for the symbolum must be hacked out of the way so that one experiences language as a living organism, because much is to be experienced within language. Someone recently told me that there are certain things in language which only need to be pronounced and one is surprised at how they reveal themselves as self-evident.

The Greeks recited in hexameter. Why? Well, hexameter is an experience. A person produces speech, as I've already said, in his breathing. However, breathing is closely connected to other elements of rhythm in the human being; with the pulse, with blood circulation. On average, obviously not precisely, we have

18 breaths and 72 heat beats; 72 equals 4 times 18. Four times 18 heart beats gives a rhythm, a collective inner beat. In a time when man sensed in a more primordial and more elementary way according to what was taking place within him, man experienced, when he could, in uttering the relationship of the heart beat to the breathing, bring the totality of himself into expression. This relationship, not precisely according to time, this relationship can be brought to bear; you only have to add the turning point as the fourth foot (reference plate 3 ... not available In German text) then you have a Greek hexameter half-line, in the ration of 4 to 1 as a pulse beat to breathing rhythm. The hexameter was born out of the human structure, and other measures of verse were all born out of the rhythmic system of the human being. You can already feel, when you treat language artistically, how, in the process of treating human speech in an artistic way, language is alive. This makes it possible to acquire a far more inner relationship to language, yet also far more objectivity. The most varied chauvinistic feelings in relation to language stops, because the configurations of different languages stop, and one acquires an ear for the general sound. There are such things which are found on the way to gaining the power of creative speech. It does finally lead to listening to oneself when one speaks. In a certain way it's actually difficult but it can be supported. For various reasons it seems to me that for those who are affected by it, it is also necessary not to treat the Scripture in the way many people treat it today. You will soon see why I say these things.

In relation to writing, there are two kinds of people. The majority learn to write as if it's a habit of staking out words. People are used to move their hands in a certain way and write like this: in the majority. The writing lesson is very often given in such a way that one just comes to it. The minority actually don't write in the sense of reality, but they draw (a word is written on the blackboard: "Kann" [meaning can; be able to]). They look at the signs of the letters simultaneously as being written, and as an artistic treatment of writing, it is far more an intimate involvement. I have met people who have been formally trained to write. For instance, once there was a writing method which consisted in people being trained to make circles and curves, to turn them and thus acquire a feeling of connecting them and so form letters out of them. Only in this way, out of these curves, could the letters come about. With a large number of them I have seen that they, before they start writing, make movements in the air with their pen. This is what brings writing into the unconsciousness of the body. However, our language comes out of the totality of the human being and when one spoils oneself by writing you also spoil yourself for the language. Precisely the one who is dependent on handling the language needs to get used to the meditation that writing should not be allowed to just flow out of his hand, but he should look at it, really look at what he is writing, when he writes.

My dear friends, this is something which is extraordinarily important in our current culture, because we are on our way to dehumanizing ourselves. I have already received a large number of letters which have not been written with a pen but with the typewriter. Now you can imagine the difference between a letter written with a typewriter or written with a pen. I'm not campaigning against the typewriter, I consider it as an obvious necessity in civilization, but we do also need the counter pole. By us dehumanizing ourselves in this way, by us changing our relationship towards the outer world in an absolute mechanistic and dead manner, we need in turn to take up strong vital forces again. Today we need far greater vital forces than in the time in which man knew nothing yet about the typewriter.

Therefore, for someone who handles words, he must also acquire an understanding for the continuous observation, while he is writing, that what he is writing pleases him, that he gets the impression that something hasn't just flowed out of a subject but that, by looking simultaneously at it, this thing lives as a totality in him. Mostly, the thing that is needed for the development of some capability is not arrived at in a direct but in an indirect way. I must explain this route because I have been asked how one establishes the power for speech formation. This is the way, as I have mentioned, which comes first of all. As an aside I stress that language originates in the totality of mankind, and the more mankind still senses the language, so much more will there be movement in his speech. It is extraordinary, how for instance in England, where the process of withdrawal of a connection with the surroundings is most advanced, it is regarded as a good custom to speak with their hands in their trouser pockets, held firmly inside so they don't enter the danger of movement. I have seen many English people talk in this way. Since then I've never had my pockets made in front again, but always at the back, for I have developed such disgust from this quite inhuman non-participation in what is being said. It is simply a materialistic criticism that speech only comes from the head; it originates out of the entire human being, above all from the arms, and we are — I say it here in one sentence which is obviously restricted — we are on this basis no ape or animal which needs its hands to climb or hold on to something, but we have them as free because with these free hands and arms we handle speech.

In grasping with our arms, creating with our fingers, we express something we need in order to model language. So it has a certain justification to return mankind to its connection with language, bringing the whole person into it, to train Eurythmy properly, which really exists in drawing out of the human organism what is not fulfilled in the human body, but is however fulfilled in the ether body, when we speak. The entire human being is in movement and we are simply transposing though the eurhythmic movements, the etheric body on to the physical body. That is the principle. It is really the eurythmization of something like a necessity which needs to be regularly brought out of the human being, like the spoken language itself. It must stand as a kind of opposite pole against all which rises in the present and alienate people towards the outer world, allowing no relationship to be possible between people and the outer world any more. The eurythmization enables people in any case to return to being present in the language and is on this basis, as I've often suggested, even an art. Well, if you take into account the things I've just proposed, then you arrive at the now commonplace speech technique basically under the scheme of pedantry.

The great importance given to teaching through recitation and that kind of thing, only supports the element of a materialistic world view. You see, just as one would in a school for sculpture or a school of painting not really get instructions of the hand movements but corrects them by life forces coming into them, so speech techniques must not be pedantically taught with all kinds of nose-, chest- and stomach resonances. These things may only be developed though living speech. When a person speaks, he might at most be made aware of one or the other element. In this respect extraordinary atrocities are being committed today and the various vocal and language schools can actually be disgusting, because it shows how little lives within the human being. The formation of speech happens when those things are considered which I mentioned. Now if the question needs to be answered even more precisely, I ask you to please call my attention to it.

Now there is a question about new commentary regarding the Bible, in fact, how one can arrive at a new Bible text.

You see, the thing is like this, one will first have to penetrate into an understanding of the Bible. Much needs to precede this. If you take everything which I have said about language, and then consider that the Bible text has originated out of quite another kind of experience of language than we have today, and also as it was experienced centuries before in Luther's time, you can hardly hope to somehow discover an understanding of the Bible through some small outer adjustment. To understand the Bible, a real penetration of Christianity is needed above all, and actually this can only emerge from a Bible text as something similar for us as the Gospels had once appeared for the first Christians. In the time of the first Christians one certainly had the feeling of sound and some of what can be experienced in the words in the beginning of St John's Gospel which was of course experienced quite differently in the first Christian centuries as one would be able to do today. "In the primal beginnings was the Word" — you see, today there doesn't seem to be much more than a sign in this line, I'd say. We come closer to an understanding when we substitute "Word," which is very obscure and abstract, with "Verb" and also really develop our sense of the verb as opposed to the noun. In the ancient beginnings it was a verb and not the noun. I would like to say something about this abstraction.

The verb is quite rightly related to time, to activity, and it is absurd to think of including a noun in the area which has been described as in "the primal beginning." It has sense to insert a verb, a word related to activity. What lies within the sentence regarding the primal origins is however not an activity brought about by human gestures or actions, because it is *the* activity which streams out of the verb, the active word. We are not transported back into the ancient mists of the nebular hypothesis by the Kant-Laplace theory, but we will be led back to the sound and loud prehistoric power. This returning into a prehistoric power is something which was experienced powerfully in the first Christian centuries, and it was also strongly felt that it deals with a verb, because it is an absurdity to say: In the prehistoric times there was a noun. — We call it "Word" which can be any part of speech. Of course, it can't be so in the case of St John's Gospel.

In even further times in the past, things were even more different. They were so that for certain beings, for certain perceptions of beings one had the feeling that they should be treated with holy reserve, one couldn't just put them in your mouth and say them. For this reason, a different way had to be found regarding expression, and this detour I can express by saying something like the following. Think about a group of children living with their parents somewhere in an isolated house. Every couple of weeks the uncle comes, but the children don't say the uncle comes, but the "man" comes. They mean it is the uncle, but they generalise and say it is "the man." The father is not the "man"; they know him too well to call him "man." In this way earlier religious use of language hid some things which they didn't want to express outwardly because one had the inner reaction of profanity, and so it was stated as a generalization, like also in the first line of St John's Gospel, "in the beginning was the Word." However, one doesn't mean the word which actually stands there but one calls it something which has been picked out, a singular "Word." It was after all something extraordinary, this "Word." There are as many words as there are men, but children said, "the man," and so one didn't say what was meant in St John's Gospel, but instead one said, "the Word." The word in this case was Jahveh, so that St John's Gospel would say: "In the primal beginnings was Jahveh," so one doesn't say "God," but "the Word."

Such things must be acquired again by living within Christianity and what Christianity has derived from the ritual practice of the Old Testament. There is no shortcut to understanding the Gospels; a lively participation in the ancient Christian times is necessary for Gospel understanding. Basically, this is what has again become enlivened through Anthroposophy, while such things have in fact only risen out of Anthroposophic research. We then have the following: In the primordial times was he word — in primordial time was Jahveh — and the word was with God — and Jahveh was with God. In the third line: And Jahveh was one of the Elohim. — This is actually the origin, the start of the St John Gospel which refers to the multiplicity of the Elohim, and Jahveh as one of them — in fact there were seven — as lifted out of the row of the Elohim. Further to this lies the basis of the relationship between Christ and Jahveh.

Take sunlight — moonlight is the same, it is also sunlight but only reflected by the moon — it doesn't come from some ancient being, it is a reflection. In primordial Christianity an understanding existed for the Christ-word, where Christ refers to his own being by saying: "Before Abraham was, I am" and many others. There certainly was an understanding for the following: Just as the sunlight streams out of itself and the moon reflects it back, so the Christ-being who only appeared later, streamed out in the Jahveh being. We have a fulfilment in the Jahveh-being preceding the Christ-being in time. Through this St John's Gospel becomes deepened through feeling from the first line to the line which says: "And the Word became flesh and lived among us." Even today we don't believe a childlike understanding suffices for the words of the Bible, when we research the Bible by translating it out of an ancient language until we penetrate what lies in the words. Of course, one can say, only through long, very long spiritual scientific studies can one approach the Bible text. That finally, is also my conviction.

Basically, the Bible no longer exists; we have a derivative which we have put together more and more from our abstract language. We need a new starting point in order to try and find what really, in an enlivened way, is in the Bible. For this I have suggested an approach which I will speak about tomorrow, in the interpretation of Mathew 13 and Mark 13. You will have to state in any case that even commenting on the Bible makes it necessary to deal with the Bible impartially. If it is stated that something is mentioned which had only taken place in the year 70, therefore the relevant place could not have been mentioned before other than what had happened after this event, this could be said only if it is announced at the beginning of the Bible explanation that the Bible will be explained completely from a materialistic point of view; then it may be done like this. The Bible itself does not follow the idea that it should be explained materialistically. The Bible itself makes it necessary that the foreseeing of coming events is first and foremost ascribed to Christ Jesus himself, and also ascribed to the apostles. Thus, as I've said, this outlook is what I want to enter into tomorrow on the basis of Mathew 13 and Mark 13, by giving a little interpretation as it has been asked for.

Another question asks about the reality behind the apostolic succession and the priest ordination. This question can hardly be answered briefly because it relates deeply to the abyss which exists between today's evangelist-protestant religious understanding and all nuances of Catholic understanding. It is important that in the moment when these things are spoken about, one must try to acquire a real understanding beyond the rational or rationalistic and beyond the intellectualistic. This is acquired even by those who have little right to live in the sense of such an understanding. In the past I have become acquainted with a large number of outstanding theosophical luminaries, Leadbeater also among them, about whom you would have heard, and some other people, who worked in the Theosophical Society. I have recently had the opportunity — otherwise I would not have worried about it again — to experience, that some of these people are Catholic bishops; it struck me as extraordinary that a part of them were Catholic priests. Leadbeater in any case had, after various things became known about him, not exactly the qualification to become a Catholic bishop. Still this interested me about how people become Catholic priests. One thing is observed with utmost severity, which is the succession. In order for me to see which people have the right to be Catholic bishops, I was given a document which revealed that in a certain year a Catholic bishop left the Catholic church, but one who was ordained, and he then ordained others — right up to Mr Leadbeater — and ordination proceeds in an actual continuation, in an absolutely correct progress; they actually have created a "family tree" by it. I don't want to talk about the start of the "family tree" but you must accept that if it would be a natural progression that there once was an ordained bishop in Rome who dropped away, who then however ordained all the others, so all these Theosophical luminaries would refer back to a real descent of their priesthood to that which once existed. Therefore, awareness of this succession is everywhere present and such things are, according to their understanding, taken completely as the reality.

Something like this must be taken as a reality within the Roman Catholic Church. The old Catholic church more or less didn't have the feeling — but within the Roman Catholic church it is certain accepted this way — that the moment the priest crosses the stole he no longer represents a single personality or attitude but he is then only a member of the church and speaks as a representative, as a member of the church. The Roman Catholic Church considered itself certainly as a closed organism, where the individual loses his individuality through ordination; they see it this way increasingly.

Now something else is in contrast to this. You may think about what I've said as you wish, but I can only speak from my point of view, from the viewpoint of my experience. I have seen much within the transubstantiation. Today in the Catholic Church there is quite a strict difference according to which priest would perform the transubstantiation, yet I have always seen how during the transformation, during the transubstantiation, the host takes on an aura. Therefore, I have come to recognise within the objective process, that when it is worthily accomplished, it is certainly fulfilled. I said, you may think about this as you wish, I say it to you as something which can be looked at from one hand, and on the other hand also as a basic conviction of the church being valid while it was still Catholic, when the evangelist church hadn't become a splintering off. We very soon come back to reality when we look at these things and it must even be said within the sacrament of mass being celebrated there is something like a true activity, which is not merely an outer sign but a real act. If you now take all the sacraments of mass together which had been celebrated, you will create an entirety, a whole, and this is something which stands there as a fact. It is something which certainly touches things, where the evangelical mind would say: Yes, there is something magical in the Catholic Mass. — This it does contain. It also contained within it the magical part, one can experience in the evangelist mind as something perhaps heathen. Good, talk to one another about this. In any case this underscores it as being a reality, which one can't without further ado, without approaching the bearer of this reality, celebrate a mass. I say celebrate; it can be demonstrated, one can show everything possible, but one can't celebrate with the claim that through the mass what should happen at the altar will only happen when it is read without any personal imprint, in absolute application.

You see, it is ever present there where one works with the mysteries; it is simply so, when one works with the mysteries. Just as no Masonic ceremony may be carried out by a non-Mason in the consciousness of the Freemason, nor may a non-ordained person in true Catholicism work from out of Catholicism and perform with full validity the ceremony in consciousness.

This is where we are being directed and must consult. I want you to take note that in this case the Catholic rules were actually very strict. Please don't take things up in such a way as if I am saying this towards pro-Catholicism; I only want to point out the situation. It isn't important for us to be for, or opposed, to Catholicism, because it's about something quite different. Particular customs were very strictly adhered to in the Catholic Church — not at all what is today in Rome's mood and procedure. If a priest became so unworthy as to be excommunicated, then his skin would be ripped off, scraped off from his fingers where he had held the sacred host in his hands. His skin would be scraped off. Sometimes such things are referred to but legally it is so, and I know such processes quite well, that after the priest's excommunication the skin of the fingers which touched the host, were scraped off. You can certainly set the objective instead of the succession that goes from the apostles through the priesthood to the priest celebrating today. You can set that which goes through consecration and through the sacraments themselves. You can exclude priesthood, but you can only exclude that by taking things objectively, right to a certain degree, objectively, that the priest no longer may have skin on his fingers when he is no longer authorised to celebrate the sacrificial mass.

Isn't it true, if you have Catholic feeling, it is something as definite to you as two plus two making four? It is something definite according to religious feeling. When you don't have that then you as modern people must have a certain piety, which says to you the Catholic church has also just preserved the celebration of mass and if this is carried outside the circle to which it had been entrusted — other circles have not preserved the sacrifice of mass — if it is being performed in other circles it is pure theft. Real theft. These things must also be understood from such concepts. I believe to some it appears very difficult to understand what I am saying but in conclusion it has as such a certain validity which needs to be achieved through understanding. We don't have to worry about it here because you can experience the mass according to what there is to experience. As far as the training of a new ritual is concerned, it would not be disturbed at all by this, that the Catholic mass regards the mass to be something so real that it may certainly not to be removed from the field of Catholicism.

This is firstly something which I wanted to say during our limited time. When I speak about the mass itself, and I will do so, I will still have a few things to add.

PRAYER AND SYMBOLISM

Lecture given in Dornach on 30 September 1921.

My dear friends! It is important that the question which we had yesterday and actually have been considering during the past days from the side of Anthroposophy, we now approach from a religious side, but again I don't want to do it through definitions and explanations but in a more concrete way. It is important in fact, as you have probably already sensed, to find a way which must come out of religious experience. What belong to religious experiences are the reality of prayer and the reality of the examination of the word, first becoming visible for us in the examining of Gospel words. We will have to draw on the more inner elements of religious life, but we will adhere to these two, prayer and the examination of Gospel words, through examples that are far better than concepts.

Regarding prayer, my dear friends, one can from a religious standpoint say that a person who does not pray in our present time, cannot be a religious person. Certainly such a statement can be doubted from this point of view, but we don't want to enter into an abstract discussion but approach from a positive point of view, and this must always have some or other basis. So I would like to start from a kind of religious axiom, which for many can consist in feeling that without the possibility of praying it is not an inner religious experience, because in prayer a real union with the Divine must be sought, which interweaves and rules the world. It is important now to examine prayer.

We need to be clear that despite the general human differentiation in humanity, the care of a spiritual life also appears, according to the varied callings of different people. If prayer is also certainly something general and human, one can say that a special prayer is then again necessary for those who want to be teachers in the field of religious life, and this will bring us to the Breviary absolving. We want to speak about all these things because they are for you, namely young theologians, of imminent seriousness for the tasks that you are to set yourself, I'm not saying now, but which you can set yourself according to the demands of the time.

Regarding prayer, in order to reach clarity, I want to speak about the Lord's Prayer and inner experiences of the Our Father. It is important that we may not take our starting point today from experiences of ancient Christianity by examining the Lord's Prayer or bringing it to life inwardly; our basis must be about contemporary man, because we want to speak about the Lord's Prayer in a general human way. Yet one must be aware of the following. Let's accept we will start to say the Lord's Prayer according to the style in which we say the first sentence: "Our Father who art in Heaven." It is important *what* we feel and experience in such a sentence and what we can feel and experience with other sentences of the Lord's Prayer, for only then will this prayer become inwardly alive. What we are talking about here, in fact, first of all, is to have something like an inner perception of such a sentence, not really just something that appears in the symbols of the words, but something that lives in us in real words. The heaven is basically the entire cosmos and we make it perceptible when we say "Our Father in Heaven" or "Our Father who art in the Heavens" or "Our Father, You are in the Heavens," so that in saying these words they are permeated with the spirit; we are turning towards the spirit. This is the perception of what we need to visualize, when we say such a sentence as "Our Father in the Heavens." Such a similar experience is what we need with the words "Your kingdom come," because within us there needs to be, more or less as an intuitive feeling, the question: What is this kingdom? If we are Christians, we will gradually, in our striving, approach a perception of this kingdom — or expressed more appropriately, the kingdoms — and be reminded of what was mentioned yesterday, we are reminded of Christ's words which sound and ends in "the kingdoms of heaven." Already in the 13th chapter of Matthew's Gospel, the Christ wants to speak to the people on the one hand and to the disciples on the other, about what the kingdom of heaven is. There has to be something lively about the phrase "Your kingdom" or "May Your kingdom come to us." When will the right thing come to life in us? The right thing will only become alive in us when we take such a sentence not as a thought, but when we make it alive as if we actually hear it within us, as if we apply what I have more than once spoken to you about recently. A path must be made from the concept to the word, because there is quite a different kind of inner experience when we, without outwardly saying the words, inwardly not only hold an abstract concept, but a lively experience of the sound, in whatever language it might be.

The entire Lord's Prayer becomes, so to speak, reduced out of the specificity of language, also when we in some or other language not only imagine the thought content but what is contained in the sound. This was stressed much more in earlier times regarding prayer, that the sound element becomes inwardly alive, because by the sound content becoming alive within, the prayer is transformed into what it should be, as an interactive conversation with the Divine. Prayer is never true prayer unless there is an exchange with the Divine, and for such an interactive conversation with the Divine, the Lord's Prayer is suited in the most immanent form because of its structure. We are so to speak outside of ourselves when we speak such sentences as "Our Father who art in the Heavens" or "Let Your kingdom come." We forget ourselves the moment we really make these sentences audible and alive within us. In these sentences we erase ourselves to a large extent simply by the content of the sentences, but we take hold of ourselves again when we read sentences of a different structure or make them inwardly alive. We take hold of ourselves again when we say: "hallowed be Your name." It is then actually a lively exchange with the Divine, because it transforms itself immediately as an inner deed in "hallowed be Your name."

On the one hand we have the perception that in "Our Father who art in Heaven" nothing is happening unless the sentence is thoroughly experienced. By us directing ourselves to inner listening, it enlivens our inner hearing for the name of Christ, like it did in pre-Christian times when the Jahve name had caused it, in the sense of what I had mentioned earlier about the beginning of the St John's Gospel. If we utter the sentence "Our Father who art in Heaven" within us in the right way in our time, then Christ's name mingles into this expression, then we inwardly give the answer to what we experience as a question: "Let this name be sanctified through us/ be hallowed by your name."

You see, it takes prayer to live correctly into the Lord's Prayer; it takes on the form of an exchange with the Divine, even so when we in the right way experience the perception "Your kingdom come." This kingdom can't primarily be taken up in the intellectual consciousness; we can only take it up in the will. Similarly, when we lose ourselves with the sentence "Your kingdom come to us" we discover, taking hold of ourselves, that the kingdom, when it comes, works in us, that the actual Divine will happens in the heavenly kingdoms, and therefore also where we are on earth. You see, you have an exchange with the godhead in the Lord's Prayer.

This conversational exchange prepares you firstly to have inner dignity in relation to the concerns the earth, and to bring it into a relationship with what has happened in this exchange, by connecting that to earthly relationships. Obviously to some of you it might appear that when I say "Hallowed by Your name" there's an enlivening of the Christ name. However, my dear friends, it is precisely here where the Christ Mystery lives. This Christ Mystery will not really be recognised for as long as St John's Gospel is not really understood. At the start of St John's Gospel, you read the words: "All things came into being through the Word and nothing of all that has come into being was made except through the Word." By ascribing the creation of the world to the Father God, you go against St John's Gospel. In the St John's Gospel you hold on to what you take as sure, that everything which exists as the world had been created through the word, thus in the Christian sense through the Christ, through the Son which the Father had substantially created, had subsisted, and that the Father has no name but that His name is actually that which lives in Christ. The entire Christ Mystery lives in these words: "Hallowed be your name" because the name of the Father is given in the Christ. We will still speak about this enough on other occasions, but I wanted to refer to it today, how in prayer a real inner conversational exchange with the Divine should be contained in the prayer itself.

Now we can go further and say: Nothing is given to us from the natural world merely by taking our daily food, our bread. We take our bread from nature with the conditions which I've mentioned; by our digestive processes, through regenerative processes we become earthly man on the earth, but that can't really live in us because life in God is different, the life of God lives in the spiritual world. After we have entered into a conversation with the Divine in the first part of the Lord's Prayer, we can now out of this mindset which has permeated us within, release the negative and say positively: "You give us our bread, which works in our everyday life, today." With this it means: what has been nature's processes and work in us as processes of nature, this is what should, through our consciousness, through our inner experience, become a spiritual process. In this way our mindset should be transformed. We should become capable of forgiveness towards those who have done something to us, who have caused damage. We would only be able to do this when we become conscious of how much we have damaged the Divine spiritual, and therefore should ask for the right mindset in order for us to handle what we have become guilty of, in the right way; we can only do this if we have become aware that we are continuously doing harm to the Divine through the mere nature of our being, and continuously need the forgiveness of those beings towards whom we have become guilty.

Now we can add the following, which is again an earthly thing, something which we want to link to the first thing we have related to: "Lead us not into temptation," which means: Let our connection to You be so alive that we may not experience the challenge to merge with mere nature, to surrender ourselves to mere nature, that we hold you firmly in all our daily nourishment. "But deliver us, from the evil." The evil consists of mankind letting go of the Divine; we ask that we are freed and let loose from this evil.

When we ever and again have such experiences of the Lord's Prayer as our foundation, my dear friends, then we deepen the Lord's Prayer actively towards an inner life, which enables us to create the mood and possibility in us which allows us not only to act from one physical human to another physical human but that we act as one human soul to another human soul. In this way we have brought ourselves into a connection of the Divine creation in others, and we learn through this, what it is to experience such words as: "The least thing you have done to my brothers, you have also done to Me." In this way we have learnt to experience the Divine in the earthly existence. However we must in a real way, not through a theory, but in a real way turn away from worldly existence because we become aware that earthly existence, as it was first given to mankind, is actually no real worldly existence but an existence stripped of the Divine, and that we will only have a real worldly existence after we have turned ourselves to God in prayer, having created a link to God in our prayer.

With this, my dear friends, the most elementary steps, the stairway, can lead to the conscious awakening of religious impulses in human beings. These religious impulses had to a certain extent been instilled in the human beings since primordial beginnings, but it concerns becoming aware of these impulses within, and that can only happen when a real exchange with the Divine in prayer comes about. The first meaningful discovery which one can make about the Lord's Prayer is that within its inner structure lies the possibility for a person to directly, with understanding, enter into a conversational exchange with the Divine. That is only a beginning, my dear friends, but it is so, however, that in the beginning, when it is really lived through, it is taken further and just when the question is taken religiously, it concerns wanting to find in our experience of the first steps, the strength to continue with the next steps through our own inner being.

It is quite different to speak from the point of view of knowledge than it is to speak from the religious viewpoint. When one speaks from the side of knowledge, one deals mainly with the content; when one speaks about Anthroposophy as a religious element, my dear friends, then we need to pay attention to Goethe's words: Not *What* we think, but more *How* we think! — and for this reason I said yesterday, Anthroposophy inevitably, as is its character, leads to a religious experience, it flows into a religious experience through the *How, how* its content is experienced. However, when one speaks from the religious angle, it is necessary now not to look first at *What* it is which lies in the spread ahead of us, but that one goes out from this *How*, one comes from the human subject, one has to illuminate this human subject.

When you have found the attitude of prayer, you can now go to the other side and find it in the reading of the Gospels as well. The meaning the Gospels have for religious development, we will of course still speak about. In any case, real Christians need to remain within inner childlike feelings today in order to understand the Gospels in a believable way, also without criticism. When as a theologian he applies criticism, he has to, because he comes from the Christian angle, be able to understand the Gospel without criticism. At least he must firstly become strong in his experiences of the Gospels, and then, armed with this strength, he only then applies criticism. That's actually the basic damage in Bible criticism and actually in the Gospel criticism of the 19th Century; people are not initially religiously strengthened before they apply criticism to the Gospels. As a result, they have arrived at a Gospel criticism which is nothing other than done in the modern scientific sense. Nothing is more clearly felt regarding this modern scientific sense, my dear friends, than the Gospel words of St Matthew 13, for in Matthew 13, I could say, the pivotal point of the whole chapter are words which encloses a mystery, and that perhaps in the entire evolution of Christianity it could never have been felt more deeply by religious people than today, when they come up against the world. It is in the words: He answered and said: for you it is possible, to understand the mystery of the Kingdom of Heaven, but for those, whom I've just mentioned, the people around, it is not so. — To this an actually deep puzzle is connected: To him who has it, more will be given ... but he, who does not have it, nothing will be given: what would have been given to him, the little he has, will be taken from him. — These are extraordinarily deep words. Perhaps nowhere else in the evolution of Christianity can these words of giving and taking be so deeply felt — when one can really feel in a religious way towards the world and people — how just today, science has taken over nature and in the widest circles gained ever more authority; accepted to take away everything which could give the possibility of being able to spiritually hear with his ears or see with his eyes. This is not what man is supposed to do, in the scientific sense. Spirit should be obliterated in the sense of science, in the mood of our modern times. When we speak in the same way as modern theology speaks to people who are raised in scientific terms, we take away that little which they could have in religious feeling. When we counter what is done in the Faculty of Philosophy with what is done in enlightened theology today, we remove the last bit of what is religious.

This needs to be felt, experienced in deep profundity, because the mood of the time is such has made it necessary for theologians to eradicate the religious. It is very necessary that we listen in a lively way to these words of the Matthew Gospel. However, this leads us to the next question: How can we discover the truth content, the vital content of the Gospel in the right way? We must find the correct way so that we can find the truthfulness also in the details of the Gospel and with this truthfulness directly illuminate the content of our lives. You see, in the way I'm saying this, I'm formulating my words in a particular way. I'm thinking of Paul's' words "Not I but Christ in me" and see how it should be spoken now in relation to the understanding of the Gospels, and when the word is within the heart of truth: "Not I, but Christ in me," the Christ said, in order to align the people in the right direction: "I am the way, the truth and the life." — We may express the words of Paul, "Not I but Christ in me," and then we will approach the Gospel in a way which leads to the right way to access the truthfulness and through this find the vital content in the Gospels. We have to climb up to a certain level in order to bring to life Paul's words: "Not I, but Christ in me." We must try to ever and again let it be spoken out, when we want to understand the Gospel. My dear friends, if Christ had spoken in the theologians of the 19th Century, then quite a different theology would have resulted, than it did, because a different Gospel view would have resulted.

Having indicated the first steps to experiencing it further and continuing with the Matthew 13 Gospel, I would like to say a bit more. I stress clearly that this is the start of something we need to continue within ourselves, and here I want to again call your attention to the words "Think *what?* Think more *how!*"

By taking the 13th chapter of St Matthew's Gospel as our example, we must understand the situation: as soon as we approach the Gospel, we must renounce intellectualism and find our way into the descriptive element. Let us go straight away into the descriptive element and let's look at the verses leading up to this, in the verses 46, 47, 48, 49, 50 of the 12th chapter. These indicate how Christ Jesus is addressed: "See, your mother and our brother stand outside and want to talk to you" — and how he lifts his hand and points to his disciple and says: "Behold, in those souls live my mother and my brothers." — We want to go even deeper into these words, but first we need to clarify the situation. What we bring with us through birth into this life, the feeling which one can in the profoundest sense refer to as a child-like feeling, or as a brotherly feeling, this which we receive through the utmost grace, this is what is referred to here. Immediately the transition can be made towards which the most important aspect of Christianity is to lead; that we learn to extend, as best we can, the child-like, the brotherliness, to those souls with whom we have a spiritual connection. Wrong, it would be completely wrong, to feel this is somehow negative, when it is felt that only in the very least would that which lies in the childlike and brotherly feeling would be loosened and put in the place which lies in the feelings to the disciples. This is not what it is about, but it is rather about the human feeling lain into mankind as brotherhood, firstly only found in nature, therefore in that which we are born into this world as our first grace, in the feelings to our parents, to those we are bound through blood. We place ourselves positively towards it, and what we find in it, we carry over by ensouling it, towards all those with whom we want to have a Christian connection and want to live in a Christian community.

This is what comes over into the 13th chapter of the Matthew Gospel. With it we are immediately in a starting position. If we take the content from the 53rd to 58th verses of the St Matthew's 13th chapter of the Gospel, and lead it over to the following, then we find that the greatest importance is the Christ Jesus now returns to his hometown, and through the experience of being in his hometown, express the words which appear in the 57th line of the 13th chapter: He says: "A prophet is nowhere less accepted than in his hometown and in his own house." The 58th verse now continues with the line: "And he was not able to do many deeds of the spirit there, for the sake of their unbelief." When we understand this situation, we are immediately led to see how Christ Jesus stands amidst people who have not understood the words: "Behold, in those souls live my mother and my brothers."

They failed to understand these words; as the words were not understood in their time; they also don't lead the way to Christ Jesus. The way to Christ Jesus has to be looked for. At this point it is indicated in the Matthew Gospel which people would find the way and who would not be able to find it, but also, how it can be found. We really need to understand that for those who are unable to ensoul the feelings of blood relationships given through grace to mankind, would not be able to find the way; those who only want to be part of their fatherland and not part of God's land, will not be able to find their way to Christ Jesus. So we are placed between two concrete experiences in Matthew's Gospel, chapter 13, and out of this situation we must expect that in this 13th chapter of Matthew's Gospel the relationship between the folk and Christ Jesus is stated, and how Christ Jesus as such can be discovered again by the folk.

Let's enter more deeply into this situation. Already in the first sentence we are drawn more intimately into the situation. It is important firstly, to be able to enter right into it. You are already standing in it if you take what leads up to it and away from it; it is important to stand completely within it: "On the day of Saturn Jesus left his home and sat down at the lake." — If this is read without a lively engagement and purpose, then the 13th chapter of Matthew's Gospel is not actually being read. First of all, what is happening there is on the day of the Sabbath, the day of Saturn. We will discover, my dear friends, that the enfolding of the liturgy is found throughout the year but it is not indifferent regarding how a priest applies the Gospel; we will see that the Gospels are placed in the course of the year in such a way that people can find a connection in the Gospel to what can be experienced in nature, otherwise you will not really give the words of the Gospels their correct inner power.

We will still talk about the details of the year's liturgy, but we need to get closer to these things. If you look at it spiritually, the 13th chapter of Matthew's Gospel speaks about the end of the world, that means the earthly world, and it is clearly indicated that it will happen in the manner of the prophecy. In the 35th verse it says: "That it might be fulfilled, that which is spoken by the prophet, who says: I want to open my mouth in parables and speak about the mysteries of the world's primordial beginning." — Here in the 13th chapter the end of the world should be spoken about. Christ Jesus chose the Sabbath because earlier people turned to it when they wanted to understand the beginning of the world, to compare it to the truths about the end of the world. The reception of these words needed an inner peace, it is indicated directly by the time setting. The effort of the preceding days must have taken place for man must be in need of rest in order to understand what would be said in the 13th chapter of Matthew's Gospel. He goes out of his home because he has something to say which goes further out than what can be said at home; this is the immediate recovery of verses 53 to 58. At home he couldn't have said anything. The writer of the Gospel is aware of indicating this in conclusion. You can't get close to the Gospel if you don't have the precondition that every word of the Gospel carries weight; it can't be indicated outwardly, you must try to let it enter into your inner life.

"He sat down beside the lake." You only realize what it means to sit beside the lake, how we are led in the wide world of experiences, when you sit at a lake and you are led away from everything which binds you to the earth. With the sensation of airspace, we already have too much abstraction which escapes us. Of course, experiences in the air spaces of the spirit leads us away from what chains us to the earth, but as human beings there is firstly something which escapes us.

We now have him sitting down beside the lake. Here he now gathers the folk, and speaks to them of the Kingdom of Heaven, in parables. The disciples start to understand that when Christ Jesus speaks to the people in the way in which he addressed the disciples, in the examination of the parables, then people would also be deprived of what they have, at least. He could give the people nothing if he gave them the solutions to the parables. So what does he have to do first of all? To start off with, he should not speak of a spiritual world content, but firstly speak about world content, spread out before the senses. He needs to speak about the grain seed, leading them through every possibility in the destiny of the kernel. He must lead them to the possibility that the seed can't develop roots, or only weak roots, or hardly any roots, and can be lamed by opposing forces to fully develop its roots.

My dear friends, you need to understand that you must speak in this way to people, because people first need to become inwardly alive towards what is usually thoughtlessly passed by. Their souls need to be lit up for the observation of the outer world. The soul remains dead and un-kindled if what lies externally, is not stirred up in inner words. People go thoughtlessly and wordlessly through the world. They look at the seed, which wilts. They see the seed which bears fruit, but they don't connect their seeing in such a way that it becomes alive as an inner seeing, an inner hearing. Only when we have transformed the experience of outer world into an inner image, only then do we have what can become preparation. The soul needs to be kindled by the external, the soul needs to revive itself in the external world. If you speak only about the meaning of nature, then you will firstly be speaking to deaf soul ears and blind soul eyes, and you will also take away the least which people have. You only give them something when they understand that you are speaking to their soul, speaking to their soul in the same way as Christ Jesus could speak to the disciples, having enlivened their souls through their participation in his life. The soul needs to be stirred, made to come alive towards the outer world and only after this enlivening is accomplished can you speak to the souls regarding interpretations placed before them as parables of nature. In this sense you link people initially to natural processes and try to transform the natural processes into images. Enliven everything which you can experience around you, imbue it in a sunny way.

From the moment we wake up in the morning, to the evening when we bring ourselves to rest, we are surrounded by sunshine. As unprepared individuals we have at first no inkling of what surrounds us in sunlight, which floods around us. We see sunlight reflected on single items, we initially see colours mirrored, but whether this imbuing sunshine floods through us as human beings experiencing colour, particularly activated and enlivened, we have no inkling of. We simply find ourselves in light from waking to going to sleep, and then we turn in a moonlit night to the moon, with open human hearts, and see how it is surrounded by stars that accompany it, and now return to the first experience which we could have that when you look at the sun, just when it is most lively with its light flooding around you, your eyes become blinded. The intensity of sunlight is so strong that it could, without hesitation, change eyes into suns.

If I look at the moon, then the moon throws the sunlight back to me, it sends the light back in such a way that I can take it in. The dazzling sunlight takes away the discretion. This discretion only remains while I'm looking at moonlight. The rays of the sun have such a majestic intensity that they do not have to rob me of my discretion when I turn towards them. I can turn to them when they are given again by the moon. How can I make this into an inner experience? I may and can, as a human being, unite myself with what the moon returns to me; I may, when I place it as a symbol in front of myself, have something with which I can unite myself. I can, with what I encounter in the moonlight, make myself an image with which I can unite myself. In other words, I may make an image of the sun, which has presented itself through the moonlight, and that is the Host, which I may consume. However, there is something so intense, so majestically great, that I can't be allowed to expose it immediately.

When I imagine this in images, I must present it in another way. I must determine a relationship which is not only visible as a similarity, and place it there, by becoming the nourishment for what the journey is allowed to become (the Host) surrounded with that which may only be looked at, with the monstrance (receptacle of the Host) [a drawing is done on the blackboard] and I have my relationship to the world born out of a dualistic comparison, a twofold kind, which I make into a kind of image with the inclusion of the monstrance. In the nourishment for the way, in the Host I have something with which I can unite. In what surrounds the Host I have an image of the weakened rays of the sun. Through communion there must appear in me what appears in the experience of the weakening, which I sense in moonlight, which I couldn't feel as a direct sun process, otherwise I would be blinded. In between both these is the communion: I place myself in the world context.

Plate 4   8. Lecture   30. September 1921, in the morning

What the sun and moon have to say to one another, this is what is found in human beings, the human being stands right in it and enlivens it through communion.

So you can see, further than just the mentioned comparison, it is distilled into a symbol which can be experienced. If it is experienced in the right sense, that means, experienced in a way as one does with others, with the full understanding of the words

"And he pointed over to his disciple and said: See, that is my parent and my brother," then to a certain extent the human community is placed within the sense of these words, then one works towards community building and this teaching, how community building can be achieved, we will discover again when we move forward in the interpretation of Matthew 13.

My dear friends, it is from inner knowledge — which an anthroposophical overview can give of human evolution — it is from my complete conviction that it would be especially bad for the present if we were to ignore the signs of the times today in order not to want to surrender to them. Just think, just when you allow your soul to look at Matthew's Gospel 13, you notice the following: the Catholic Church remains primarily fixed at the symbolism; what appeared in their community building was tied to the symbolism, the symbolism which lets you experience the kingdoms of the heavens. It didn't occur to anyone during the first centuries of Christianity's propagation, to speak about patience, that people could wait, and so on. I am obliged to say this. They were completely filled with the need for action, because they found the efficacy of symbolism and contribution of the symbol itself, as community building. They found within the symbolism what Christ wanted to indicate through the words which record the seven parables of the kingdom of God. They wanted through the symbolism make ears to hear and eyes to see before they started with the proclamation; you are standing within the living world of symbolism.

Today we are standing in a completely changed time. We read in Matthew's 13 Chapter that initially explanations of the parables would only be given to the disciples. This we can't do today. It would be impossible today because the Gospels are in everyone's hands and the meaning of the parables can be read by everyone. We really live in a completely changed time. We don't really notice this at all. We must in a new way understand what the Matthew Gospel Chapter 13, contains. In the sense of our time, we must consider the structure of Matthew 13. Firstly, we have Christ sitting in front of the people, he delivers the parables to them about the kingdom of heaven, and from the 36th verse it is written: "Then Jesus left the people and came home, and his disciples approached him and said: Explain the parable of the weeds on the fields. And he explained it to them."

Let me clarify this situation completely. Firstly, the Christ speaks to the people in parables, which are clothed in outer events. He points to these parables for his disciples. He utters during these explanations meaningful words of mystery, which I have tried to bring closer to you. After he has returned home and spoke to his disciples about the parables of the weeds, he spoke to them about a number of other parables — about the treasure in the field, the priceless pearl, and some of the discarded fish found in the fishnet. Thus, he spoke about other parables to the disciples, after he had left the people. This all belongs to this situation: in the Gospels everything is important. We also have — let us place this clearly before our souls — the Christ at the lake, sitting in front of the people, telling them about the parables, then turning away, turning to the disciples, leading them into the situation in which he utters important mystery words, speaking to them alone away from the people, explaining the parables with the help of other parables, then, after he had again led them to the spirit-godly revelations, he asks if they had understood. Their answer is "Yes." Now the very next conclusion is — because everything else is just an introduction -: "Having been initiated into the scriptures you will conduct yourselves like a man who is master of his house, who takes out of his treasure that which he has experienced, but that part of what he has experienced which he has filled with life inwardly, so that he can add something new to it and then be able to present it to his listeners."

I wanted to show you the way towards understanding Matthew 13, and tomorrow we will speak further about the content of truth and content of life, which can be found in this way in the Gospels. I have only indicated as an insertion how symbolism is found in this way in a central symbol from which certainly everything has to be believed, my dear friends, that it should also become a central symbolism for those who want to bring it into the ritual in pastoral care. What is needed is something visible as a symbol, which is more than just a product of nature, and for this, words are necessary which are enlivening; and action is necessary which is more than a mere action of nature. In the context of our civilization today we have dead words, not enlivened words. We only have actions, also human actions, which only contain nature's laws. We have neither living words, nor actions permeated by Divine will. To both of these we need to come through prayer and in reading the Gospels on the one hand and real fulfilling of the ritual on the other hand.

More about this tomorrow.

RELIGIOUS FEELING AND INTELLECTUALISM

Lecture given in Dornach on 30 September 1921, afternoon.

Emil Bock: I would like to introduce today's discussion hour and assume I have your understanding when I ask that yesterday's questions which have remained open, will, where possible, be considered again today. I believe I have your support for this. If you want me to clarify this request on your behalf, it will be to deal with the complex of questions regarding the apostolic succession coming into the question in future, where the need for the establishment of a new tradition must be expected, so to speak. In relation to this the question is important, how we, who are mostly Protestants, would relate to the work and personality of Luther, and go back to Luther's stance on the sacraments and to the whole Mystery content of Christianity. If I'm properly informed, that was the question which now appears to us as the next one, and I would very much like Doctor Steiner to enter into these questions as far as he considers possible.

Rudolf Steiner: My dear friends! I will try to continue with what was implied in this relationship started here yesterday in such a way that the many questions, which actually have to come out of such an examination, from the most varied sides, can then be considered further, because for this program of the Dornach course, it would be of the utmost necessity that as far as possible, no doubt and uncertainties would remain.

I would endeavour to go into the actual complex of questions and through this we will perhaps reach what underlies them, for further discussion. In fact, everything that licentiate Bock has just said is actually connected, so I may say it is important what opinions rise up among you now, regarding the position of Protestantism and Catholicism. I believe I can accept that you have come here from quite a positive foundation, namely to find a way out of today's religious turmoil. I myself don't want to say that it is obviously my wish to influence this towards the one or other side. Indeed, it doesn't concern some or other knowledge, but is about decisions of will, and these must rise out of inner convictions, being able of course to be motivated in the most varied ways, so we must actually discuss the possible motivation of their willed decisions. For example, a lot will depend upon your decisions of intent with regard the abyss that gapes between Catholicism and evangelical Christianity, between Protestantism and so on. Isn't it true, your resolution will be substantially different — I am now referring to the resolution of the majority of those present here — if you take into account that the Christian impulse, considered as widely as possible, in for example community building, can become that which the Christ wills for the world. However, regarding Catholicism — where I now separate Catholicism strictly from the Roman-Catholic Church — you could not find in Catholicism a possibility to bridge the abyss to the evangelistic side, if you don't gain a mutual understanding about the sacramentalism anchored in the Catholic world.

Naturally you could also be of the opinion: we are not concerned at all, we want to create a life-filled church-based movement and then show how this viable church movement asserts itself in the world. — You could also take on this point of view: that doesn't require such a strict understanding of Catholicism as such. However, you could only gain support in the judgement regarding this direction, after you have found clarity in some historic foundations about the basis for the opening of this abyss. Today the situation is actually like this; if a person has remained within Catholicism, is standing within practical Catholicism, then he actually can't understand the evangelical mind. Neither will someone who has grown up in the evangelical-protestant tradition, who is really connected to the various nuances in modern views anchored in the Protestant churches, be able to find the way over the abyss easily. It is precisely the reason for this question that must be understood before a decision can be reached.

Catholicism carries within it that view which has disappeared from modern consciousness, actual modern consciousness from which has disappeared, one could say if you want to be precise, since the 15th century. It was quite appropriate — but again connected with Roman political impulses, which then allowed the appropriate background to come in — it was quite appropriate, in a certain way, to keep Catholicism in mind and make it a duty for the Catholic clerics to return to the philosophy of Thomas Aquinas, in other words, the philosophy promoting the culmination of philosophical thinking before the 15th century. One can say that to live without this philosophy, one can actually find no theory of knowledge for the justification of sacramentalism, as practiced in the Catholic Church. By contrast the protestant-evangelical consciousness lies within this development which was only imposed after the 15th century. If you want to live through the wrestling of these two currents you can look at the work of Nicolaus Cusanus, who already in the 15th century, one might say, with all intensity, raised the question for itself: How does the past and the future stand beside one another in my soul? Cusanus, by going back to certain soul experiences, connected with the name of Dionysius Areopagita, and was able to build a bridge for himself.

I said yesterday that the Protestant quite rightly sees something magical in the way the Catholic performs Mass, and that is certainly correct. Because of our adaptation of the modern-day educational material, we are incapable of admitting to this magic. If you come with a modern consciousness you would not be able to find any difference between a sacrificial Mass as presented in the continuity of Christian evolution and a sacrificial Mass which is simply presented in words, symbols and gestures, perceptible by outer senses, as taking place in the Mass. Beyond the understanding of the content lies the understanding of that which is the sacrifice of Mass for the Catholic; this is connected with the unifying understanding of the world which has got lost for modern humanity, the unified understanding of the world which is understood on the one side by the spirit and on the other side from nature. I could say the route of knowledge has turned more to the side of nature while insight into the spiritual world has disappeared, and as a result of this, the possibilities to perceive certain mysteries. With this I don't want to say that in the consciousness of every Catholic priest there is also a substantial content about the sacrifice of the Mass. Still, in the Catholic community there is an awareness of this substantial content of the sacrifice of Mass to such a degree that one can still speak about the reality of it in the present.

I can't make anything presented here, clearer to you in any other way, than through the view of knowledge. Everything, my dear friends, which is woven into our discussions during these days, what is presented in the Elaborat of Dr Rittelmeyer and the Elaborat of Dr Schairer, regarding the determination of the religious and the differentiation of the religious point of view from the point of view of knowledge, all this is incomprehensible to the Catholic. It basically doesn't exist for him. When he considers it as a modernist or someone like that, then he is basically already accepted by Protestantism even within Catholicism. For the Catholics none of these things give rise to some or other question; for them you can't formulate questions in this way. For true Catholicism, the assumption is that there should be a mere emotional human relationship to God, without a religious dogmatic content, something quite incomprehensible; the religious dogma should connect itself with the supersensible world. Certainly, you could say, the Scholastics do this, making a differentiation, as Protestantism adopts in a different way, regarding what one can know and what one should purely believe. However, the Scholastics don't make this differentiation in the same way. For the scholastic the difference lies between truths, acquired simply through human reason, and those truths which lie at the basis of revelation, basically only relate to the various ways people come to the content; but it is still not a fundamental difference. For scholasticism it is true that the *Preambuli fidei* are certainly there, acquired through ordinary reason, above which lies the truth of revelation, but the truth of revelation also has a real content with which one can have a thinking relationship, like the scientific truths, which also promote a relationship through thinking. Therefore, one's relationship to the revelations is the same kind of relationship one has to scientific truths. There is only a difference in relation to the way people arrive at the truth, not a fundamental difference as we have been discussing here, these days. There is something extraordinarily important here, and from it comes the basis of the abyss.

You see, in order to clarify the sacramental and mass aspects to you here, I have to approach through the content of knowledge. If you look today at the two outer poles of human existence, the birth with the embryo and conception — I want to place these three in a unified term of "birth" — with birth on the one side and death on the other, so you understand what happens for the physical human being, even according to the order of scientific events. Today's human being, even if he is a theologian, speaks about birth and death as if they are scientific facts, involving physical man. That's exactly why in this day and age the wall between faith and knowledge has been so ruggedly erected, because one wants to keep something which has been taken away through purely scientific knowledge about birth and death, as one admittedly doesn't want for religion, to classify it in terms of knowledge.

How does a person regard birth today? It must seem a peculiar thing that I speak to you about birth, when I want to speak about Mass, but I would not be able to speak about Mass, without also speaking about birth. People see birth according to the study of embryology and ask: What happens to the embryonic germ through the fructification? — Then they ask:

How is the male and how is the female substance of inheritance absorbed, and what actually goes on there, scientifically observable, from the forefathers to the child? — Today's man must, with all the antecedents of his scientific education, certainly take this point of view. This point of view exercises such a colossal suggestive view on modern man, that if this point of view is not according to science, it is regarded as nonsense. Everything which is brought up in the human being and is thereby entangled with his thinking habits, leads the human being to phrase his question in this way. Then he can, when he says: 'This question can be answered by science' — at least add: 'Faith remains the way in which the body and the soul may unite.' Yet, it is actually not so. Here lies one of the points where you can make yourself quite demonstrative; for Anthroposophy it is quite important to connect with science and develop it further. Through anthroposophic research it is shown that the concept of matter, as it exists in the human organism, becomes fully disabled in its mode of action. If one looks at a fertilized female egg and its further development, one actually is looking at something which through conception, has excluded itself from all possible earthly events. In the fertilized egg a chaos is created in which all processes available to science, are initially excluded. If I present it schematically it will end here. (A drawing is made on the blackboard.)

FOUNDATION COURSE

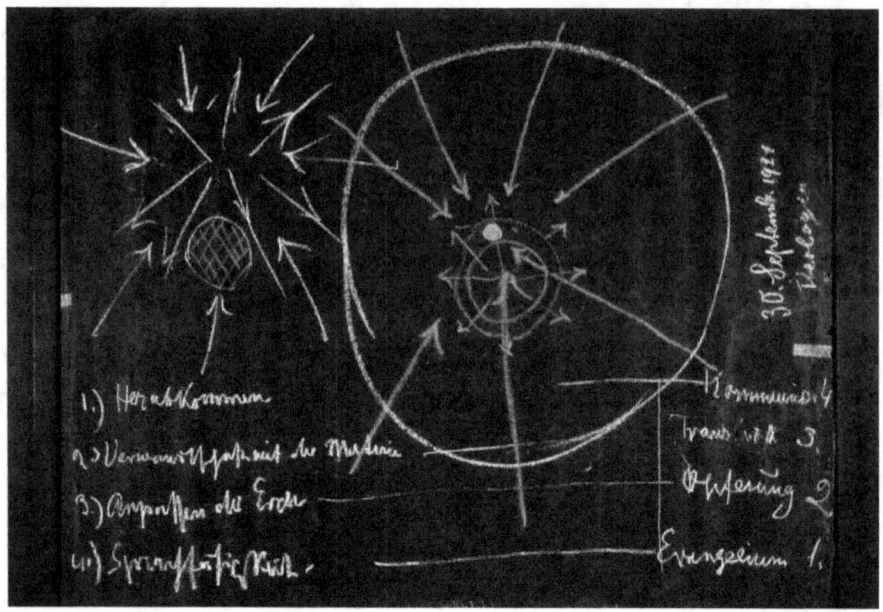

Plate 5   9. Lecture   30. September 1921, afternoon

Through the fertilization, as far as it happens in the human being, a place is created within earth's processes, where everything stops which could be accessible to natural science. Through this exclusion the possibility is created, at this point, for cosmic activity to take place, peripheral cosmic processes. Within this place something happens which is not accessible to material science.

Here I'm drawing the earth, here is the realm of human beings, this is the periphery beyond which you can go, far beyond measure. While most of us, actually in the realm human beings have the earth's processes, also with the father and mother, we have here — in this circle which I'm drawing — effects from the periphery, from the immeasurable expanse, so that, what is happening here, may be transferred and enter into the scientifically given world. It is an imagination which is quite far away from modern man, because it has been lost since the 15th century.

When you are in the proximity of Nepal and walk over the earth, you only need to put a flame to a piece of paper and light it, to see how it smokes out of the earth. Those of you who have travelled in Italy would have seen this: it smokes out of the earth. Why does this happen? It is because what would rise from within the earth is usually held by the air pressure; by lighting a piece of paper the air pressure is reduced and what is below, in the earth, now pushes out.

Through the fertilization the earth processes are excluded, and this enables the heavenly processes to be active. The reverse is what you can demonstrate with a volcanic vent. While we just examine earthly phenomena we have mainly to do with centralized processes, in other words that which rays out from the earth's centre, basically in the direction of gravity, whereas when we consider embryonic processes it is in relation to peripheral processes, which to some extent come from out of immeasurable widths, working in towards the centre. They become effective the moment the earth's effectiveness is excluded. If we go into what is taking place here, then with human embryonic development we need to examine what the participation of the entire cosmos has in the origins of mankind, and not look at precursors which are earthly. Secondly it happens — and it happens further along the embryonic development — that it enters into a relationship with physical matter. Thirdly, what happens is that which has come to the human beings out of the spiritual world and entered the physical world and all that can be in its emerging, everything which had come from the cosmos as periphery-central, in contrast with central-peripheral, now comes into the centre. Through all of this, only now earthly processes come about, man's utilisation of the earthly. The fourth event, the last one, is the preparation for inner human love which only appears when the individual has learnt to speak. So we can say that the precursors which take place through birth are the following: the human being's descent from the spiritual community: if you like the word, it could be "excommunication," meaning the descent, the coming down. *(He writes on the blackboard.)*

1. **Descent.**

    The second is the entering of the relationship with matter. *(Writes on the blackboard:)*
2. **Relationship with matter.**

    The third is entitlement to the centralising forces of the earth: adaptation to the earthly. *(Writes on the blackboard:)*
3. **Adaptation to the earth**

    And the fourth is perceptibility, the ability to speak which however only emerges after the birth, to the extent of what embryonic activity took place. *(Writes on the blackboard:)*
4. **Ability to speak.**

    We come closer to the mystery of birth in quite another way if we look at it like this, my dear friends.

    How can we come closer to the mystery of death which is the other pole of human life? If we now go in reverse, and we begin with the Ability to Speak *(Writes on the blackboard:)*

Gospel 1

Then we create in contrast to the entitlement of the centralising earthly forces, the resurrection, the re-adaptation of the periphery: this happens in the sacrifice of smoke. The opposite of "three" is what we are doing by taking what we receive and adapting it to the earth, to the smoke counteracting the earth's centralizing forces. *(Writes on the blackboard:)*

Offering 2

In other words, what are we doing here? We first speak the Word in the Gospel, and we become conscious that we express this Word in such a way that it is not our word in the sense as I've said yesterday, but that it goes over into objectivity. We relinquish the Word to the smoke — smoke which is capable of adapting the form of the words. Certainly you may say it is suggestive, but still, only suggestive. The Offering consists in the expressed word, which creates waves, being trusted to the smoke, carried up in the smoke. Our word itself becomes carried up. If we turn the relationship to matter around, then we arrive at the dematerialization in the transubstantiation, in the transformation. *(Writes on the blackboard:)*

Transubstantiation 3

In our becoming a child out of the periphery of the cosmos and drawing in our 'I,' in death we withdraw, and we have for this the sign of the transubstantiation, the de-materialization. Where does this power come from? See, just as the peripheral forces work towards the centre when we speak about birth, these forces which we have called up in the offering, work outwards into the world. They work because we have entrusted our words into the smoke. They now work from out of the centre and they carry the dematerialised words through the power of the speaker and in this way, we come into the position, to fulfil the fourth, the opposite of the descent, the merging with the Above, the communion. *(Writes on the blackboard:)*

Communion 4

Now, however my dear friends, we are not only born in the beginning of our lives but forces active at birth continue to work in us. These forces, however, do decrease when we are separated from our mother's body into the outer air. They become subdued but continue working to a lesser extent. The most obvious continuation lies in the creation of languages from the embryonic forces, also in relation to the rest of the organism. Besides the forces creating language, embryonic forces continue to work and do so most strongly from the moment of going to sleep to that of waking up. Thus, embryonic forces work more strongly during sleep than when people are awake. It is only an extract which had been working during the time of being an embryo, yet during hours of restful sleep these embryonic forces continue to work. Forces of death also work in us continuously. Every moment we are born, and we die. Death forces are working. The reverse processes which had descended to work in the development of language continue to work in us; this process works in us, which come from the Gospel through to communion, from the speech up to the union with the Divine-spiritual. However, that which is a sacrament in the Mass, is fulfilled in an outer process which continuously counteracts what is being born in us. This is what amounts to the continuous perpetual forces of death in us.

You see, this sacramental process would have been fulfilled in the old Mysteries. Why could they have been accomplished in the old Mysteries? They could have been fulfilled because a certain inherited spiritual perceptivity was available for them.

The very moment when a person who lived before the Mystery of Golgotha, pronounced the corresponding words, therefore expressing what we have in the Gospels today, these words were taken into account by the Divine-spiritual. With the ceremony the people surrendered their continuous dying process to the Divine-spiritual forces. These Divine-spiritual forces left the earth during the time of the Mystery of Golgotha. It is only a historical prejudice to believe that the earth is in a continuous development. This is not so; it is certainly not. If the Mystery of Golgotha had not been fulfilled then we could not fulfil such a ceremony, then what dies is given over to the etheric and astral worlds and not, however, to the world where our 'I' belongs. It was not like that before the Mystery of Golgotha.

Here we touch on something, dear friends, which people with their intellectual education can't believe at all because they don't have the antecedents to it. They can't believe that fire, air, water and earth since the time of the Mystery of Golgotha are different from before. It only appears as determined by a time, not that the following could be answered: What would have happened to the earth if the Mystery of Golgotha had not taken place? — So let's just switch the Mystery of Golgotha off, and we can ask ourselves: What would have become of this ceremony if the event of the Mystery of Golgotha had not happened?

It would be a procedure that, driven by the process of death, would only have conserved our being up to our astral body. The physical body would lose itself into the earth, the ether body would become indistinct in the etheric seas, and the astral body would enter into the astral world, but the I would be corrupted; the I would have to reach its end in some or other incorporation; the I could not go through the portal of death. That is the secret of earth evolution, that, before our time calculation began, the human being retained something which could have been redeemed by going through the gate of death, and which could be made clear through this ceremony. This ceremony, had the Mystery of Golgotha not intervened, would have become what it could have, if the last of the spiritual beings who still had a relationship to the human I, had departed from warmth, air, water, earth, and as in warmth, air, water and air only those beings remained, which still had a connection to our etheric, who have a further relationship to our astral, but no more with our human I.

This, my dear friends, was the huge fear for the demons when they recognised Christ, who had descended on to the earth. They believed they could now take on the control and eradicate the human I from earth. It is clearly expressed in the Gospels, how the demons behaved when they recognised who had arrived. They knew their plan for the world was crossed out, they had hoped — from out of the spheres where they had originated, they could hope for it — to take the earth's rulership into their own hands. Christ stepped on to the earth and that which the Christ had brought down from the spiritual worlds into earthly events, gave the ceremony its new content, and in this ceremony the presence of the Christ Being took place.

This is something which certainly can be accessed through spiritual science. You really need to take this up in yourselves, what I have, in a way, only drawn in threads, sketched, as if given in a little drawing. The human being needs to start arriving at a real understanding for the mystery of birth, which appears in nature as a sacrament itself, because it is supernatural, and an understanding must be created for the sacrament within the sacrifice of Mass, which becomes supernatural through the presence of Christ. For those who can't reason, as I've just spoken, for those who can't understand the actual process in the outcry of the lower demons when they saw the deeds of Christ, and only regard this outcry of the demons as a comparison, taking it as something exhausted in the meaning of words, don't understand anything about sacramental deeds, and in particular, the central sacramental ritual of the sacrifice of Mass.

Unfortunately, humanity has forgotten that they could speak about these things since the first third of the 15th century. Today we are confronted with not only what is customary in the country, but also what has become customary on earth, to appear like a maniac when words are uttered considering the outcry of the demons as a real event when they saw the Christ. We often have the experience: What is wisdom before God, has become foolishness to the world. Then again what is foolishness before the world, in present times is so often wisdom before the gods.

So the time has arrived when the sacramental element is not at all able to penetrate, because intellectualism is seizing all circles with such power — it works firstly on our religious and scientific areas — that it also seizes the religious and above all, things concerning theology. It's connected to external events, my dear friends, that took place, and you can see it resulted in what had actually developed out of church schools as a teaching for humanity, first preserved in the universities. If you want to continue taking this further you can study the way universities continued from the 14th century onwards, where the spiritual evolution gradually became removed from human evolution, how they gradually became secularized and how in due course what was within the spiritual led to the worldly. Make a study of how state waged war with the church, and how the state — because the church insisted on it — at most left the teaching content within it as an enclave but otherwise the spiritual has been taken out of humanity's evolution. This historical evolution you have to experience, you must even be able to feel it. We stand today in the presence of many cold hearts in historical development. We have completely stopped feeling religious at least as far as historical development is concerned. How can we gain from the Gospels at all, while they have emerged out of quite other states of evolution, when we have stopped feeling religious towards historical evolution?

You see, here you have a real transition from out of the earthly life, into the spiritual life. Through birth a person descends in four steps into the earthly existence until the moment of speech, through the death process he ascends from speech up to communion. He would have died today, also his I, if he had not taken up what lies up to communion in the whole ceremonial process, if he has not taken up Christ, who redeemed from within the physical, the etheric, astral and conserving the I, so that he can retain his I even after death.

With the sacrifice of Mass people are snatched away from the power of the demons, from that power which entangles us in contradictions which are primarily shaped by intellectual concepts with sharp outlines. However, life is not made up of sharp outlines, life can only live within our consciousness in a conceptual way, if a concept organically evolves into another concept. With the inorganic, where we have detached concepts, they are merely clothed as dead in our consciousness. We need concepts which can evolve from one into another, which are alive and capable of metamorphosis; only *these* concept are not pushed away when we take them up inwardly, these concepts would be propagated and would be capable, through the offering, through transubstantiation up to communion, to become re-united with the Divine, through which we are released here on earth.

Whoever adapts the standpoint of modern consciousness, my dear friends, takes on the standpoint which had to be accepted on the one side from the 15th century, if one goes with the progress of the human race. One actually has to simply go with progress; it gives a certain viewpoint of consciousness, by which we can't remain standing still. Even if we are to fall into an abyss, we would have to go with the progress of the human race, but we must simply find the possibility to return from the other side of the abyss so we may continue. What has been happening since the 15th century has of course been necessary. The evangelistic-protestant consciousness has permeated what had been necessary in the evolution of humanity since the 15th century. You can see how, as the point of this development approached humanity, the most varied discussions regarding the transubstantiation and the Last Supper came to the fore. As long as one takes the point of view of the sacramental, such discussions won't arise, because such discussions stem from the invasion of intellectualism in the sacramental way of thinking. From before the 15th century, we in Europe were at the same standpoint on which Hinduism stands today. When a Hindu participates in intellectual development, he is in this intellectual development as free as possible, in as far as he remains a true Brahman. The Hindu participates in the ceremony, in the ritual; it connects everyone, and those who participate in the ritual is a true Hindu believer; he can think about it as he wishes, in it he remains completely free. Dogma, which is captured by thoughts, or a content of teaching, basically doesn't exist. Schools can emerge that interpret things in a hundred different ways. All of this can exist in orthodox Hinduism, if only the ceremonies are recorded as something actual and real.

Humanity in Europe also reached this standpoint before, around the time of the 15th century. At that time the invasion of intellectualism, which promoted sharp, outlined concepts, would simply not comply with sacramentalism, because with the commencement of discussions there was actually nothing to discuss. If there had been such a person as Scotus Eriugena, in other words a person who stood amidst the conception of the first Christian centuries presenting the discussion of later — one could even say that they were in front of him in a certain sense, it works that way ahead, it is after all in the others ... — (gap in notes). If you study this in Scotus Eriugena you could say he spoke out of the fullness of life, by contrast the later discussions can be compared to my experience with a school friend who had quite radically wriggled himself into materialism, and during our dialogue about one thing and another, he became quite angry and interrupted with the words: It is nonsense to speak about something other than brain processes, to say anything other than what moves in the brain are mere molecules and brain atoms, because those are the only things that happen in thinking and feeling. — So I answered: So, tell me, why are you lying? You are continuously lying when you say, "I feel" and "I think" and so on; you will have to say, "my brain feels," "my brain thinks"; in order for you to be correct, you have to say it like that. — Because he had developed completely into materialism, he criticized people one day in their very foundations. He said: A human being is a being who, instead of standing properly on a surface, moves by oscillating on two legs in a constant search for a position of equilibrium: it is simply nonsense to regard the way he moves, in any other way. — From his point of view, he spoke correctly because he criticized the living from the point of view of intellectualism. Somewhat in this way it would appear to an old confessor of sacramentalism, if one spoke from an intellectual critical viewpoint about sacramentalism and criticized religious life in this way. Since the 15th century it has become a matter of course and all of what is modern religious consciousness doesn't know just how much it has become entangled in it.

So one can say: we have on the one side the Catholic Church, which, if it feels its living nerve rightly, does not allow intellectualism to enter into it, and we have on the other side the evangelist-protestant consciousness having developed in a cultural milieu which no longer experiences the reality of sacramentalism, as I've indicated today. That's why the abyss is so enormous. The Catholic has stopped in the human evolution presented in the impulses of the 15th century; he developed his religion only up to this point. Cardinal Newman's connection to Catholicism therefore was so difficult, because his approach was out of modern consciousness. For the Catholic, religious life has come to one side, while modern science took the outer side. You can't read a scientific work that has emerged from Catholicism without experiencing how the most learned priests and most learned Catholics work with science in such a way that it is regarded as outer phenomena, and only that which they bring in feeling, in fervour from their Catholicism, can give them strength. However, science is a different matter to what is done within the religious, and the scholasticism of Thomas Aquinas was the last product of intellectual development in that it still included the philosophy as organic in its world view. As a result, it basically had to be discussed again for the philosophical fortification of Catholicism. The Protestant consciousness felt obliged to take up intellectualism, to process intellectualism. Thus, they became alienated from sacramentalism; as a result, it became necessary to take on an ethical character, it was necessary to relinquish everything which somehow formed foundations of knowledge for the religious life. It was for instance necessary to insist that, instead of adding a mystery to birth, to substitute it with the scientific mystery of birth which meant connecting the soul with the body, achieved without an opinion possibly gained from it. The Mass, the inverse ceremony of birth processes, which are dying processes, would be mindlessly given over to historical development, and abandoned. This all relates to the time of intellectualism when the human being could no longer directly find the spiritual within the physical. So it can be seen, that if religious content is to be saved at all, it would be to formulate it in such a way that it has nothing connecting it to a content of knowledge. This will always stand as a gaping contradiction for anyone who does not, in theory, want to ignore the practical impulses of the soul's life.

However, humanity could never have entered into the age of experiencing freedom without having participated what had been brought to fruition in the 15th century, because freedom can only be gained within the culture of intellectualism. Only intellectually are we able to depend so much on ourselves that we may have the inner experience, which I have portrayed in my book "The Philosophy of Freedom" (later translations called The

Philosophy of Spiritual Activity) regarding the experience of pure thinking as the foundation of freedom. All discussions prior to this regarding freedom, are only preparatory, because freedom is not to be discovered within a view which basically only contained necessity, like the view which had remained before the 15th century. So let's pose the fundamental question which can be solved in the present: How do we, despite recognising the blessings of intellectualism, rediscover the sacramental out of freedom?

Without a deep grasp on this question, we will not be able to understand it. The help of historical evolution needs to be taken into account in order to understand these things. If you can't let go of what I've now come to terms with, if you don't understand Luther's soul struggle inwardly either, but only in a certain sense only outwardly, intellectually, you will see in the next few days that we have already, with what has been said today, started moving the building blocks together for the understanding of Luther's soul's struggle. With this I want to close today.

(Afterwards Rudolf Steiner admitted he would be willing to enter into eventual questions and Licentiate Bock asked him to shortly clarify again the connection between Mass and birth.)

Rudolf Steiner: It concerns the ability of speech, therefore life through words, which is the last capability given through the powers of birth, come to the fore in this direction (reference to table 5 — see outline below). Now, we develop the ability for language which we receive here, in the most comprehensive sense, which we apply in the Gospels, in that we proclaim the words of God, so that we are carried from birth up to the words which turn back again. So the way goes from "descent" up to the words, Logos, and then back again. I only wrote "Gospel" on the blackboard, to place the Mass as a reverse ritual in the ceremonial process. When we look at the sacrifice of Mass — I'm letting go of the introductory processes, they are all preparatory — so the first real action is reading the Gospel, the sounding out of words, that means all which is directed towards birth, we allow to sound initially in the sacrifice of Mass. The Gospel which is read, is actually the first process of the Mass, and sounds out as word. Now, after intermediate processes here again, which do not represent the essential, the offering begins. The altar is smoked. This has the meaning that the word, which is sounded, unites with the smoke and rises from the altar. Then a time follows in which the offering continues up to the transubstantiation, when we also come back to the final material. Finally, there's the communion, which is the reverse of the descent, which is to be taken upwards. If we have understood the totality of the processes, then we first have the word, then the offering with smoke, then the word is carried into it through the power of dematerialization in the transformation and to the unification through communion. Yes, so be it.

1. *Descent* — *Communion 4.*
2. *Relationship with matter* — *Transubstantiation 3.*
3. *Adaptation to earth* — *Offering 2.*
4. *Ability to speak* — *Gospel 1.*

COMPOSITION OF THE GOSPELS

Lecture given in Dornach on 1 October 1921, morning.

My dear friends! At the end of this lecture I would like to explore the arrangement of the material which we want to consider in the time remaining available to us. Today I want to start by continuing what I had begun yesterday. This will make it easier to reach clarity quite quickly regarding the effects of the teaching when the necessary basics are there in the sense I have imagined them and added them to this. For these basics to be more solid, we need a little additional time.

If we consider how to enter into the Gospels in the sense of working with the Gospel processes, then we first of all discover before our souls how in a most particular way the Gospels can be related to, and it is of course necessary, regarding this point, that everyone approaches them from a personal perspective. You then generally understand the content when such a perspective is asserted. For this reason, you may allow me to say something personal in today's lecture. I'm urged to do this because it is the best way for you to receive the following.

When I approach the Gospels, it often happens that I have quite a distinctive feeling that within the Gospels, as far as they can be understood, what has been thought and said about them — and you could even, I say this explicitly, however often you approach them — always encounter something new. You can never know enough about the Gospels. Learning about the Gospels is linked to something else; it is linked to the fact that the further you occupy yourself with them, the more your admiration grows for the depth of the content, for just that, I could call it the immeasurable, into which you can become immersed, which calls for the actual experience, that there is no end to this immersion into the depths, that this admiration increases greatly with every deepening of the Gospel involvement.

There are however difficulties along this path which come to the fore when some strides are made into the Gospel — I stress the words "into" — that make you stumble over the inherited content. For actual spiritual researchers this creates less of a disturbance, because such a person would place the primordial Gospel into, what one could nearly call, a wordless text, and that makes it easier not to stumble over the inherited content. Admiration as a basis for reading the Gospels, seems to me an indispensable element for individuals, as a foundation for their religious learning processes. I once more need to stress that it is not important to characterise religious life in general, but to supply a foundation for the teaching process, in any case for religious processes as such.

This admiration you develop for the Gospels actually connects to everything, including details in the Gospels, and follows something else which will probably surprise you, but as I said, I'm speaking from a personal perspective; as a result of this admiration there is the feeling that you are never completely satisfied with just *one* of the Gospels, but you would only be satisfied with a combined harmony sounding through all the Gospels in a lively way. For instance a great deal of meaning can be found if you let the 13th chapter of Matthew's Gospel work on you and strive to enter into it as I've tried to indicate yesterday and want to continue with today; then again taking the parallel position, but now with Luke's Gospel, into your soul, where approximately the same situation is described, then you will have quite a changed impression of the experience. The impression becomes quite different; one arrives at quite another synopsis to one which one usually experiences, compared with an inner, lively synopsis.

You see, when you have occupied yourself with such things for a long time, you have had all kinds of experiences in life, and these experiences could seem quite important in as far as having started as a youngster and entering into these teaching processes which you wanted, in the majority.

I once encountered a man with a New Testament. For this New Testament he had acquired four differently coloured pencils and then he had with one pencil, I think it was the red one, underlined everything carefully which appeared as common content in all four Gospels. That meant, as he showed me, very little. He had taken St John's Gospel. There were four pencils; the other three he had applied to delete what only is contained in the Matthew Gospel, and then, what only was in Mark's Gospel and finally that which only appeared in the Gospel of Luke. In this way he had in his way created a strange analytical synopsis about which he was extraordinarily proud. I objected, saying such attempts were often made; we also know about it within German literature — it was an Englishman who held this achievement in front of me — where these attempts are made with corresponding places indicated next to one another in columns and blank intermediate spaces left where it can only be found in one of the Gospels. He was a priori convinced that his synopsis was the best.

It is exactly the opposite way to what can be found with the choice of the spiritual route. Here the different Gospels' content doesn't fall apart in contradictions, but they are enclosed into the totality of the deed, together; the coming-into-admiration is an experience which has to be had, an experience which is resisted in the most imminent sense by our present spirit of the time. For the spiritual scientist, however, it turns out that what I cannot even ask you to accept is still there, it turns out that there is no other way, than that the content of truth must appear other than just by the harmony between the four Gospels. It would, even if one would create an external synopsis as in Tatian's sense, which are not contradictory within certain limits, it would not result in what is found in the four Gospels as a concrete harmony.

You need to allow all four to work on you and then wait to see what comes out of this, not by first prescribing what the unopposed abstract truth should be and then only look for all which you can eliminate which contradicts the abstract truth. The truth needs to be experienced, and the Gospels themselves are such written works in which truth can be experienced; however, you need to have patience in order to experience this truth in the Gospels. You can of course object and say, you will never actually be able to experience the truth within the Gospels. I have to agree with your point of view because I still never presume to believe that I have found the truth of the Gospels completely; by continuously making further progress I have the decisive feeling that remaining patient in waiting is the basis, because the certainty of truth does not diminish, but becomes increasingly bigger. You can calmly feel the truth as an ideal placed before you at an immeasurable distance yet with the awareness that you are on your way towards it. These are the things you need to place in the soul with Gospel reading, and shape in your heart, otherwise you would actually never be able to cope with the Gospels in a real way. Of course, you could ask: Should I do this? — It will be shown in the next few days, that yes, one should do this after all.

Now I must say, it was quite an inner rejoicing for me when I came across something in the Gospels which someone else probably have found as well, but I came across it through spiritual research into the Gospels. I came across an image which really should be grasped with the eyes of the soul; an image of the three Wise Men or the Three Kings — kings were in those days initiates, inspired by wisdom — how the three Wise Men according to their knowledge discovered in the stars, clearly saw the starry script in the heaven leading them to the Star of Christ, and they came to worship Christ. They actually saw that Christ had to come, according to the prophecy in the stars. For those who know out of scientific foundations what is called star wisdom, can actually only honour this image in the right sense, because they would know that star wisdom is in the most imminent sense different from what we call astronomy today.

What we call astronomy today is mathematical and, at most, of a physical nature. If we talk about astronomy today, which is a science of calculations, and we talk of astrophysics, which is a mechanical science, also when we as religious individuals come from a different basis to our feeling towards the cosmos, we speak out of our time spirit and feel and think within it. However, prophetically predictive star wisdom of the Tree Wise Men is something quite different.

Star wisdom was at that time not taken like earth wisdom. Star wisdom was called something which could not be calculated purely by mathematics or physics, it was regarded as something that must be read like a scripture which had to be learned. The starting point was the twelve fixed signs of the zodiac, and then to look what changes the planets experienced in their positions — seven were accepted, as you know — in relation to the fixed signs of the zodiac. These curved movements were taken up by man; just as we read letters, so man saw signs in the curves, signs giving through the planetary positions in the zodiac, and with their own observations of the stars, to each was added a plane. These planes were differentiated according to how man experienced the world-all from the physical point of view: (draws on blackboard) north, south, east, west, with which you could intensively think about the depth of the dimensions, with nothing added, but everything that was found in the dimensional depth, projected on this plane. By looking at these fourfold differentiated planes as the table on which you read what is shown in the starry worlds as revealed, resulted in a feeling as if you read in the cosmos, and there were specific tasks, which one attains through this reading of the cosmos.

COMPOSITION OF THE GOSPELS

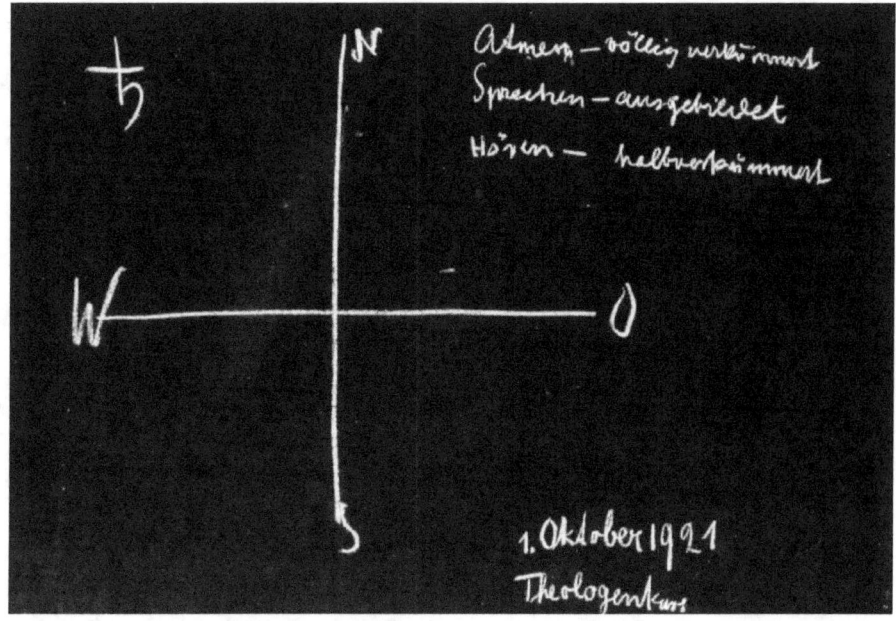

Plate 6   10th Lecture   1. October 1921, in the morning

One such task was that you said: Shift yourself particularly into seeing, into your inner seeing and understand how you feel yourself within it, and by understanding yourself in this inner positioning, you now follow the moon's course, follow therefore what can be placed here (demonstrates on blackboard), and you will understand as earthy man, the secrets of Saturn.

I initially just want to indicate how such things came about. These were once lively human occupations and through this reading in the heavens a certain amount of knowledge was gathered. Today's astronomy and astrophysics by comparison appear as someone describing the letters, but in the astronomy under consideration here, I'm not even talking about the letters but about reading the text. That's the difference. With this I wanted to characterise how wisdom was created for humanity from which the wise men rose up out of the Orient in search of Christ: this wisdom directed them to the Christ.

My dear friends, what has actually arisen in our souls with this? What is placed before our souls is that the highest wisdom which could, at that time, be reached in the world, was leading towards the Mystery of Golgotha, the highest wisdom. To a certain extent in this lies the thought of the proclamation: May you obtain the highest wisdom; the highest wisdom which can be gained from reading the stars, proclaiming the Mystery of Golgotha to you.

This image appears in the Matthew Gospel when you are in the position to fully engage in the Matthew Gospel, in its own time epoch. This experience forms itself in such a way that it really turns into admiration for the depictions of the Matthew Gospel.

Now you leave this image for a moment. Going on to Luke's Gospel you find the verse of the shepherds in the fields. In contrast to the Three Wise Men from the Orient, who have the highest knowledge, you are taken to the simple-minded shepherds in the fields, who know nothing about knowledge, who can't for a moment sense the knowledge possessed by the three Wise Men from the Orient. The shepherds, through the natural relationship they have with their consciousness, only have an inner experience in which the announcement is given: The Divine is revealed in the Heights, so that peace may come to all mankind — only out of their uncomplicated, simple-minded experience this manifests as an image, not a mere dream image, but a picture of an imagination of a higher reality, a higher actuality. We are led to the hearts of these shepherds, who out of this human simplicity, in the absence of all knowledge, come to the decision to go and worship the Child.

Let's now place these two side by side. We don't look at them as something about who said this or who said that, but we place them side by side as the complimentary experience towards the complete truth. What do we get then? We have the direct, enlivened conviction: The Mystery of Golgotha has appeared in such a way that it is revealed to the highest of knowledge of that time *and* the most simple-minded hearts, if they are open to it in a selfless way. On the one hand, hardly anything can be seen with greater illumination and on the other hand experienced with greater depth in the soul, than the feelings in the Mystery of Golgotha.

You have to have the boldest of modern intellectualist minds towards experiences, well founded in present knowledge and not only in an outer content of old wisdom, but in the soul constitution of the old wise ones, if you want to behave like modern science behaves towards these things. Just as deeply as the cosmic reading resides within the starry worlds, so deeply are the simple-minded shepherds in the fields certain of the strong validity of the announcement. Today, mankind no longer knows how the soul constitution has changed in the course of time, humanity doesn't know how, what can be read in the outer knowledge of the stars, can be experienced inwardly in the human soul as it was experienced in olden times, how astral truths were heart-felt experiences, and how we as human beings, in order to gain our freedom, were led out of these stages of consciousness, and after gaining our conscious freedom, we can again return to this earlier stage. My dear friends, we must be able to acquire this selfish feeling. To achieve our freedom, we must go back so far, let's say from 20 December to 6th or 7th January just as abstractly as people with our souls, as we do, for example, when we (abstractly) experience Easter time. Let me express this particularly clearly — as I've said, these things even take root in life's experiences — I once attended a small gathering where the discussion was about a reformed calendar, a reformed calendar to be developed from modern needs. A modern astronomer who was highly regarded in the astronomic scholarly community, was also present. He obviously was an expert witness and pleaded for the uniformity in the Easter festival being determined as always being on the first Sunday of April, that it would be at least purely outwardly, abstractly, fixed. He had no understanding at all that mankind had to look at the alternating relationship between the sun and moon in order to determine the Easter festival. To speak like this in such a gathering would of course have been complete foolishness. We are so far away from our inner religious experience of what current humanity can understand of the cosmos, which, just when it's at the highest point of its particular chapter of scholarship, they see it only as normal for mankind.

Among the reasons given at the time to determine the Easter festival, there was also introduced the disorder which had to be put into the annual accounting records, when the variable time of Easter had to be placed into these books, they no longer preserve anything other from the old religion than inserting the words "With God" on the first page. This was recorded in the accounting records. I ask you to please go and look for yourselves, how much of this expression is observed in the pages that follow.

You need to understand such things thoroughly, as expressions of the spirit of the time. If you don't grasp the spirit of the time even into the details, how will you then sense the actual impulse for religious renewal? You have to be able to say to yourself with certain seriousness that this "with God" should prove true on the pages of the General Ledger and Cash Book or Journal. Just imagine what power is needed to encounter the forces active in today's social life, to really bring religion into life. This has to be sensed constantly in the background, or otherwise the drive to religious renewal is not serious enough, as it should be today. So, a feeling must develop for change in the soul constitution. You must understand that in olden times the soul constitution was such that when the earth was frozen and the stars appeared in its extraordinary aura in the second half of December, inner mankind was so contracted that they came to visions which allowed them to inwardly experience what in reality was outwardly read in the stars by the exploring astrologers.

From the same source did the poor shepherds on the fields and the astrologers (for that was they were, the Wise Men) come to worship the Christ infant. They came from different sides to the same place. The ones from the periphery of the world-all, the others from the centre of the heart of mankind, and they discovered the same. We must learn while doing one thing or another, to also really find the same, we must, particularly as religious teachers do this, so that our words gather content, content of such a kind as the content in the words the Tree Wise Men brought from the Orient.

In the same way as the shepherds went forth in the fields, we must go, because only then will words become as powerful as they need to be. We need content for our words, and we need power in words. We attain such content for our words when we deepen ourselves in something like the Matthew Gospel; and we attain the power when we deepen ourselves in something like the Luke Gospel. These two Gospels — we will still come back to the others — stand to a great extent as complimentary opposite each other. It is what anyone can give and taken into their being, just as if we break through what is given as religious teaching content coming from of the depth of the human soul.

So you see, we can only really speak in this way through Anthroposophy. Just try for once if you can find the possibility somewhere, to speak in this way. Where you will find it, Anthroposophy is actually subliminally present; it doesn't always have to be called dogmatic, it is not meant that way.

Now, as soon as we approach such feeling and experiences as we find in the 13th chapter of the Matthew Gospel, my dear friends, then first of all we will find — by just taking the words, as they are expressed — that their experienced content is not the same as what we so easily have in the awareness of our time — we discover first of all an elevated admiration for the entire composition of the 13th chapter of the Matthew Gospel. The entire composition can only leave one filled with admiration.

First of all, we have the parable of the sower. After this parable we have three parables, from the sowing of the herbs and the weeds which should grow until the harvest, we have the mustard seed parable and the parable of the sourdough. Between these parables we have certain instruction of the disciples who should listen differently compared to how other people listen. Then come the dismissal of the people and more parables which are addressed to the disciples only. During the course of the chapters we are led through parables spoken to the people, and to instructions given to the disciples regarding the parables which had been given to the people. Then follows the disciples being taken into, I'd like to call it, the secrecy of the parables which only the disciples share, followed by the question: Have you understood the parables? — and the answer: Yes, Lord. —

This is a wonderful composition and it becomes even more admirable when we go into details. First of all, we simply have the parable of the sower. After introductory words having been said, we are told what the sower sows; that birds also eat the sown seeds, some seeds fall on stony ground where they can only have weak roots and get too little inner strength, others fall on good earth. This is clearly put to us; and after this has been given, the next parable already starts with the words: "The Kingdom of Heaven is like ..." The parables that follow and that are also spoken to the people, begins with "The Kingdom of Heaven is like ..." The people are therefore thoroughly prepared, by first having the facts established and then they are softly led to what is said as facts, facts aimed at the nature of the kingdoms of heaven. That's all the people will be told, then they will be released.

The following parables are taught to the disciples: the parable of the treasure in the field, the parable of the precious pearl, the parable of the fish caught in the net from which many are thrown out, and the good ones gathered for nourishment. These parables are only spoken about to the disciples, and they are asked whether they have understood. They answer with the word "Yes," which in the context of the Gospel would mean the same if today we could acquire the right feeling for it, and say: Yes,

Amen. — In this the wonderful composition lies, which does not have to be looked for because it comes across in a natural way.

Sceptics may well say: this layout means nothing, as it is put down. — However, my dear friends, if you let yourself live into the Gospels, you will not be able to do anything other than experience these things; and it will have its reasons why we must experience them so, as to live into the wonderful composition, in order to really notice all the details, the Gospels have to reveal. Here you have a wonderful composition.

Let's try and enter into this wonderful composition. Let's go to the three parables only told to the disciples about heaven. According to the total sense in which the 13th chapter of Matthew's Gospel is expressed, out of the spirit of Matthew's Gospel of Christ Jesus, this is not said to the people. Listen carefully what I emphasize: in the spirit of the Matthew Gospel this would not be told to the people. Try to remember exactly what is said in these parables which are only told to the disciples. Firstly, there's the parable about the treasure in the field, discovered by a man who then sells all he has in order to buy the field with the treasure in it, so he may own it. Actually, it comes down to this, that he sells everything in order to acquire this treasure; that he gives up everything so that he may have the treasure. This relationship of Jesus to his disciples may not be expressed to the people. Why? Because it contains a certain danger; that of becoming egotistic, the danger of reward-ethics. One could not, without damaging the people, without further ado speak about egoism. Egoism is addressed when one urges good deeds with reference to the reward of the Eternal. Reward ethic, which fundamentally is still present to a marked degree in the Old Testament, this reward ethic is rejected by Christ Jesus.

That is why he speaks about this parable — for which the unprepared would look for as reward — only to those who had already progressed far enough that there would no longer be a danger for this parable to indicate its egotistic meaning. The disciples who through their communal life with Christ Jesus had gone beyond egoism, to them this could be said as it is in this parable, to them the heavenly realms could be compared with a treasure. In the disciples the urge for selfishness was not agitated. To the people in this sense of the Matthew Gospel it could not be said, just as little as what follows, which is structured accordingly with the parable of the merchant who sells everything in order to acquire the Heavenly realm. Because Christ Jesus knows he may speak to his disciples in this way, he can speak to them about the last, the most dangerous parable. It is the parable which must have a terrible effect on unprepared people, the parable of everything which is in offensive, evil or sinful, will finally be burnt in the furnace of fire, and only the good be gathered for Heaven. This can only be tolerated by minds which have learnt to be un-egoistic; otherwise it would anger their minds regarding such a parable.

What is it actually, that should be avoided with such an instruction, which Christ Jesus gives his disciples? Becoming angry should be avoided, that people should become angry with the way of the world and about being human. The entire 13th chapter of the Matthew Gospel is an instruction to make people patient regarding their destiny; for this reason, it can only be revealed at the very end, as to what will happen at the end of the world. So these final parables are the ones which could only be spoken to the disciples in secrecy because in they were — whatever the Christ Jesus may also say, as the most terrible thing, at this moment, in this immediate present — to be found in unselfishness. For this reason, they could say: Yes, Amen.

After we have tried to have an experience of these particular parables addressed only to the disciples, we can go back to the others. A person can only be prepared for a selfish notion of something if he approaches something which exists outside of him in nature, without agitation of his judgement. If a person dwells on the contemplation of the four processes of the seeds — if a person doesn't think of anything other than: the seeds which fall on to the ground are eaten by the birds, the seeds that fall on stony ground, fall under the thorns, and some on good ground — by simply spending time with these observations, one can actually not be engaged with oneself: one is drawn into selfless observation. After one has, in this way, presented the outside world to the usually selfishly dominated mind, then only can something happen. What is it that can happen?

Now you see, here we again come to an important detail of the 13th Matthew Gospel chapter. I can do nothing towards someone finding this examination of details as perhaps pedantic; for me it is not pedantic, it is certainly a reality. From out of the time consciousness of the epoch of the Mystery of Golgotha important differences are made between ears, errors in hearing, and eyes which are slumbering, sleeping and not awake. The explanation is given that the evolution of mankind should be discovered through the inaccurate hearing and that the eyes should be awakened.

You see, this leads us to, as at that time — which we know about from other anthroposophic foundations — a clear differentiation made between the organisation of hearing and the organisation of seeing. People in the present day clearly know nothing about this. They don't know for example, that the total organisation which stream out from the rhythmic, goes up into the head organisation, and encircles an inner organisational harmony between hearing and speech. Hearing and speech belong together. Hearing and speech is to a certain extent combined in a single organ complex, which today's physiology doesn't list. When I show you my wooden sculpture group you will be able to use this practically demonstrated physiology — but which it doesn't want to be — to see how it appears these days, out of anthroposophic foundations, that they are a unit: breathing, speaking and hearing. These three are also present in seeing. Take this for example (writes on blackboard):

Breathing
Speaking
Hearing

I could also have written: speaking, breathing hearing — the sequence is unimportant. Take these three as the members of a single deed. The three members are also present in seeing. Also in seeing it is there on the one hand, something driven through breathing into the brain, the breathing process participates in seeing. All this is so quietly indicated in the human organization that we are able to say: This here (note on blackboard: *breathing*) is completely atrophied in human consciousness; what we are still able to observe, when we speak, and thus look at our breathing, we don't notice in the visual act; it is completely atrophied. (Beside the word *Breathing* he writes on the blackboard):

- *completely atrophied*

With the act of seeing there is also something half atrophied that links to hearing. (Beside the word *Hearing* he writes on the blackboard):

- *half atrophied*

That is partially atrophied, it remains quite in the shadows of the subconscious. The only thing which is expressed in seeing, corresponds to speaking. (Beside the word *Speaking* he writes on the blackboard):

- *developed*

In conjuring up the images around us through our eyes, we speak etherically. However, the other two members which otherwise clearly diverge, which diverge while listening and speaking, are hardly present with seeing, but atrophied; here mere formation of the image overwhelms us. Because this connection is not perceived, today's tricky physiological foundation lies in epistemology. All epistemological theories, or at least many of them, start from the physiological foundation of observation, which are equally described for all the senses; they actually have no meaning other than an act of seeing. What you can find in the physiological foundation only really fits the act of seeing and is therefore unclear, because people can't see that some things are atrophied. One could say that these physiological views, which dominate there in relation the sensory physiology, are the most dreadful, able to depress the human mind: one is forever being bothered with things said about the senses in general while each sense must be treated concretely, individually. In many cases it is so that a sensory unit theory is taken as a basis.

Such a science as we have developed in Anthroposophy was of course not available at the time of the Mystery of Golgotha. How we can discover the truths about things today essentially depends on our admiration for the Gospel content. Today there's been talk that one must apply great efforts to reach into spiritual research, and that we must regard seeing differently to listening. With listening one must say: People can actually only hear in error because listening is fully developed as a single act. We also have ears that are open during sleep; we have no wilful influence on our auditory images. Our 'I' doesn't quite flow into them and form what is heard, but only in such a way that it can penetrate them with erroneous judgements. Hearing can become incorrect. Seeing has caused hearing to become half atrophied. Seeing has only developed what corresponds to it in speech. Added to this one must be awake, the eyes must be awakened just as people need to learn to speak.

Without it being explicit knowledge in the time of the Mystery of Golgotha, it would have been simply correctly spoken and understood out of the inner soul constitution of the people. I'm not saying something like the Christ having learnt Anthroposophy — that sounds very amusing — or to those he had spoken, had learnt about Anthroposophy. He spoke in such a way because he was aware how the other, by listening, would have understood. Yet also there he had to speak in such a way, as one spoke at that time, regarding seeing, and regarding hearing, from out of the most inner soul constitution. Because of me you use the expression "out of the subconscious" which is a term often misused today in an inconvenient way for these things. In order to have this understood in the right way, you can also understand the third which is also contained in the Matthew Gospel: to understand it with a person's whole being; his concentration, understanding through the heart. Understanding with your whole being is quite a different kind of understanding; one must speak to the heart of the person if you want to explain the parables. You can't speak in a different way to the heart if it is not functioning in such a way that the eyes are made to see in the right way, the ears to hear in a right way. This is how you have to distinguish: you must awaken the ability to see and make the ears hear in the right way. The ears don't need to be awakened, they only need to hear correctly.

In the total style of the 13th Matthew Gospel one's first attention is directed to the full human being; to the focus of the whole human being in his heart, perceiving through his senses, if he is to approach the interpretation of the parables. In the following way Christ Jesus makes it understandable to his disciples: after he has gone through from quite an objective observation given in the parable of the sower, he can no present further active parables and allow these to lead towards the functions of the heavenly realms. First, we have the parable of the plants and the weeds which point out that the good seeds could not flourish, without evil next to it. Then again one could say this is being expressed in a wonderful, quite scientific knowledge, because we know in a certain sense that plants can be damaged if the weeds are taken out in the wrong way. Likewise, we would harm mankind if we were to eradicate sin, for example, by not leading sinful men spiritually to the righteous, but by eradicating them before "the harvest," that is, before the end of the earth. This is approachable to people; what works in plants or in weeds, can be placed before their souls. It can be taken further, placed there objectively, how the world is spread out in the wide-open spaces, and how to carry what comes from the world, to the heavenly kingdom. The kingdom of heaven is the mustard seed, which is small compared with other seeds, then again it becomes a bigger tree compared with other plants.

This too, has to be pointed out to people, how it needs to be seen that the sprout is less visible to the eye than the grown-up plant, the heavenly less obvious than the worldly. Then awareness is drawn to how the kingdom of heaven works like sourdough, but all permeating, also working — at that time this imagination was far more obvious — as something spiritual. At that time this imagination could be uttered without introduction: Look at the sourdough as it is taken by the woman who leavens the bread with it; look at the bread which it spiritualises, behold the kingdom of heaven as it spiritualizes the world. You could not say to the people: Sell everything! The people had to behold what is indicated here, otherwise if you said: Sell everything! — in their selfishness they would really sell the whole world in order to buys something which is in the heavenly realm.

So we see in the 13th chapter of the Matthew Gospel the construction and composition of the truth because the truth is not simply stated as an abstraction, but the activity of truth consciously works from one person to another, that one needs to feel all the time, how one should speak. This is not the teaching of a hierarchy, this is simply the result of what becomes necessary through reality. It is in fact necessary, my dear friends, to speak to you in a different way because you want to become pastoral workers, than I would have spoken to non-pastoral workers, who are only believers. This content of the truth we find in the 13th chapter of the Matthew Gospel comes to us as a direct life experience which we can have in our time, which calls such a strong feeling within us, that it actually has something of a religious character.

You see, for those who have the sense that a way must be found to the truth, the truth must turn into such an inner component that it exists among people and that people can experience the truth — they would feel that university education, as it lives in writing books, is actually something hostile. Today something exists in our writing of books; when we write a book, we don't really feel like a human being among other human beings, for it is conceived as an abstraction; while writing the book it is without regarding who would be acquiring the book. This even produces the desire particularly when spiritual supersensible things are spoken about, for things that can stand alone in a book, and that, because it is ignorant, can only give something very deficient to unknown crowds of people, also again jointly experience the truth with the people in the manner and way these people are prepared for truth, while much is given in the preparation of the truth and less to the ignorant formulation of the truth content. This gives one a clear and strong experience of what I yesterday called the vital content of the Gospels. The vital content of the Gospels must also not be understood abstractly, as many do today. People do not believe, when they as religious teachers allow their words to a certain extent to flow together, that words are permeated with feelings; they firmly insist that in what one calls sacramental, they believe they should find something flowing forth out of the abstraction.

This is not the essential thing; the essential is the sense of feeling oneself a person among people, by experiencing truth with other people. This is after all Christian. For this reason, it is necessary to believe in Christian community building, not only Christian proclamation. It is very necessary to believe that everything must necessarily flow towards real community building: this means not merely thinking about what others are saying, but to communally feel and act together. In community building the foundation must be for the community feeling communally, and act communally. It must be a real soul-spiritual organism built by the community. We will talk about this further.

The following list was given for the material to be discussed:
1. Preliminary conditions
2. Foundation of teaching activity
3. The way to experiencing the truth
4. The essence of the breviary, the sermon
5. Building the ritual
6. The treatment of the Community.

INSIGHTS INTO MYSTERY OF GOLGOTHA, PRIEST ORDINATION.

Lecture given in Dornach on 1 October 1921, afternoon.

Prayers were said from various sides before the start of the lecture, and a particular wish was expressed to hear more closely about the battle of Luther's soul.

Rudolf Steiner: Yes, my dear friends, if I want to continue exploring which what we started, in various directions, it is important that I firstly touch on what existed in ancient Christianity, and then what unfolded out of the various forces working from ancient Christianity leading to the rise of the Evangelical-Protestant experience. We must be quite clear that during the time in which the Mystery of Golgotha took place, those people who would at least have a tendency to accept Christianity, were still of a totally different soul constitution, than what was later the case. The Mystery of Golgotha took place in the human evolution during a time in which it had basically nothing at all to do with, I could call it, pursuing the objective course of the world in a spiritual-scientific way. This is quite extraordinary. When you try to deepen yourself particularly into the objective course of the world, as it is presented in its totality, incorporating the physical, soul and spiritual, you have a strong impression regarding the development in the 8th century before Christ. Once again, you will get this strong impact — this can already be noticed in outer knowledge — regarding the time which I've often spoken about, in the 15th century.

The time epoch stretching from the 8th century BC to 15th AD creates roundabout an epoch in which humanity's development, if you follow this development spiritual-scientifically, was unfolding and can be called the Mind- or Intellectual Soul; in other words, it was the epoch of the Mind- or Intellectual Soul development. In its purest form it comes out of the Greek people's evolution. I call it Mind Soul but ask you, please, not to connect an intellectual concept to this term. Should you want to study the Mind Soul today, as it had developed out of Greekdom, then you need to study such individuals who had in a certain sense some kind of clairvoyance, not schooled clairvoyance but an atavistic one; inherited clairvoyance which can still pop up in some people at present. You can see that the content of the world appears to such people as imaginative, made up of images. If you should ask them to describe their pictorial impressions — of course only if no physical deformation disorder is involved, but when the whole thing is pure — you discover an extraordinary amount of understanding in the images thus depicted. They describe some processes in the spiritual world in pictures. They receive the images, but they get the sense of them as well. They can't help it if they include understanding in the images they receive because they take place together. Up to the 15th Century the soul constitution of many people were still not as developed as the mind is today, but they were inspired by their minds, they could have revelations in the mind. Only after the 15th Century did intellectualism develop which means that the mind had to be actively laboured with inwardly in the soul. Logic had to be developed, it was something to be worked at; it was not, so to speak, just given to the soul. That is the essential difference in the soul constitution of more modern people in comparison with those in this earlier epoch.

When you go still further back, to the evolutionary period of mankind, before the 8th century BC, then you arrive at an epoch where such pictorially filled imaginations initially developed as involuntary imaginations. You get to an epoch which reached back to the 3rd century and find that just this reading in the cosmos which I've described for you this morning, unfolded and appeared in the human soul as pictorial imaginations, still existed in the time of the Mystery of Golgotha, in naive and simple mind natured people. By contrast we have an epoch since the 15th century in which human consciousness must veer to freedom, and this can only happen when people create their own thought forms, out of themselves.

If we simply study world processes objectively, we initially have no reason to believe in the Mystery of Golgotha. We need to attain intuitive knowledge in the sense in which I've depicted in my book "Knowledge of the Higher Worlds and its attainment," and then you get the idea that the Mystery of Golgotha can be seen as falling out of the entire remaining course of the world view. *(Writes on the blackboard.)* If I namely have 8 centuries BC before here, the 15th century, then we have a particular process which must be considered as flowing together, and now gives a particular impact in our years of one or zero.

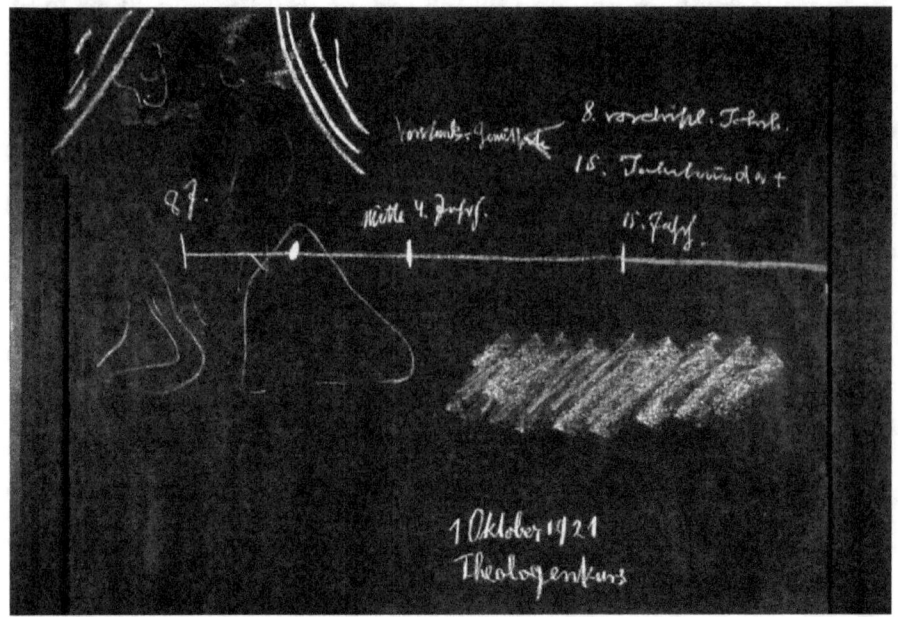

Plate 7   11th Lecture   1. October 1921, afternoon

To a certain extent we can research from the oldest times the evolution of the earth and man, and we will reach a certain stage in the development, but we do not arrive at seeing the Mystery of Golgotha within this research. We definitely come through research of this evolution, if we do *not* look at the Mystery of Golgotha, to the feeling: we are moving to the end of the earth, as human beings we must find our grave in the earth. — This way we arrive at quite a decisive conclusion of the earth dying away. Then we can turn our gaze to the Mystery of Golgotha and so we will find that the earth was renewed, fructified by the Mystery of Golgotha, that a new seed from the expanse contained up to that moment evolutionary streams, and that this new seed, having arrived through the Mystery of Golgotha, forms the foundation for the renewal of the earth. This is primarily the meaning of the Gospel's words which I mentioned yesterday when I said: The spiritual beings who remained on the earth would have perished with the earth (if the Mystery of Golgotha had not taken place): The demons screamed when they saw the Christ, because he stripped them of their rulership. This is certainly a real process. You can be quite certain it isn't merely about accepting some or other event given in the Bible, but it is about a clear observation of the processes.

The Mystery of Golgotha does not even fall in the middle of these time slots (between 8 BC and 15 AD), because the middle of this time is in about the middle of the 4th century. Therefore, this event doesn't even fall into the middle, so one could say: The event of Golgotha is something which took place in contrast to the world of necessity, taking place through divine freedom entering into the earth. It is a deed of freedom coming out of the divine worlds, it certainly was given to humanity from outside, as a gift from the divine world order. As a result, it can't be understood by those who want to observe the continuous historic processes, they may not be able to discover something within it like the Mystery of Golgotha.

To suggest that, I often express it this way: If, let's say, a Mars inhabitant came down to earth, he would find much he can't understand, but he would be able to start understanding something when he looks at something like the painting of the last supper of Leonardo da Vinci. To this extraordinary image and what is intended with the Christ, he would be able to see something which would indicate the central point of earthly events to him. That is obvious only through comparison, but it is a comparison which I've often had to make to indicate what is important here.

Particularly for those who had a strong feeling for the sense of the Mystery of Golgotha as fallen out of the ordinary earthly course, like all that the Roman Catholic Church has gradually become, still a kind of departure came about from the original meaning of the Mystery of Golgotha. It has crystallized into an historic anecdote. When Leonardo da Vinci was appointed to paint the Last Supper, he worked slowly, for a long time. Actually, he needed more than ten years. Then a new Prior arrived and wanted this painting chap to finish off the thing at last. The painting had been completed up to the figure of Judas when the new Prior asked when it would at least be complete. Leonardo said that up to that point he had not been able to complete the painting because he had no model for Judas. Now however, he had in the Prior a model for Judas, and he could complete the painting.

With this anecdote there is definitely a crystallization of the feeling which in the Roman Catholic Church had as a departure from the original sense of the Mystery of Golgotha, how one would far rather take a Prior and make a Judas out of him than anyone else.

This attitude of mind can be studied up to the middle of the 4th century, and then again, how it prepares itself for intellectualism from the middle of the 4th century onwards. For example, you can already see, when you study the writing of Scotus Eriugena, how in the 10th century on the one hand, the tendency plays in towards intellectualism that would later fully emerge, and on the other hand in what one could call the gifts of understanding out of higher worlds. This appeared strongly in that time in which it prepared itself from the middle of the previous epoch up to the 15th century of our present epoch. It is conclusively quite different before the middle of 4 AD; it continues into the 5th century, the times are not so strictly separate. You always find strong experiences towards the Mystery of Golgotha present in the first centuries after the event, as the supersensible spiritual plays into the earthly. This permeation of outer spiritual into the earthly became ever more difficult for the ordinary state of mind. We are just seeing in the centre of this previously mentioned period, a personality wrestling with every possible thing, just to get along. It is with such a turn that the one side of the human state of mind really changed, and on the other side a new kind of understanding necessary for the Mystery of Golgotha. This personality, as you know, was Augustine.

Within his soul, Augustine just couldn't come to terms completely with how the spiritual worked into matter. Augustine for instance sought amongst the Manichaeans for a possibility of how to recognise the spiritual in the material. He didn't manage; he actually only managed by withdrawing completely into himself, in order to depend on the self-assurance of his human I, which made him one of the precursors of the famous Descartes declaration: "Cogito, ergo sum." (I think, therefore I am.) This principle is found with Augustine already. However, on the other hand he was confronted with a certain doubt about the teaching, and this doubt was eating him up. One can certainly understand out of the configuration of the time, why Augustine felt this way. How the old heathen point of view of the church fathers, namely Clemens von Alexandria, was still completely accepted, so that in the oldest Christian times they were totally overtaken by the pagan in Christian teaching, and this Augustine could no longer accept, because in his human soul constitution it was no longer appropriate. The teaching content was also shaped in such a way that, essentially in the time of the Council of Nicaea, it had been brought as abstract dogmas which could then be absorbed by intellectualism. So the human soul in Augustine's time, I can mention, was already driven towards intellectualism. From then on Augustine could do nothing other than accept the dogmatic Catholic Church content, in order to find a teaching content.

Through this, a great crack came about in the Catholic Church. What appeared from the ceremonial of course could not correspond to a soul content. Humanity didn't come in the same way to the undermining of the ceremonial content, as it came to the drying up of the soul content. So it happened in the Catholic Church that the soul content dried out dogmatically, while the ceremonial content actually sustained itself. This ceremonial content of the Catholic Church didn't come out of Christianity, but it came out of far older ceremonial processes. Out of such times it stirred, from a time in which people still had a living reading of the cosmos in which, as a sacrificial offering, it could be accomplished from the reading in the cosmos. What was drawn from the ancient ceremonies of the mysteries, was then Christianized. The Mass offering is also certainly taken from the ancient mystery ceremonies and Christianized. However, what remained as symbolic in the act of sacrifice, is what actually continued within the Catholic Church.

The Catholic Church was actually on this point always consequential, also when it became a worldly establishment under Constantine, as it went over into the political field. It was, one could say, really ironclad in its consequentiality. It has maintained its ceremonies in the most conservative way and in order not to go under, suffocated its soul content with dogmatism. No wonder that the ceremonial content became more and more strange as an experience, because people had no lively relationship to it anymore, and the dogmatic content was experienced as something obsolete — while it had been lively knowledge in olden times, knowledge experienced by a different soul constitution. The dogmatic content could not hold true compared with what came out of purely worldly knowledge. However, the Catholic Church had to remain absolutely consequential, and it has remained in its conserved state right up to the present. It has remained conservative by not participating in the state of mind/soul constitution residing in the present day. It has remained so, that it demands faith in preserved dogmas, which corresponds to a knowledge of an earlier soul constitution so that what is learnt about the Catholic Christ in the Church today is completely bound up with a dogmatic content which believes it presents a level of knowledge which mankind had actually reached at the end of the 14th century AD.

What Anthroposophy wants to developed is regaining the supersensible substance of knowledge; the kind of supersensible knowledge which has died in dogma; Anthroposophy wants to enable the achievement of a new understanding for the Mystery of Golgotha, because the dogmas of the Catholic Church can no longer penetrate into an understanding of the Mystery of Golgotha. This is extraordinarily important, that the dogmas of the Catholic Church no longer can allow the understanding of the Mystery of Golgotha to come through. The ritual of mass lets the souls penetrate to something different, to taking an interest in the symbols of the ritual. It is already so, that the Roman Catholic Church has remained in line with its ironclad consistency even into the 19th Century. Some things appear as quite strange if you examine the dogmas instituted by the Catholic Church before the 19th Century. I would like to give you an example so you can see what a kind of abyss exists, in order for you to reach an insight as to how such an abyss can once again be bridged over.

Once I had a conversation with a very learned theologian regarding the *Conceptio immaculate*, the immaculate conception, which was only instituted in the 19th Century. You perhaps know that this doesn't deal with the immaculate reception of Jesus himself, but of the immaculate conception of Mary; that means St Anna conceived Mary in an immaculate conception. This is actually the dogma laid down in the 19th century. The other dogma — that of the immaculate conception of Jesus — had existed already for a long time. As a "singular grace" it can be seen by those who can even see the emergence of dogmas from the imaginative content, even if they can't approve of it at all because its content is deadened by it — but one can see it.

So, in my conversation with this theologian, I said to him that it was impossible to reconcile the idea of the immaculate conception with modern conscious. I said to him, one isn't compelled to lead the modern consciousness over into dogma in relation to the individual case; one is not compelled to apply logic in an individual case because the singular also, according to scholastic opinion, evades follow-up. The moment you assume a series of facts, in other words a backward looking of a series of facts, where you rise up from the immaculate conception of Mary to the immaculate conception of St Anna, it is necessary to continue and then you, out of necessity, must accept an entire generation line of immaculate conceptions. — Now the theologian turned to me and said that is not correct, because then we come back to David — this is how he expressed it — and then the story would be quite disastrous, and that could not be allowed.

You see, with today's consciousness this has a certain stroke of frivolity, but it certainly is something which can be made known, how within the Roman Catholic Church the entire relationship to the truth is something quite different.

In this depiction of our conversation I wanted to firstly stress the kind of perception of truth we lived in during the middle of the 15th Century. The Catholic clergy was not experiencing the perception of truth like modern consciousness does, but a truth-conception corresponding to an earlier time epoch. They were not aware of the view of truth that reckons with the consequences of truth for the inner life of a human being. Quite a different attitude to the truth existed, and as it had changed from olden times, was not clearly understood. We need to look back at the evolution of humanity which means that the soul constitution essentially has changed. Basically, there is no incorrect expression other than that nature had made no leaps. Nature in fact makes continuous jumps. Take for example a green foliage leaf to the coloured flower petal — that is a jump. In the same way we have leaps in the course of time, apparently quite a sharp advancement from one soul state into another. However, people don't always grow in the same degree but allow old points of view to continue and as a result their souls atrophy, as we are able to notice if we look at the enormous leap which has come about in modern human soul constitutions and which has not been participated in by a large number of people.

Now we must clearly see that such an inner kind of experience, as can be describe as an historical consciousness, which can be acquired, stands out particularly strongly in a person who, through a certain education in the Church, it can especially be applied, when we think of a case like Luther's. If you want to understand Luther's soul then you must be clear that be comes out of the after effects of Augustinism, and that it is precisely in his time, just a bit after the beginning of the intellectualist age, that he is confronted with one of the most serious soul conflicts imaginable. Why was this so? You must just imagine: Augustine had come to an agreement on the recognition of the Christian-Catholic dogma, but for him this was connected with his living within something which was still alive, and even more alive among the Manicheans with whom he had met. What was still full of life in his time was the observation of original sin, in general the consideration of higher processes taking place in relation to lower earthly processes. People still have trouble today to make such things comprehensible.

If we position ourselves at the beginning of earth evolution, we can gradually enter into an imagination of the origins of what we today call a human being. There were higher beings who were in a certain way connected with earthly evolution. The Old Testament indicates one such higher being having become the snake, a being who we call Lucifer today. This higher being, so it is described in the Bible, actually initiated the original sin. In the beginning of earthly existence, this being was there and the original sin was actually due to the calculation of man's precursors of his ancestors, who then appeared as the serpent of paradise. What this pre-human being had begun by the seduction in paradise was transferred on to the human beings. During that time, what played into human thoughts, existed there as primal guilt, within which man got trapped and later dragged it along, because he originally had become entangled and then in fact he now transferred it from one generation to the next through the blood.

As a result of this primal sin the Christ appeared on the earth — I am speaking in the consciousness of this time period — in order to gradually heal people from their dying through what Lucifer had done to them. That we outwardly know so little about the constitution of consciousness, is a result of the really innumerable things proclaimed by the Roman Catholic Church, which is based on this ancient tradition. Above all, everything Gnostic was eradicated and also later the reproduction of anything that still had an older soul constitution was made exceedingly difficult. You know the writing of Scotus Eriugena had been lost and only later rediscovered, and for centuries people knew nothing about Scotus Eriugena because all copies of his writing which one could get hold of, had been burned. It is certainly so that it deals with looking again at an event which took place in the supersensible world and into what human beings had become entangled.

Among the impulses of such observations, I could say something worked behind human events, active through superhuman events of other beings who actually were also involved with human evolution, in order for Augustine's teaching regarding predestination, to develop. Augustine saw the incarnation of people on earth as something much rather, if it could be expressed it would be by saying: The human being is actually the result of the battle of superhuman beings. — This meant individuals had no intrinsic worth; that only happened in the middle of the 15th century. Augustine believed it quite possible to think of human development as beyond their will, accomplished by the destinies of superhuman beings. His teaching could only be alive in him if a part of the human being, not the sinful part, but a part, be destined for demise and another part of the human being destined for bliss, the teaching which is not usually presented in all its meaning, when it is to be experienced. Today this can't be experienced in devotion, which was possible for Augustine. Into this soul constitution something also played that one can call original sin, which is balanced out by the Mystery of Golgotha. People in Luther's time still expressed it in this way, but they lived in another time of a soul constitution as in the time of Augustine. It was quite impossible to find one's way into these ideas with all of one's soul. In this way Luther experienced the illumination through his soul, as an Augustine monk.

Now I must speak to you about my conviction which is based — even though it is called a conviction — on knowledge. For me it certainly is knowledge. I am not in the position to speak in the same way about chance or coincidences like other people because coincidences also belong to an order of things which is usually ignored. I can't attach it to an actual incident in Luther's life, I can't be indifferent to a lightning strike in a tree beside him, but I can see it, according to my knowledge, only as the effect of a truly supersensible intrusion. You can think about it in any way you like, but if I speak sincerely and honestly, I certainly regard part of Luther's soul constitution as this pointing in, if I may call it so, of God's finger, not out of belief but out of recognition. Luther's state of mind or soul constitution became something quite different under the influence of such a deed; it happened so that certain inner sources were opened. These sources, or better said, the effectiveness of these sources, had already been prepared through the wrestling with misunderstood lore. It could not rise up, it was like a turning point in the soul itself, but it could not consciously show itself. Then it rose up into consciousness and became a turning point for only that which was happening. If I want to express myself roughly, the body has been softened, so to speak, and what had been prepared in Luther for a long time, permeated through a soft body.

Now Luther gradually became aware of all the dangers in which modern man lives. It isn't easy to say in how far this went into Luther's clear consciousness, and it's also not that important. In any case this position of modern man played into Luther's soul on the one hand as a streaming from earlier times, and on the other hand, what man should be since the middle of the 15th century. The entire dangers of modern man flooded Luther's soul. What did this consist of? It consisted of — I'm speaking in a Christian way — man being afflicted with the deeds or the sequences of deeds of superhuman beings in which he had become entangled. Through what had been an entanglement of original sin in the lower human being as inherited traits, man entered into the next epoch in a different manner than he would have if there had been no original sin through the Fall. As a result, that which should appear in humanity as intellect came through in a far more abstract measure than how life used to be in former times, when it was afflicted with something subhuman through original sin. To a certain extent, what man was to experience intellectually became diluted, more abstract, which in earlier life had been more dense, more natural, than it should be for mankind. It was only now that man was basically condemned to fall away from God through his intellectualism. The whole danger of intellectualism which pushes too far to greater abstraction, lived itself out in Luther's soul, and Luther really experienced it with such vehemence as described in his vicious battle at Wartburg Castle.

We have two opposite poles which can clearly be determined in the newer evolution of mankind. On the one hand is Luther, positioned in the great spiritual battle after the middle of the 15th century — of course a little later — and now as a result, while he wanted to loosen himself from intellectual dangers, first renounces the intellect and seeks justification outside the intellect which can lead him to the divine, as it were, beneath the intellect.

The other pole is Faust. He took on the intellect with all his senses, resulting in his deteriorating into the dangers of the intellect, as he entered into all the individual dangers of the intellect. It is not for nothing that these personalities are a kind of landmark for modern mankind: on the one side Luther and what he connected to, and on the other side Faust, and what he associates with. It was truly no small deed of Goethe when he wanted to reshape Faust in such a way that he would not perish. Lessing already thought about it. If freedom is to be achieved for humanity, the intellect needs to be engaged with, but humanity should not be pushed away from the divine. The Faust fragment of Lessing ends with the words (of the angels to the devil): "You shall not prevail!" which Goethe remodelled. He said to himself there should be a possibility not to be separated from the divine when mankind engages with the intellect — but he needs it for the development of freedom. In this terrible battle Luther stood. He saw how the intellect contained within itself the danger that man also strangulates his soul from the divine, how man succumbs to the death of the soul. That which is devoured by the intellect — in anthroposophy we call it "becoming Ahrimanic" — which totally enters into the intellect, becomes devoured, it is cut off from the divine. This is what Luther felt for modern man.

Historically it was so that on the one hand there was the Catholic Church where people were absolutely not within the intellect, it even wants to save people by preventing them from entering into the intellect, it wanted to preserve them from progress made in the 15th century onwards by conserving such dogmas like the one which claims infallibility, such as the dogma regarding the immaculate conception, as I've mentioned earlier. They couldn't manage consequently in the Roman Catholic sense without the infallibility dogma because they even deny its intellectual meaning, declaring it unfit for development and incapable of understanding the spiritual world. A reinforcement was needed for what people had to believe, indicating the sovereignty of the Papal Command for the Truth. There is nothing more untimely, but basically nothing greater than this determination of the dogma of infallibility, to completely contradict all consciousness of the time and all human desires for freedom. It is the last consequence of the secularization of Catholicism in an iron clad consequence of tremendous genius. One must say if you take, on the one hand, the ironclad consequence of the Roman clerics in their determination of the infallibility dogma, and on the other hand the kind of polemics of a Dollinger, the latter is of course philistine in the face of tremendous ingenuity — you could even call it devilish — something is carried out, because it was once the consequence to that which Rome has come to since the secularization of Christianity by Constantine.

So it happened that in the bosom of the Roman Catholics, two souls could live next to one another. On the one hand was the submission to the rigid dogma, which no human being could touch save the infallible Pope — because the Council had lost its power since the determination of the infallibility dogma — and on the other hand the unhindered care of outer science as an external manipulation to which one is devoted and partake off, but don't attribute any meaning to the actual content of religious doctrine. Just consider from a modern consciousness, what the justification of the Roman Catholic doctrine looks like. I suggest you read for instance such writing as "The Principle of Catholicism and Science" by Hertling, the previous German Imperial Chancellor.

Firstly, you'll discover that it was a world historic mistake for this man to have become the Imperial Chancellor but on the other hand you will learn something about the unusual thoughts modern people had and how these two souls could justifiably live in the same bosom. It is also remarkable that this writing on the principle of Catholicism appears in French. It is therefore extraordinarily interesting that the writer of this work, whose name doesn't come to my mind at the moment, has a perpetually logical conscience and therefore he has to make a differentiation between the Roman Catholic teaching material and what constitutes the content of outer science. That is why he proposes two concepts next to each other, the idea of truth and the idea of science, which he always sees as two disparate ideas. He says something can very well be scientific, but truth is something else; what is true does not need to be scientific. In some or other way he comes to the conclusion that science doesn't have anything to do with what one acknowledges directly as containing truth. So on the one hand things worthy of contemplation are mentioned, but are already beaten, on the other hand the most grotesque somersaults are being beaten in order for these two souls to become reconciled with one another.

So, on the one hand we have the continuation of symbolism, the symbolism that led to the enormous upswing of art in the Renaissance period in central Europe. Art Historians need only dig deep enough to discover that without the Catholic symbolism the entire artistic development of Giotto, Cimabue, from Leonardo to Rafael and Michelangelo would have been impossible, because the artistic development is certainly a propagation of Christian artistic subjects and belongs so strongly in Christianity that people can't, for example, understand why the Sistine Madonna looks like she does.

Look at the Sistine Madonna, she is magnificent. As far as one can see there are images of clouds which transform purely into angelic heads, and how the Madonna herself, with the Child, condenses out of the angles who reside in the clouds. It is as if the angelic forms have condensed out of the cloud images and have descended down to the earth, yet everything is wonderfully lifted into the spirit. Then the two curtains (*he sketches on the blackboard*) and below that a coquettish female figure and a terrible priestly figure, all things which absolutely do not belong to it. Why is this so? It is simply from the basis of Raphael having initially intended with this image, to give a soul experience with the picture of Mary on a certain feast day of Mary — now this is on the Feast of Corpus Christi -where people walk around in a procession with a picture of the virgin Mary that is carried under a canopy and comes to the altars where people kneel down. This is why there are these curtains (*points to sketch on blackboard*) with the kneeling female and male forms in a chapel, in front of the picture of Mary. Well, that is the kind of elementary school way of looking at what Raphael painted. What is actually meant here stands right in the Roman Catholic cult — absolutely right inside it.

Basically, everything contained in this Roman Catholic ritual is what Luther saw in Rome. Isn't it tremendously symbolic, historically symbolic, historically symptomatic, that Luther saw only corruption in Rome, not being actually touched deeper by what flowed out into depictions in art, how he was not deepened inwardly by art, but that he only saw moral corruption? Here we see how the soul in fact was positioned through his particular development in the historical becoming of mankind, he was like a soul at war, thrown this way and that, searching for a way out. Despite all this, like the doom of Lutherism in particular, comes the big problem: How do we as human beings absorb intellectualism, so that we are not doomed but that we overcome the fear of becoming doomed, because it is necessary for human freedom to integrate us?

Modern intellectualism presses strongly into our human consciousness. The evangelical church reckoned with it for centuries, the Catholic Church kept itself completely distanced from it. The evangelical church gradually withdrew back on to faith because with intellectualism, as it developed in the world, it didn't agree, so it increasingly withdrew from knowledge by depending on belief; it now rests within a faith in which the doctrine content is to be sought. The Catholic Church had doctrine content, but it was allowed to dry up. From the intellectual point of view the way to individuals can't be found, who see themselves isolated from those superhuman forces which could still be felt as being connected to Augustinism.

Basically we in humanity stand right in this battle today, only, if I could put it that way, we have come to the cutting edge, so that we simply stand there and say: We need a pure concept of faith so that we have a religion opposite intellectualism, because we can't take up the old Catholic doctrine, for it has dried out. — With this dried out dogmatic content the evangelical church rejected the ritual in the most varied forms. This is what started with Luther, putting us today on the knife edge; we must become aware of the seriousness of this position. It is a struggle for the power of faith in the soul, who wants to save the faith at the cost of not having the existing doctrine content at all. However, without content we can't learn, and it appears impossible to simply rediscover a bridge to what Catholicism has secularised.

Now my dear friends, I come to the question of how we should proceed. It is like this: you see, with all this there was also an evangelical consciousness introduced in the evolution of humanity, in the individual human development, because the earlier evangelical consciousness to a certain degree entangled man in the supernatural, superhuman processes and acts of superhuman beings. With Augustus it was expressed somewhat differently, that the progress of humanity was permeated with the superhuman element ... (*gap in notes*). People saw the superhuman battle raging as something like Christ fighting against the enemy who wants to lead him into the temptation of appearing super human; that the one who drew near to the Christ was one to whom original guilt was traced back to, and it is shown how Christ turns against the original sin. This understanding has now come to an end. Earlier, this understanding had been adhered to, for what was supersensible-divine permeated earthly matter, and there already has been an intention present for specialization to make a dividing border between the supernatural, and that part of man entangled in sensuality.

This dividing border is done through consecration. Consecration is actually the separation of the human being, or that part of the human being, from being entangled in the earthly. The ordination of the priesthood is only one part because there are also implements and so on; everything possible is consecrated. Once during a war, the Pope consecrated the bullets but that is only due to the secularization of Catholicism.

Do you see that consecration is really the dividing boundary between two worlds, and there is certainly the awareness in Catholicism — even if it is not present in individual priests — that a consecrated priest is active in another world when he does something, that he is also speaking from another world when he speaks of the Gospels, even though all his ordinary actions are in the earthly world. This differentiation could not be understood since the 15th century. In historic Catholicism, throughout, was this strong differentiation where, in circles of ordained priests, it was consciously stressed. Only now and then some bishop, by mistake, will bring something non—Catholic into Catholicism, namely modern consciousness, and that leads to absurdities. There was for example a pastoral letter written which claimed that the priest in the fulfilment of the sacrament at the altar would be more powerful than Christ Jesus, because he forces Christ Jesus to be present in the sacrament; Christ Jesus has to be present when the priests demands it; the result is that the priest is now more powerful than Christ. — This is the content of a pastoral letter of not long ago. You can come across such things when out of modern consciousness something is understood which should be understood in quite a different mood, namely that which lies beyond the earthly sphere and separated from it by the consecration.

The principle of consecration comes from far, far back. It already existed in the oldest oriental religions and it was particularly developed on (the Greek island of) Samothrace. Catholicism took it over from ancient times but for the newer consciousness it was totally lost.

Tomorrow I will try to add further elements to it, so that you can come to a full understanding of the principle of consecration, and also priest ordination, without which the apostolic succession won't be comprehensible.

FOUNDATION COURSE

PROPHECY, DOGMA AND PAGANISM

Lecture given in Dornach on 2 October 1921, morning.

My dear friends! Today we need to pursue what we had started yesterday, by adding details to some of the requests. Above all questions, as difficult as they may be — be it in the religious sense, or anthroposophic sense — will be those related to knowledge which reaches into the future. Such knowledge into the future can only be understood if one is able to discuss all prerequisites for such knowledge, so to speak. You know, of course, that outer materialistic science also has certain knowledge of the future which is quite possible.

Solar and lunar eclipses can be predicted to the second, and these predictive calculations depend upon having a definite insight into the details of the phenomena. In outer materialistic science it relates to this insight of the context of the phenomena being hidden, because it is presented in formulae; the formulae are learnt and one no longer really knows where they came from; they actually originate from observations made in the very same area to which they are applied. Nobody would be able to calculate the solar and lunar eclipse predictions if solar and lunar eclipses were not originally observed, forming a basis for observation and formulas obtained from these, which now continue as based on the belief of a regularity applied to these phenomena. The psychological process which takes place here is far more complicated than one is often aware of today. Things start becoming particularly complicated if they are not applicable only to outer, spatial mechanical or mathematical kinds of laws, but if they deal with what happens inwardly, in the intrinsic sense, in the course of the world. Because these questions are based on the prerequisites of modern consciousness they can barely be studied, that's why we find modern Bible explanations — and the priest must also be a Bible explainer — so difficult, like chapter 13 of the Mark Gospel and everything relating to this chapter. Besides that, in later translations this particular chapter has become extraordinarily difficult to understand because it relates to circumstances which have become the most corrupt.

Now I would like, before I proceed into the situation of this chapter, to say something about the predictions in the Christian sense. You have the feeling that within the development of Christendom there had already been, especially in olden times, references to future events, and future events of the most important kind had already played a major role. You also get the feeling that present day people hardly believe such indications, and that they actually can hardly reckon with such indications being anything but illusion. One always gets the feeling, when such things do happen — in modern language use it would be called prophesy — that something else must play along, other than real knowledge of what will happen in the future. You must however make yourself familiar with it, it is after all also present in our time, in the time of intellectualism — and rightly so in this time — it has eradicated certain traditional, inherited, atavistic clairvoyance. There are clairvoyant people of the older kind who are still serving certain theorists, also of the 19th century, as examples from which they wanted to prove the existence of a supernatural world they could not experience for themselves. We only need to consider such a type of prediction, then we will see — quite equitably, whether we believe it or not — what is actually meant. Such cases could happen, and it has, if I take it as typical, and still occurred numerous times in the course of the last century, whereas in the present time it shows a certain decline. Such abilities are still common in country people. It could happen that someone sees in an advantageous moment in a dream, how he, riding a horse, falls and hurts himself. Such seeing is certainly a sight into the future and one can, even by being careful, find out everything with all the scientific chicaneries that exclude an influence on following events, one cannot speak otherwise but admit a true looking into the future exists. This is something which had been recorded by the most earnest theorists everywhere, up to the middle of the 19th century. You can find this writing originating from otherwise quite serious natural scientists from the first half of the 19th century, discussed in numerous journals. As I've said, whoever observes people today must see that such atavistic abilities have gone backwards and become drowned out by intellectual life; a condition which completely excludes looking into the future.

Now, as we've said, we must at least familiarise ourselves with such abilities which can be called looking into the future, abilities present in ancient times and certainly understood in the surroundings of Christ Jesus, when he spoke in a certain way about the future. In order not to be misunderstood, I want to call your attention straight away to something else.

When you take literature which appears as Christian literature according to the actual Gospels, according to the letters of Paul and others, of direct disputes attributed to the disciples, and you take the later literature of the so-called church fathers — under 'church father' it is meant those who were still students of disciples or at least scholars or the apostles not too long ago — when you take the literature of the church fathers, then you will often discover three characteristics.

The first characteristic is that these writings have become dried up of an actual living understanding for the Old Testament. You will clearly notice how everywhere in these writings, up to the "Shepherd of Hermas," the craving comes to the fore to depict the Old Testament intellectually, in this case interpreting it allegorically, therefore it is pulled out of a real encounter to a mere concept, into what is, so to say, intellectual. The restyling of concepts into allegory puts up with the tradition of the Old Testament as a tradition of facts, told as facts — in reality these are to be understood through the intellect. That is the first essential characteristic.

The second essential characteristic is that the Second Coming of the Christ is clearly mentioned everywhere in the writings, that is to say, exactly what is referred to in the 13th chapter of Mark's Gospel in the most delicate sense of the word. It was certainly, one must admit, the belief in the entire spirit of the church fathers' writings from the 4th century that the Second Coming of Christ can be predicted in the near future. They called people's attention to how the old world would fall apart and how the Christ would reappear, and added to this, the imagination was created that Christ would appear in a similar way, in the most wonderful way, strolling over the earth, as it had been the case before.

The third element in the writings of the church fathers is what actually contributed a great deal to the church doctrine. Everywhere a kind of legal element developed, a warning to obey the bishops, the dogmas, to submit to the constitution in the developing church. So everywhere something was taking place which one could be referred to as this: To the believers it was said that they will fall into bad luck if they develop anything which comes from within themselves, while they are searching for a religious path. — The religious path given by the church's constitution and the legal constitution, which ordered obedience to the church, was something that has continued particularly in Catholicism to the widest extent, which even as an experience today can still oppose one very forcefully.

I once, for example, had a conversation in Rome with a priest brought up in quite the Jesuit manner — it was very hard, to get this conversation going — indicating all the sources which gave him the basis of his teaching and also showing the way in which he was to arrive at the teaching content. He pointed out that one then had the written words containing the dogmatic church content, and those were all things which needed no proof, they simply had to be believed, in as far as dogma was concerned. He pointed out that only interpretation was allowed, one was not to criticise or prove anything in the Gospels, while reading them again and again; one had the church tradition which flowed into the breviary, and then one had a living example of the life of the saints.

The former could not very well form the subject of a discussion involving this cleric because one had to admit that what the Catholic Church wanted to protect was presented in such an ingrained sense, that there was no way around it. But the latter, the relationship of the Catholic clerics to the saints, that of course is something which creates certain difficulties even with the Catholic clergy when they think about it, and here an objection could be used. Saints are fixed personalities valued by the church for their faultless manner in their direct, vital relationship to the supersensible worlds, either through the understanding of how they had found the revelation out of the supersensible world through their inner experience, or that they performed deeds which can only be understood through accepting these deeds as having been performed with divine assistance.

You may know that such a canonization in the Catholic Church requires a very detailed ceremony, preceded by the exact determination of how the relevant person lived and what he thought, a process which should not last years, but centuries. Further, this examination must end with a ceremony which exist of all those who come forward, who have something well founded to present regarding the living exchange the personality has in relation to the divine, and to some extent always enter into what is said in such a way, that the so-called Advocatus diaboli, the representative of the demonic world, who has to refute everything that the other side has to say for the relevant canonisation, is brought to attention. So there will be an extensive trial, at which the being who should be regarded as the Diabolus, the devil, will have on the other side, the Christ representative, for the Christ-like will always be drawn into the discussion with the devilish representative, when a saint is to be recognised.

Now of course I could have interrupted this conversation with him, regarding the church always admitting to the possibility of lively exchanges with the divine, so that supersensible experiences were possible. It is however the dogma of the Catholic Church that such supersensible experiences which could take place, are devilish and that they must be avoided, one must be forced to flee from them. Of course, it is certainly the Catholic Church's dogmatism which says that all of Anthroposophy is objectionable from the basis that it claims to touch on insights in the supersensible worlds. For this reason, Anthroposophy is rejected because such an insight can only be arrived at with the help of the Devil; it is therefore evil. That is something which is judged by the Catholic Church as quite necessary, quite consistent. Things are already such that they must not be blurred. Whoever thinks reconciliation between Anthroposophy and the Catholic Church can without further ado be brought about, is mistaken. The Initiate knows, for the Catholic Church to be consequent from their side, it will regard Anthroposophy as devilish, and more than ever, the Catholic church today has allowed such consequences to become its custom.

As an answer from the priest I received his claim that any exchange with the supersensible worlds may in no way be wished for; if it happens in this world it must be made clear that the divine principle has been besieged by the devil. — So, I said to him: If you now have such an exchange with the supersensible worlds, would you consider that as devilish? — He answered: Yes, he has on his side the talent to merely work with literature of the saints in order to know that something like that exists; but he doesn't desire to become a saint himself. — This is now the last sentence which would be expressed by these people, this person also did not express it because if he did, then the last sentence would be that he says: To regard me as a saint, the church has the right to wait for two to three centuries.

We can draw all kinds of conclusions from this. You could for example connect all kinds of evil thinking habits to it which is relevant particularly at present, when someone says that everything which can be said about the causes of the war, one would only really know about after decades when all the archives have been combed through. If you have any sense for reality you would know that in a couple of decades everything would be so blurred that no truth would be discovered in the archives in order to determine something as some tradition, and you would know that one, I could call it, very insidious step could renounce what has been said out of the consciousness of the present. This is also something which must be considered more deeply, but it only belongs in parenthesis here: I only want to draw your attention to it, that with the proclamation of a saint, waiting for such a long time, things in question could have become thoroughly blurred, and you can have insight into the Catholic Church's extraordinarily difficult burden towards its real progress.

These three characteristics you will find in post apostolic literature during the first four centuries: the allegoric explanation of the Old Testament, the reference to the Second Coming of Christ and the destruction of the old world, and the admonition of obedience to the superiors. We need to focus our present interest primarily on the middle one, the reference to the Second

Coming of Christ, because to this reference we need to link line 6 of the 13th chapter of the Gospel of Mark: Many will come as though they came in my name and say: I am he, and will lead many astray. — In this chapter you find a remarkable reference; many will come and appear in the name of Christ, and they will forthwith be referred to one or another person who also designate themselves as Christ. Here you see something extraordinary. On this basis it is extraordinary to see — I will speak more closely about these things but I'm leading up to it — that already at this point in the Mark Gospel the reference is linked to the view of the church fathers of the post apostolic time. By presenting it thus, that the Christ will reappear in this way, it is at the same time the fulfilment of the prophecy that tempters will come who all want to be designated as Christs; and this is what also happened in the first centuries, in this sense many came to the fore, who actually referred to themselves as Christ. An astonishing amount of literature has been lost in the first centuries — these things can actually only be found through spiritual science.

So we must say — and I have expressly spoken about it — if we look at the totality of facts, the Christian church fathers lived in a misunderstanding of the Gospels, perhaps even a really bad misunderstanding of the Gospels. When we actually bring our feelings into the Gospels, as I have shown you yesterday, when we really with our whole heart and entire soul find ourselves with ever more wonder towards the Gospels, then we would find it inordinately difficult to find our way with our intellect to the first church fathers. We discover with the first church fathers that we relatively early come to the end of understanding because the Gospel itself leads us into immeasurable depths, and we very clearly experience that in a certain way we actually feel uncomfortably touched when after our wonder at the Gospels we now turn to something which appeared in the church fathers.

Now, this leads us on to something else. Later we will talk about the justification of prophecy but now we want to find our way into the situation in terms of contemporary history and so it appears to me, that if we want to understand the 13th chapter of Mark's Gospel, before anything else, we need to pose this important question: Can the fulfilment of the prophecy be asserted from a correct pursuit of the facts? Surely you first need to be able to understand in what way the prophecy should be fulfilled, and then you could ask, what are the facts? Then, isn't it true, that with something like the destruction of Jerusalem it is easy to raise a question, but when it comes to the destruction of the world which we are still expecting, and regarding the coming of the kingdom of God, modern thought only has information that it still has not happened, that under all circumstances it must have been an illusion, that you had in all cases to do with false prophesies; and then you only have the choice to either interpret these things out of the Gospels, or to follow what the first church fathers did with the Old Testament through allegorizing, or even to do anything as long as it is abstract. All of this is being done against the total feeling which is necessary in relating to the Gospels, which does not arise here. The most important question seems to me to be the impact of the prophecy, because that helps towards understanding the process of prophecy.

I tell you, my dear friends, for me, the destruction of the world and the coming of the kingdom of God have simply already been fulfilled. We must swing around to look at the world in such a way that we learn to represent this statement as having been fulfilled. Towards this we certainly must penetrate more deeply with spirit into the words of Christ Jesus, as opposed to what usually happens.

Those who were around Jesus knew exactly, just as the poor shepherds in the fields knew in their inner sight: Christ had arrived. They still knew precisely that the entire life of human beings on earth would have been different in ancient times and it would become something different at this historical moment, even if little by little. Gentle feelings are still around at present, but only gentle feelings. I have such a quiet feeling about it but that must be trained in an intensive manner, for example, as found in the art historian Herman Grimm, and perhaps it will interest you to look into something like this as well because psychologically it leads to what we need to attain, little by little.

The art historian Herman Grimm had roughly the following view: when we go back with our examination of history, from our time to the Middle Ages and further back to the migration of peoples, back to the Roman empire, we still may have the possibility to understand the history. We have such feelings today, we could say, through which we can understand the roman imperial age and roughly the roman republic. We are still capable today, to understand this. When we go back into Greek history with the same kind of soul understanding then we enter into the highest form of illusion if we believe we can understand an Alkibiades, Sophocles, Homer or someone similar. Between grasping the Roman world and the Greek world there is an abyss, and what has been inherited from the Greek world, so Herman Grimm says, is basically a fairy tale; here starts the world of fairy tales, a world into which we no longer can enter with our present day understanding. We must be satisfied with the inherited images presented to us, but we must take these in a general sense as a world of fairy tales, without intellectual understanding. — It still has a soft echo of something which human beings need to create; an inner feeling towards the historical development of mankind.

This sensitivity of feeling will of course become completely distorted by those whose opinions are according to modern evolutionary theories, which simply go back from the present and consider modern human beings as the most perfect now than what was initially achieved. Here one arrives at a perspective from which one no longer can understand those who were around Christ. One also understands why, out of what soul foundations, such experiences and imaginations of today have become clothed in the scientific view when for instance you look at the answers the imminent thinker, Huxley, gave an archbishop; his words are quite understandable according to the modern perspective. The archbishop said the human being descended from this divine being; the godhead placed him without sin in the world, and that's who has descended into the present human condition. — This archbishop's opinion couldn't but let Huxley reply to this sentence with: I would surely be ashamed as a human being if I have descended so far from my divine origin, but I can be very proud from my animal standpoint of how far I have worked towards who I now am. —

Here you can precisely see the moral impulses entering into what we call objective science. The need to revert to moral impulses is everywhere for those who tinker with science, if this tinkering it is to be believed.

You must be very clear about the ancient human being before the time of Christ, the heathen person, who without sin, was aware that everywhere, when he observed nature or when he looked into human life, he encountered the divine and nature simultaneously. In the rock spring he didn't just hear the rushing sound we hear today, but he heard what he perceived and interpreted as the voice of the divine. In every animal he saw something that had, so to speak, been brought about from a supersensible world, but despite its deep fall from the supersensible world, if one really understands it, still totally leads back to the contemplation of this supersensible world. In this way the ancient people could not imagine the supersensible world without the divine, being part of it.

In Judaism, quite an intense feeling came to the fore. It was this: In whatever form or way the divine appears, man may not claim himself to also have the divine appearing in himself in a perfect form, but only at most as an inspiration, but not in its complete form. This was something the orthodox Jew didn't even want to touch in his thoughts; that which he still permitted for the rest of nature, that everywhere the divine may be revealed, and what he considered facts in his Old Testament, this he didn't allow to happen in people. For the surrounding heathen world, for the old way of observation, it was self-explanatory that the mineral kingdom, the plant and animal kingdoms were consequentially built on one another, and so, just like the rest of nature was divine, so also the human being is an incarnation of the divine. At the same time thousands had a firm belief that the human being was ever more losing the possibility through his outer life, to realize God within.

So, it had been an original human ability to create the divine within, but people gradually lost this ability. Those who surrounded Christ experienced that the divine, which had been in humanity earlier and which also appeared in the outer world, this divine element no longer could appear in humanity; it was given to the earth, it appeared everywhere through the Son of God but stopped appearing in mankind and can no longer appear in human children. It must come once again from elements outside the earth so that the last incarnation of the divine, which actually becomes a new time, can catch up, but it must come from outside — if I might express myself roughly — from the stock out of that which the earth had originally loaned.

From this point of view — knowledge, at that time, my dear friends, was filled with feeling, which as such took place in immediate experience — from this point of view those around Christ looked on with feeling at that which had invaded the Roman Empire and was now being fulfilled in Asia. What was this, which was accomplished through the invasion of the Roman Empire into Asia? You need to look at what actually penetrated the consciousness of that time. The ongoing war was at that time outer events which in their final dependency were also derived from divine will. However, this was not the most important aspect; the most important thing was that those who sat on the thrones were Roman Caesars who through religion presented themselves as incarnations of gods, and that, as lawful. Caesar Augustus was according to law a recognised incarnation of the godhead. Some Caesars tried, through ceremonies which had been fulfilled in ancient times, to bring about a ritual action which was so close to human truths, to inner human truths, that the Caesars could allow these ceremonies to be fulfilled but transformed into earthly existence, in order for the divine to actually act, for the divine to be made real.

Penetration of these secret divine mysteries into the world can perhaps not be more strongly symbolized than through relating the story of (the Roman Emperor) Commodus, (son of Marcus Aurelius) when he searched for initiation and allowed the ceremony to be fulfilled, because the ceremony also included the symbolic slaughter of an uninitiated person; at his mystery initiation a man was really killed, murdered. In brief, one felt that by this penetration of the Roman Empire, the divine disappeared, and the divine is presumed to be that, thus in the presumption of the divine there is an incarnation of the ungodly, for man must incarnate into something. The divine was not incarnating, it had stopped, so if the divine was not incarnating then in meant the ungodly was incarnating, the enemy of the divine. You could interpret it as you wish, but you will only be right if you understand that those who surrounded Christ Jesus, had said: In the Roman Empire, which is spreading in the world, is the incarnation of the enemy of the divine.

This is elementary, this is truly a discerning feeling and discernment in Christianity for those who were around Christ Jesus. Never again, from the Christian point of view, would that which had developed further as a dependence on the Roman Empire, be seen as anything other than an earthy bound realm, an empire of the world in opposition to the realm of Heaven. This means in other words: this world which existed then, the divine world, perished, it went under due to the Roman Empire. The downfall was accomplished in the first three centuries up to the middle of the 15th century, as I've mentioned to you. The downfall was accomplished. It is a perished world that now exists, a world that is no longer divine, a world that only gives news of the divine. One must turn to the last, who had become the first, to the divine incarnation of Christ in Jesus, who through his own power gave the possibility, through the handling — if I could use such an expression — through the handling of that which is associated with the fulfilment of the Holy Spirit in one, not by nature, but in a direct way to reach the divine-spirit world, which one can also find in nature when one has found the following of Christ Jesus through the spirit.

The world is coming to an end. The Christ is no longer coming as an earth dweller, but out of the clouds, out of the cosmos he will come again. In this way he comes to everyone who has the awareness of what was meant by the world before, which perished with the Roman Empire.

My dear friends! It is an unpleasant truth for those who want to be within today's consciousness; they don't know what to do about it; it is an unpleasant truth certainly for those who from an erroneous view want to apologize for Christianity before the present time. It is an extraordinary chapter in the involvement of today's world when people come and say Christianity is impractical, Christianity is something which allows escape from the world, Christianity has a mystical atavistic element which makes it unworldly. Then others come along who want to excuse Christianity by discussing away what some are saying who considered the world in a strong spiritual light and who still have a relationship to the world. The excuse is given that things don't need to be understood, they are really not meant so badly regarding fleeing from the world and with it coming to an end, it has continued its progress from the first centuries up to now; the world is just and anything some fanatical priest or fanatical pastor claims about the downfall of the world from God, is really not so seriously meant, it has only come about through the Catholic influence; one must wipe it out.

In brief, my dear friends, the largest part of pastoral and theological work exists in this. Place your hand on your heart and learn through it, feel out of your heart what I have said regarding the necessity for the renewal of Christianity, for the Christian impulse, because the biggest part of what is being preached and discussed exists in the continuous retreat from the recognition of gross intellectualism and the piecemeal eradication of everything out of Christianity, which actually should be understood in a profound way through strong thinking, through such a powerful thinking that the world finds God through Christ, and when God has been discovered through Christ, which can also become practical because in the discovery of the divine, the divine grasped in thought, the godless world can be included to bring about the re-introduction of the divine.

These powers must be carried in those of you who today want to speak about the renewal of Christianity, you must be able to say: Yes, today we have to look at the divinized world which started with the Roman Empire and goes back to the Roman Empire; but in this world we must not look for the divine. The world, however, can't remain without the divine. We must grasp that which does not come from the earth, something — speaking symbolically — which comes from the clouds, in a spiritual manner. We must find the Kingdom of Heaven in the place of the divinized earth kingdom. The Kingdom of Heaven has opened up and is to be found; and for this reason, we must be there to bring the divine into our earthly world. The downfall of the earth has taken place and continues to happen more and more. When we look at this earthly realm, we are then looking at the heavenly realm which Jesus Christ has brought. You must see, my dear friends, the realm of Heaven *spiritually*. We must see its arrival; we must be able to feel the fulfilling of what Christ meant when he spoke about the coming of his kingdom, the kingdom which he had to bring into the world and which does not speak out of nature; when it can however work into nature, then one can speak about this kingdom. This is primarily the feeling he stimulated in those who directly surrounded him. This is also what we must strive for in our words, when we really want to speak about these things.

We see how it is stated in about the first 3 sentences of the Mark Gospel: After Christ left the temple — the temple in which one also heard something within the outer world of the divine — one of his disciples says to him: 'Look, what magnificent stones, and wonderful buildings.' Jesus however said to him: 'You see only the large buildings. There will not be one stone left on top of another, without man taking part in the process of destruction because from now on, all of the outer, ungodly world begins to become a world of destruction.' And he went away and spoke intimately. On the Mount of Olives, he spoke either intimately by himself through teaching people how to pray, or he spoke only to his most intimate disciples, to Peter, James, John and Andrew. To Peter, James, John and Andrew he only spoke about spiritual events as observed from the perspective of divine realms in contrast to destructive events in the world facing destruction.

You see, I'm neither speaking allegorically, nor symbolically. If you felt that way, you would be putting it in my words. I'm speaking directly out of the situation experienced as it occurred, by me trying, certainly in the words of current speech, to indicate these things. I ask you to now take note of the situation. In order to experience the content of the 13th chapter of St Mark we are taken up the Mount of Olives. It ends with the word: "Awake!" — immediately followed by us being taken to the Last Supper — we are led to the first impetus for the coming of the divine kingdom through Christ placing it in front of us.

Tomorrow we will continue speaking about it. What I'm saying to you is quite new, by addressing our current consciousness. I certainly want to speak honestly, as these things present themselves to me, because I believe that by only pointing to the very first elements can one come to a true and honest conviction of what is necessary today.

FOUNDATION COURSE

THE SACRAMENTS, EVOLUTION AND INVOLUTION

Lecture given in Dornach on 2 October 1921, afternoon.

Emil Bock: There are a couple of questions, about meanings in the seven sacraments for example, then also about the difference between Luther's idea of salvation and the idea of salvation in Anthroposophy, as seen in Paul's experience of Christ.

Constantin Neubaus asked Dr Steiner to say something further about meaning in the sacraments and the consecration; he would be grateful to hear more about consecrated water, the Eucharist, the importance of the mass and prayers for the dead, and about celibacy and marriage.

A participant asked, with reference to what Dr Steiner had related, having seen how the Host acquired an aura during the celebration: how would this be if the priest did not have complete dignity?

Another participant asked for some insight into the communications of the priest with those who have died.

Rudolf Steiner: These questions will all be addressed. In what sense are you referring to this communication with those who have died?

A participant: Like you also have in the Catholic Church, in relation to the priest's help with the dead, with the sacraments of the dying.

Another participant mentioned that the question has been raised several times regarding the cosmic significance of the sun and moon standing still in Joshua.

Another participant declared he had not understood something in the morning's lecture, regarding the statement: "The human beings ever more lost the capability to manifest the divine in themselves" and he wanted to know, what this meant: the divine manifesting itself within.

Rudolf Steiner: This is only the explanation of a statement which should be taken this way: in olden times the earthly evolution of humanity experienced right into their very own form, that actually, if I could express it this way, their skin enveloped divine wisdom. This became particularly strongly expressed in the terminology being used, which is really a mystery-terminology: Man is a temple of God. — So, this immediate living-within something which originated out of the divine predecessor of human beings, was experienced in human beings. Then came the time when only a few chosen ones were ascribed with the possibility of experiencing such divinity. Actually, those who belonged to the mysteries during the time of the Mystery of Golgotha were completely convinced that people in their earthly form could no longer harbour a divine wisdom within, because of the decline gradually taking place up to the time of the Mystery of Golgotha.

Because of this, the time epoch can be characterised by saying: the earthly human being would have lost what had been its divine being in olden times, had the Mystery of Golgotha not taken place — in contrast to those with knowledge who said: the last one who comes from outside of this, to fill a human body, would become the first. — Then the earth would have been in a declining evolution, which means plunged into its downfall. This is what can be added as a clarification to the words.

However, all these things which have been brought forward now — and I ask that you make notes in advance of such questions and remarks — are actually in need of real and factual answers before we can continue to enter into the essence of the sacraments. Allow me, as if by insertion, to enter a little into the essence of the sacraments today. In this way we will possibly find it easier to discover answers regarding the consecrated water, sign of the cross, the Eucharist, mass offering and so on.

You do know of course that the Catholic Church acknowledges seven sacraments. This adaptation of seven sacraments — and we can only understand the sacramental when we approach them with such preparations as I would like to do now — these adaptations of the seven sacraments is based on the observation that we look at human life in seven stages. It is however impossible to enter into the essence of the sacraments, if you don't adapt a certain process in yourself, which has today more or less disappeared from current consciousness, a process which, I believe, also connects to that which is otherwise extraordinarily significant regarding our discussion content yesterday, because it relates to what I've only up to now fleetingly characterised as the actual foundation of Luther's soul battle.

Speaking about evolution today, you actually have a one-sided imagination of it, to a certain extent. People believe, when they talk about evolution, they must have some starting point; and this starting point, like a seed, provides the second step, and from the second comes a third and so on. In this way evolution is considered to be a process of actually always going from one previous step resulting in the next one. This evolution concept is quite one-sided in contrast to reality because evolution does not happen this way. When you look at a plant and the condition of having fully developed its leaves, flowers, right up to organs of fruit, you could kind of think how this relates to the characteristics of the evolution concept. (*He draws on the blackboard, on the left.*) But you can't imagine it in the same way if you start from the root, actually from the seed, and then look for the seed in the flower once again. You have to admit: there is a condition in the unfolding growth process where it involves a greater unfolding outward, and there is another condition where it involves the slightest outwards unfolding. Then a rhythm of unfolding alternates with the reverse, where, in a way, the essence of the thing pulls back so that the outer sense perceptible element becomes the most inconspicuous imaginable, but the full power, so to speak, is concentrated to a point.

THE SACRAMENTS, EVOLUTION AND INVOLUTION

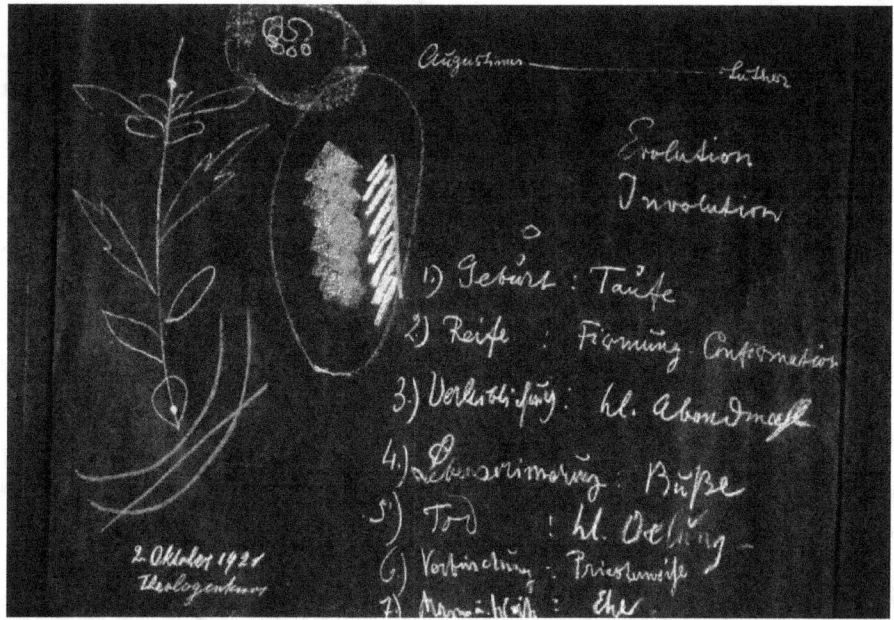

Plate 8   13th Lecture   2. October 1921, afternoon

If you want to speak in the Goethean sense, you would say: At one stage in the unfolding, the spiritual is withdrawn and the sensory aspect developed in the farthest periphery (*he draws on the blackboard*) and here where growth has been drawn inward, is where the spiritual develops and the sensory is squeezed into the most inconspicuous germ imaginable. So, we certainly have to take into account that when we speak about a concept of development, we have to speak about rhythms, but we don't come right with the development concept if we actually look at what nature is. In that moment we come up with history, things get a bit more complicated. Take for instance the course of historic development in that time span which I've characterised yesterday, from Augustus to Luther. (*He writes on the blackboard.*)

Augustus -- Luther

It is extraordinarily important to visualise everything that was contributed in this period of time, outwardly and inwardly, in the outer cultural life and the inner spiritual and soul life, towards humanity. Just imagine, that in this time epoch there was also the infinitely significant mystic ... *(stenographer record unclear, other than the name containing a B)* ... who lived at this time when the booklet was drafted which played a big role in Luther's point of view, called "Theologia deutch," and then we can think about what directly resulted after this time as extraordinary, rising from the foundation of historical development in minds like Paracelsus, and Jakob Böhme, just afterwards. When we look at these things, then we have primarily the impression — we must have an impression — that there was during this period of western development a strong tendency towards turning inwardness. Souls turned inward. If you enter completely into such arguments as sermonized by for instance Johannes Tauler, you will discover an inward striving, a withdrawal from the outer things, a waiting until, one could call it, a sparkle arose which could then renew the human mind. I have also characterised this in my booklet about the Middle Age mystics. When you look at such inner striving as with Tauler, when you notice how he, after years during the course of his life, he had become ever more mature in his internalization, how he in quite a mysterious way met a person and how this person simply through an impression from something out of that already deepened interior was transformed, so that this created the occasion for a sermon which was described in such a way that all who listened in the church were as struck as if by a blow and some fell down as if dead. People were so struck within their souls that they fell into quite a faint.

If you envisage all of this you will find that during this time, an unbelievable internalization was happening in the lives of many people in the west. If I could tell you, my dear friends, in detail, what a roll this played in the entire development, in the reading, in interpretation, yes, even the dramatic performance of the gospel action of the Gospel of Luke, this inner most gospel, and when we look at the pastoral care of this time, then we certainly find the extraordinary characteristic of internalization being poured out over this entire time period. We then discover, as this period came to a close — it had prepared itself already from the 15th century onwards and came out in Luther's time — general culture took on a certain externalisation. In everything there developed the opposite of the internalisation of the Middle Ages. The people's gaze developed towards the outside; methods of observation were directed outward, less and less care and attention was applied to the inner life. So we have — and we are still within this process of externalisation in relation to cultural development — we clearly have historically two successive conditions which differ as much as the unfolded plant does from the plant contracted into the centre. So we have the same thing, in plants as in history, that during such a period of internalisation, like from Augustus to Luther — and this period of internalisation was particularly present despite everything I mentioned this morning — all the power which was inwardly concentrated, later comes out, later unfolds.

My dear friends! Today we all work in what is outer culture, with forces which had been inwardly developed during the time from Augustinus to Calvin or up to Luther. When we look at developments in this way, then it disintegrates into an evolutionary state — that is the unfolding, it goes outwards — and a state of involution, so that the evolution is followed by involution. (*He writes on the blackboard.*)

Evolution
Involution

Only when we do an overall study of the alternate rhythms from evolution to involution, we are able to fully understand development.

The human being is a complicated being because he is actually a microcosm. What is regarded here as a concept of evolution and involution, takes on the most complicated form in the human being. This most complicated form we must first bring before our souls in a single imagination. Think for instance about birth. (*He writes on the blackboard.*)

1. Birth

If we look at the meaning of the event of a birth, regarding the relationship formed out of embryonic life, to what is brought about between conception and actual birth, we have previous steps which were initially soul-spiritual in the human being, moving into the material aspect. There is an integration of the spiritual-soul orientation into the material orientation. This is certainly a complicated process which psychology hasn't yet studied properly, regarding its deeper meaning. I can admit that the development of the germ has not been studied completely. It is usually only studied by starting with the germ cell, briefly, the evolution is followed from the first germinal cell which has been fertilized through its formative elements up to the embryo's maturity when it is then pushed out. What is not fully studied is what actually happens in the mother's body in the Chorion and the amniotic glands as organs which are around the embryo and in their way are most perfect in the beginning of embryonic development but then become more complicated and are pushed out at the birth of the embryo.

What we have here in the germinal cell is certainly the rising evolution, while the involution is through the soul-spiritual of the organs by which they are first established in the mother's body, from the Chorion, from the Amnion, and then gradually moving to the actual egg nucleus, to the actual embryo, so that we have here an involution of the soul-spiritual into matter. This matter becomes pushed out and then we have the continuation of embryonic evolution. The embryo is born and now puts forward its forces, as I've already explained to you, which it had been developing during the embryonic phase. This continues into the development of speech and still remains available in our bodies until later. We carry within our entire earthly lifetime the forces that remain inside us as remnants of embryonic development: the forces of birth. These birth forces develop within us, evolve in us like a gift of nature. This happens, if I may use this expression which sounds somewhat trivial, out of itself. However, immediately, from taking our first breath, from being in contact with the outer world, other processes come into play, processes related to those of dying. From the beginning we also have forces of dying in us. In these forces of dying our soul-spiritual becomes involved in our exchanges with the outer world.

Through observation, through thinking, we allow dying processes to be integrated into us. This is the opposite process of the developmental process at birth. Like humanity developed since the time epoch a bit before and after the Mystery of Golgotha, humanity experienced those changes of which I have spoken, and people had to a certain extent turn the involution processes into something holy, in contrast to the contrasting evolutionary processes. Evolution is natural, it is a gift of nature; that which is given to us at birth and continues to work, is a gift of nature. If we begin to feel the involution process starting to take hold of us as a dying process is, then it must be sanctified since that divination of the world which I spoke to you about this morning, which means, it must be included into what comes out of the Christ impulse. So we see since the development of Christianity something which should be added into the sacraments due to this dying process, and that is the sacrament of baptism. We will still speak about the ritual involved. In order for us to say: what is an evolutionary process at birth, the baptism should take place as a process of involution. We should add to this rhythm in which we are placed in at birth, the repulsion through the pendulum of baptism. (*He writes on the blackboard.*)

Baptism

The second evolutionary process which appears in our lives, which shows itself to great effect is when a person reaches puberty, when the physical body and astral body reach a certain development and the astral body starts in its development to introduce something quite particular, when also that which separates in the sleeping state, comes into a new relationship. During the state of sleep the physical body and ether bodies remain in bed while the astral body and ego leave. Human life consists of the intimate relationship between the physical and the ether bodies, but in a more loose connection to both the astral body and ego. While in a state of growing these four members are united, in the state of sleep the astral body and ego goes out so that their relationship is looser. However, this relationship comes into a modification, it only really matures in the 14, 15 or sixteenth year, then it comes in a real alternating process with what happens in sleep with the physical body lying asleep in bed.

The right harmony only appears around the age of 14, 15 or 16. The young person is taken hold of, by an inner strength, through which the physical body is permeated with the soul-spiritual, which means the astral with the ego-being. This is outwardly expressed in adolescence, and it is only an outer revelation while a complete transformation takes place in the whole person. This event which appears as an evolutionary process can be called maturity. (*He writes on the blackboard.*)

2. *Maturity (adolescence)*

This is the evolutionary process. The corresponding process of involution as related to maturity, just as baptism relates to birth, is confirmation. (*He writes on the blackboard.*)

Confirmation

Confirmation also has the task — and we will see with this in mind what a fitting ritual it can be — the task in the Christian sense to what can be given to the ego and astral body through which everything has evolved in a modified way between the ego and astral body, between the soul-spiritual and the physical bodily nature, having developed with the coming of maturity.

We enter with this into an age in life where we have something else in relation to development. Our soul-spiritual becomes immersed in the physical bodily nature. The physical body captures our soul-spiritual; the soul spiritual is as a result connected in a certain way with the physical body. This is the condition of our development, because we, when we want to examine it as an evolutionary process, describe it as the soul-spiritual incorporation into the human being. We could say: the third evolutionary process is the incorporation. (*He writes on the blackboard.*)

3. Incorporation

Added to this, if we now look for the corresponding process of involution, then we must above all see, my dear friends, that the human being, through the immersion of his soul-spiritual into the physical body, has evolved an admirable power in his being, continually being in the state of oscillation in which there is a return to the soul-spiritual, in the repetition of the re-immersion into the physical bodily nature so that it contains a rhythm, which threatens him to be either lost in the ecstatic soul-spiritual aspect or to fall back into the animalistic, in complete incorporation. Human beings need something which stand opposite this evolutionary process as a process of involution, and this process is reception to Holly Communion. The process of involution for the incorporation is Holy Communion. (*He writes on the blackboard.*)

Holy Communion

In our discussion about evolution and what the case has been up to now, we could say the following. It is so, that the human being in his soul-spiritual nature, confronts the physical bodily nature at every moment; at every moment the human being must take care to move in the correct rhythm so that his or her soul-spiritual nature is not allowed to sink into animalism, or that the physical is left alone and to a certain extent the unworldly rises into the soul-spiritual which would weaken the soul-spiritual. Bringing the altar sacraments into the right rhythm is what the human being must look for in the reception of sacraments.

With this, not the entire human evolution is given, because the complete human evolution includes that we not only in a single moment stand in this swing between the soul-spiritual and the physical bodily nature, but the complete development includes that we also, in time, could swing back again. We need reminders of previous earthly incarnations and earthly experiences. You only need to look at psychopathology and you will see what it means for people when their normal true recollection is ruined, undermined, somehow erased. These recollections certainly develop early and only those things connected to these recollections, intimately felt completely within, getting to complete grasps with it, only really happens after puberty. This is the difference, which today's modern psychology doesn't consider, between for instance what is present in a child's life of recollections up to 15 and 16 years of age, that it is different to what comes later when memories are again gathered so that through the recollections gathered, the I is actually firmly consolidated. In brief, we see that this becomes more and more consolidated, this which we call life's recollections. It's one of our necessities; it evolves out of our being — as humans. (*He writes on the blackboard.*)

4. Life's recollections

The corresponding process of involution is experienced in Christianity as the sacrament of repentance. (*He writes on the blackboard.*)

Repentance

Here the recollections of life are permeated with Christ; the process of recollection being permeated with Christ, lifts it into the moral realm. Not only is the person's I consolidated, but he is — through his complete lifting of his recollections towards bringing them into account in moral terms, through the process of the sacrament and developed through ritual, by developing the process towards the sacrament and asserting it through ritual worship — he is lead to the involution process of repentance. This process in the Catholic Church comprises various stages which all clearly start with a recollection. Repentance in Catholicism exists in the examination of conscience, in repentance, in the serious intention to discard the mistakes of which one has become aware in oneself, in what confession is — we still have to discuss this — and the retribution one imposes on oneself or is imposed by on one of the pastors. Through these steps, complete repentance comes about, and it is the expression for what the process of involution is supposed to be with regard to the process of the totality of memory's evolution, this means, what makes up the power of recollection in the human being.

Here we have created, my dear friends, processes involved in the evolution of the human being since birth, and then we have that which he now returns to in a natural way as an act of involution. We have a succession of evolutions. Through memory the sequence of evolution enters deeply into inner man. Memory therefore represents an internalisation of what has unfolded outwardly through birth. Here we come to the fifth of a naturally unfolding process of involution; we come to death, which concludes the life of the individual. (*He writes on the blackboard.*)

5. Death

Earlier evolutionary processes we've always contrasted with sacramental action and processes of involution; however, the evolutionary processes have gradually become similar to processes of involution. The process of involution during repentance is in a certain way the outer unfolding of quite an inner decisive recollection process; it is the process of involution which is slowly approached by the process of evolution. We need, when we now want the sacramental action for this natural involutionary process of death, to introduce it in a somewhat cultic, ritualistic form, in which something of a spiritual side of nature's knowledge can be perceived, which serve to confront the dying person and manage to do something to the dying person which is simultaneously stimulated in his soul-spiritual life, stirred by the natural processes of his physical bodily being. It shall, expressed in a rhythm, let the physical-bodily aspect disappear upon death, and the soul-spiritual in turn take shape. For certain reasons, which we will still discuss, one can always see in oils, in everything oil-like, that something leads back to the soul-spiritual. In nature as well, oiling processes are regarded as processes of salvation. Therefore, the holy last anointment is performed here. (*He writes on the blackboard.*)

Last anointment

We can add, so to speak, the process of evolution to that of involution.

Thus, we have exhausted the individual life of a human being, and there are still two human relationships left that are no longer of an individual nature. The one relationship is where the human being, standing here on earth in his physical bodily being, actually treasures a soul-spiritual relationship in heaven, so that the umbilical cord to his soul spiritual, which had been severed, so to speak, now again is reconnected to the soul-spiritual. This doesn't involve individual people; it involves the relationship of exchange with the heavenly-spiritual. This is something which is present in all people, albeit unconsciously. If we were to be completely severed from the soul-spiritual, we would never find our way back, it is a deep process of involution which is eternally present in us, quite a hidden process, even more hidden than what happens in the inner soul life when the organism passes through death; for this reason it is a process which in the course of individual lives of people do not become conscious at all. For this, an outer evolutionary process must be looked for and this evolutionary process is given in the ritual of priest ordination. As the sixth one, we have a process which is given out of itself, as I said — you could call it a connection — and corresponding as its counter impulse or the outer evolutionary process, in the priest ordination. (*He writes on the blackboard.*)

6. Reconnection: Priest ordination

Now as the seventh one we have an image of the earthly relationship given as a relationship between the soul-spiritual and the physical-bodily: this relationship is in nature's way given as the relationship between a man and a woman. For each true observation of the relationship between a man and a woman it is so, that the balance in the feminine swings more to the soul-spiritual side, and in the male, more to the physical-bodily nature. Yes, it is so. On earth, to a certain extent, the relationship is expressed between the human being and the spiritual world, and it is, I could say, that the woman has made one less step down into the physical life, than the man. One must say it actually differently, one must say: The descent into earthly life can be depicted by a definite boundary; the woman doesn't quite arrive at the boundary while the man crosses over it. This is actually the contrasting difference between a man and woman, expressed in a physical way. There is a certain boundary to reach, the woman doesn't quite manage it and the man crosses over it. Both bear a kind of imperfection within, between them a state of tension exists as a result. When this state of tension which exists naturally in a relationship between a man and woman, searches for a sacramental evolutionary value — this is a deeply hidden process of involution which we are pointing out here, when we indicate the manly and womanly — then we are given the sacrament of marriage. (*He writes on the blackboard.*)

7. Man and woman: marriage

This is what has always been in Christian esotericism in relation to sacramentalism, in so far as it is to be applied to man, that man enters this world endowed with values partly through evolution, partly through values of involution, and to this must always be added, through the sacraments, the values of evolution to involution, and values of involution to evolution. Man equally speaks out of the foundation of his experience: the human being steps with his incomplete being fully into earthly existence; he or she must first be made into a complete being. He or she expresses their incompleteness at birth, in puberty, in incarnation, in memory and in death. To these things the human being, in order to live as complete physical-bodily-soul-spiritual beings, has to add, through sacramental ways, the baptism, confirmation, sacrament at the altar, repentance and last anointment.

With regard to the social sphere, man stands in an exceptional state of priesthood, where through outer signs done in a sacramental way, also in the priest ordination, the deeply hidden value of involution is present. In the healing of marriage, the sacrament should express how that which is only given in an incomplete value as involution in a man and a woman, is to be complemented by an external sacramental action.

I ask you to take what I have initially presented to you not in a one-sided naturalistic way, otherwise you could of course say, it was all presented in a one-sided naturalistic way. If you grasp the outer natural world and the inner moral-religious world as one unit, then we always have a sacramental evolution value for an inner moral-religious value. By contrast, what we have as an expression of an outer form of evolution, is what we need to search for as a value of involution, that means, an internalisation in human beings of the outer evolution. For us it is really necessary to again accomplish the values of involution, through the sacraments.

My dear friends, why do moral and religious truths have so little power for modern man? They have little power because it is necessary that what come to man is not merely admonishment and a commandment, but that he becomes aware in this approach of an actual penetration with the Godhead taking place. This can take place in human consciousness only in sacramental actions.

So, you have asked me to speak about these sacraments. The questions asked for, today, have largely not been answered, but they were spoken about as thoughts and experiences forming the foundations of what is sacramental. These fundamental experiences and fundamental thoughts as sacramental are alive no longer, basically no longer since the time — obviously, of course, with good reason — since the sacramental has become a subject of discussions. If today it can't be somehow intentional to take up all the sacraments outside the Catholic Church, then it must be considered how to again accomplish a real cult, a real ritual, because only these, as we will still see, actually can have a community building effect.

This is what I wanted to speak about as a foundation. We will go further into the questions which had been asked.

(*Blackboard notes:*)

1. Birth	—	Baptism
2. Adolescence	—	Confirmation
3. Incorporation	—	Holy Communion
4. Life's recollections	—	Repentance
5. Death	—	Last anointment
6. Reconnection	—	Priest ordination
7. Man and Woman	—	Marriage

GNOSTICS AND MONTANISTS

Lecture given in Dornach on 3 October 1921, morning.

My dear friends! Yesterday we started by addressing a wish which licentiate Bock had expressed at the beginning of our course and we find that what we need to build on to what I said yesterday afternoon about sacramentalism relevant to today, can be discovered if we link the possible reflections, which are necessary, to the 13th chapter of the Gospel of St Mark. It is important for us to certainly try again, in all seriousness, to derive specific meaning from what is expressed in living words. To me it is impossible that pastoral care can be developed in the future, without yourself developing the application of living words and even experiencing living words. However, it is impossible for current mankind which is so strongly gripped by materialism, to be able to handle the living Word in itself, without a historical deepening. It is simply so, that in dealing with intellectualistic concepts and ideas we are only dealing with dead words, with the corpse of the Logos. We will only deal with the living Word when we penetrate through the layer in which man lives today, only, and alone, by penetrating through the layer of the dead, the corpse-like words.

My dear friends, the Catholic Church has to a certain degree understood very well how to misplace and obstruct access to these living words for those who, in their opinion, should be the true believers. In pastoral care the Catholic Church in a certain sense considers these enlivening words already, but in an outward sense. All these things will only become understood when we take what I presented yesterday and think them through deeply, and, if we can still penetrate them further, to yield clarity. I'm saying that the Catholic Church understood very clearly in this regard, to exterminate the life of the Word, because it belonged to one of the most significant epochs of all human development, and which had contributed briefly before and some three centuries after the Mystery of Golgotha, just to the civilized part of humanity.

When we ask our contemporaries about the essence of the Gnosis, for example the essence of the Montanistic heresy, then with the current soul constitution you basically can't understand anything correctly relating to it. That which would outwardly be informative in the becoming church has been carefully eradicated and the things that archaeologists, philosophers, researchers of antiquity discover from this characterised epoch, will indeed be deciphered word for word, but the decipherment does not mean reaching an understanding. All of this must actually be read differently, in order to enter the real soul content of olden times. It is for instance possible for modern humanity, to take the Deussen translation, which has exterminated all real meaning of the Orient, and, while thinking these translations are great, while mankind can't eradicate all understanding for what Deussen translated, devote yourself to such a Deussen translation. In order to understand, you need to penetrate the meaning of the first Christian centuries, more specifically the centuries before the Mystery of Golgotha happened.

GNOSTICS AND MONTANISTS

I would like to give you access, somewhat in the way I have out of Anthroposophy, by means of a presentation, which you can visualise as symptomatic of what history brings. One of the most extinct things belonging in the first Christian centuries was referred to as the Pistis, placed in contrast to the Gnosis. The Gnosis can't be understood if one doesn't know that in that time epoch, in which, let's say, you appeared in the form of a Basilides or Valentinus, people who lived in the spirituality of that time, were fighting a very terrible battle, which can be characterised by them asking a question: What do we poor people have to do on the one hand with the spirit that juts in our souls, and on the other hand our physical body into which our soul likewise juts into? In a terrifying manner this question played out in the soul battle among religious people. The two opposite poles, to a certain extent, of this battle was the Gnosis and Montanism sect.

The Gnosis was, for people who wanted to become Gnostics, being aware that within a person, where the soul resides, the spirit can only be reached through knowledge, through clear, lucid, light-filled knowledge. However, it was already during a time in which intellectualism was being prepared in the dark, in a time when intellectualism was regarded as the enemy of the human soul's relation to the spirit. To a certain extent people prophetically saw how intellectualism would push in, in the future; this arrival of intellectualism was seen as stripping the world of spirituality, wanting to completely make the world void of the Divine, like I have characterised for you yesterday. People saw this and people experienced intellectualism as a danger. People wanted to hold on to something spiritual which didn't come from intellectualism. That's roughly the soul battle Basilides fought, the Gnostic who wanted to stick to what was revealed in the course of the year. He said to himself: When a person submits himself to his forthcoming intellect, then he separates himself from the Divine spirituality of the cosmos; he must connect to what lies in his environment, which has come into being through the Divine spiritual cosmos; he must adhere to that which has the venerable image of cosmic creation in the circling of the world and thus the Divine process in matter; he must adhere to the course of the year. — Basilides did the following: He looked up — but with him it was actually still only tradition, so no longer an inner imaginative perception as in older times, which I characterised as the reading of the movement of the stars — he looked up and said: Last but not least, the spiritual gaze is lost; when we feel, that when we become aware the spiritual gaze is lost, then we talk about the unknown God, the God who can't be grasped in words and concepts, from whom the fist aeon this unknown God manifests himself, revealing himself — this concept of manifestation which later unified things as with Basilides, will be totally misunderstood if compared with what we understand today under "manifestation"; one should not say "it manifests itself" but "it is formed out of," it is individually shaped — out of the unknown God is formed the Nous, which also appeared with Anaxagoras as the first creation of the unknown God.

That is the first principle, which exists in people as a copy, when the human mind, not the intellectual mind but the lively mind I've characterised for you during these days, still existed within Greek philosophy (up to Plato), and which then appeared in a weaker form still in Aristotle.

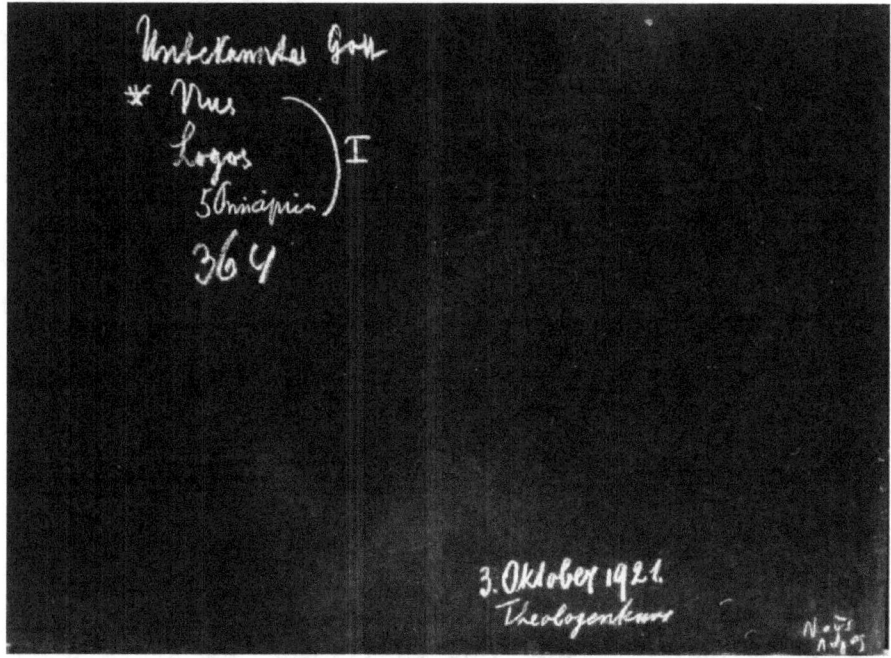

Plate 9   14th Lecture   3. October, 1921, in the morning

What comes next is the Logos, in which from the Nous we descend further down. In human beings it is expressed by perceiving sound and tone. In the neck area we find five other principles which we need not characterise in detail now. With this we have what was first called the holy days of the year, which gives people, when they read the cosmos, an understanding of the human body, leading to the human head organisation.

Besides these principles we find others in the human organization, 364 in total, which gives 364 + 1=365, the outer symbol which is expressed as the 365 days of the year. The word Day (Tag) originally was inwardly connected to God, so what Basilides, by speaking about 365 days, spoke about 365 gods which all partake in the creation of the human organism. As the last one of the gods — i.e. if you take one plus 364, and then take the last day of the year as a symbol for one God — Basilides saw the God who was worshipped by the Jews in the Old Testament. You see, this is what is extraordinary in the Gnosis, that it is in such a relationship to Jahve, the Jewish God, that he is not the unknown God connected to the Nous and Logos but with the Jewish God as the 365, as the last day of the year.

By understanding the Gnosis in this way, the experience of the soul was to be permeated spiritually. If I were to give you a characteristic aspect of the Gnosis, in relation to inner human experience it is this: that the Gnostic aspired in everything to penetrate the Highest with knowledge, so that his gaze rose above the Logos up to the Nous. The Gnostic says: In Christ and in the Mystery of Golgotha the Nous is embodied in the human being; not the Logos, the Nous is embodied. This, my dear friends, if it is grasped in a lively way, has a distinct result for our inner soul life. If you consider these things abstractly, as is in our intellectual time presented to many people, well, then it is heard that people in olden times didn't speak about the Logos in which Jesus became flesh, but of the Nous, which became the flesh of Jesus. That's the thing then, if you have pegged such a term. For a person who spiritually lives within a lively experience of concepts, he would not be able to do otherwise, than to grasp such a soul's content, as to imagine sculpturally what the Nous becoming flesh is. The Nous having become flesh however, can't speak; this can't be the Christ, can't go through death and resurrection. The Christ of the Gnostic, which is actually the Nous, could only come as far as being embodied in people; it could not die or accomplish resurrection.

For Basilides, this darkened his observation. His gaze becomes clouded the moment he approaches the last acts of the Mystery of Golgotha with his inner gaze; it clouds his gaze when it comes to dying and resurrection. His gaze is drawn to the route towards Crucifixion, the route to Golgotha of Jesus Christ, but he couldn't accomplish, out of a lively imagination, that the Christ carried the cross to Golgotha, was killed on the cross and resurrected. He regards it in such a way that Simon of Cyrene took the cross from the Christ, that he carried it up to Golgotha, and instead of Christ, that Simon of Cyrene is crucified. This is the Christ imagination of the Gnostic in as far as the image of Basilides appears and is basically the historical expression of the Gnosis.

So we see how the Christ in his final deed, is omitted by the Gnostic, how the Gnostic can't grasp the final result of Golgotha, how in their imagination the Christ is merely accomplished through the Nous, how it ends at the moment the Christ gives the cross away to Simon of Cyrene. On the one hand we have Gnosis, which is so strongly afraid of intellectualism that it did not let the legitimate power of intellectualism into human vision and as a result could not enter into the last act of the Mystery of Golgotha.

What did the Gnosis do? It stood in quite a lively way, I could say, in relation to the most extraordinary and powerful question of that current age: How does one penetrate the supersensible spirit from which the soul originated? — The Gnostic pointed away from that which somehow wanted to flow in from intellectualism and result in the image of Christ up to the point when he hands the cross to Simon of Cyrene. This is the one side of the human battle which at the time had the result of creating the influence of the great question, which I have set before you. What comes forth from this wrestling?

From all this wrestling another great question arises which became the crux for the Christian Gnostics. My dear friends, because the Gnostics regarded 365 as the Divine god of the Jews, they experienced the Fatherly and the Divine at the end of this row. When the Jews worshiped their god, they experienced it as Fatherly, while what later appeared as the Holy Ghost, they experienced the opposite pole, in the Nous. As a result, the Gnostics gave an answer to the primordial question in the first Christian centuries, an answer which is no longer valid today. Their answer was: The Christ is a far higher creation than the Father; the Christ is essentially equal to the Father. The Father, who finds his most outward, extreme expression in the Jewish god, is the creator of the world, but as the world creator he has, out of its foundations allowed things to be created simultaneously, the good and evil, the good and bad, simultaneously health and illness, the divine and the devilish. This world, which was not made out of love, because it contains evil, the Gnostics contrasted with the more elevated divine nature of the Christ who came from above, downward, carrying the Nous within, who can redeem this world that the creator had to leave un-liberated.

Christ is not essentially the Father, said the Gnostics, the Father essentially stood lower than the Son; the Son as Christ stood higher. This is the fundamental feeling permeating the Gnosis: however, it has been completely obstructed by what later occurred in the Roman Catholic continuation. Basically, we can't look back at what the big question was: How does one relate to the greater Christ in contrast to the less perfect Father? The Gnostic actually saw things in such a way that the Father of the worlds was still imperfect, and only by bringing forth his Son, he created perfection; that through the propagation of his Son, the act of procreation of his Son, He would complete the development of the world.

In all these things you see exactly what lived in the Gnosis. If we now look at the opposite side, which comes into the strongest expression with Monatunus, already weaker but still clearly with Tertullian, then we look over to those who said to themselves: If we want to reach into the Gnosis, everything disappears; we can't through the outer world, not through the contemplation of the seasons, not through reading the stars, reach the divine, we must enter into man, we must immerse ourselves in man. —

While the Gnosis directed its gaze to the macrocosm, so Mantanismus dived into the microcosm, in the human being himself. Intellectualistic concepts were at that time only in its infancy and could not yet be fully expressed; theology in today's sense did not arise in this way. What existed in all the exercises, in particular those prescribed by Mantanus for his students, were inner stories, something which was enlivened within the students as visions. These atavistic visions for the Montanists were particularly indigenous. All those who were to separate themselves from belonging to the mere pastoral care of the Montanists were allowed to practice, and all of them were allowed to practice to the extent that they could answer the question: how does the soul-spiritual in man, in the microcosm, relate to the physical-bodily aspect?

During ancient times, long before the Mystery of Golgotha, what I've just said was something obvious; had a self-evident answer. For those who lived in the time epoch of the Mystery of Golgotha, such an obvious answer didn't exist. People first had to dive into physicality. Because a fear existed of bringing intellectualism into this physicality, one entered the corporality with the power of the imagination and we get to know the descriptions of the forming of Montanist visions, which have also disappeared. In descriptions of Montanist visions — and this is characteristic — we always find the repetitive idea of the Christ soon returning in a physical body to the earth. One can't think of Montanism without thinking of the imminent return of the Christ to earthly corporeality. While the Montanist was familiar with the idea of finding the returning Christ, he strongly set before his soul what happened at the cross, what was accomplished through the death on the cross, what is involved in dying, what is involved in resurrection. The re-descent of the Christ, the physical-bodily immersion that takes place, was tinged by materialistic feelings in this view of the Montanists; they lived in the idea that Christ would come again and live in time and space. This was pronounced and those who believed this in the schools were only those who responded to the belief of the imminent coming of Christ Jesus to the earth, where he would stride along as if he is in a physical body.

This is in contrast to the Gnosis, this is the other pole: it had a different danger, the danger that all historic development of humanity is to be imagined in space and time. The urge to imagine such an idea of the world is what Augustinus for instance experienced in his exchange with the Bishop Faustus. Through Faustus a method of imagination is introduced which is completely tinged with the senses as images presented to Augustinus, and this became a materialistic experience of the world for Augustinus, from where he approached the world. Augustinus' words are gripping: I search for God in the stars, and do not find Him. I search for God in the sun, in the moon, and don't find Him. I search for God in all the plants, in all the animals, and don't find Him. I search for God on the mountains, in the rivers; I don't find Him. —

He means that in all the images there is no inner experience of the Divine, as it is with the Montanists. Through this Augustinus learnt, as it happened in his exchange with Faustus, to recognise materialism. This created his soul battle, which he overcomes by turning to himself, to faith, towards believing what he doesn't know.

We must let this rise out of history because the important things do not happen in a way, we can control it, by taking a document in hand which has lain in the archives, or by looking at the entire history of these fore-mentioned men from outside — that is an outer assessment of history. The most important part of history takes place in the human soul, in human hearts. We need to look into the soul of Basilides, into the soul of Montanus, into the soul of Faustus, into the soul of Augustinus, if we want to look into what really happened in the historic fields which one then can develop into what actually became a covering of Christianity in the Church of Constantine. The Constantine Church took on the outer life of worldly realms in which the spiritual no longer lived — in the sense of the 13th Chapter of the Mark Gospel — depicted as an already un-deified earth, a perished earth, into which the divine kingdom must again live as brought by him in its real spiritual soul form.

You see, in the course of both these viewpoints, one on the side the Gnosis which only came up to the Nous, and on the other side Montanism, which remained stuck in a materialistic conception, you see, how in these contrasts present during the first Christian century, the writer of the St John Gospel was situated. He looked on one side to the Gnosis, which he recognised from his view as an error, because it said: In the primordial beginnings was the Nous and the Nous was with God, and God was the Nous, and the Nous became flesh and lived among us; and Simon of Cyrene took the cross from Christ and thus accomplished a human image of what happened on Golgotha, after Christ only went up to carrying the cross and then disappeared from the earthly plane. — For the gaze of the Gnostic Christ disappeared the moment Simon of Cyrene took over the cross. That was a mistake.

Where do you arrive if you succumb to all thought being human and having nothing to do with the spirit? No, this is not the way the writer of John's Gospel experienced it. It was not the Nous which was at the primordial beginnings, not the Nous with God and a veil covering everything which is related to the Christian Mystery, but: In the primordial beginnings was the Logos, and the Logos was with God, and a God was the Logos and the Logos became flesh and lived among us. — So the first actions are connected to the final actions: a unity comes about when we understand it with the spirit. We wish for something which doesn't lift us above human heights, to where we must find the Nous, because that is only one perspective of the spiritual.

Just as much spirit is needed for the spiritual orientation to let people form the idea that Jesus and the Christ God is one, so much spirituality exists in the Logos. When we hold on to the Nous, we only reach Christ; when we hold on to a Montanistic vision we only reach Jesus who in an unbelievable way returns as Christ, but then again only as a physical Jesus. No, we should not turn ourselves to the Nous coming from humanity, we must turn to the Logos, in which the Christ became man and walked among us.

The origin of the St John Gospel has really come about through an immense spiritual time context. I can't do otherwise, my dear friends, than to make a personal remark here, that I need to experience it as the greatest tragedy of our time, that theologians do not experience the majesty of the John Gospel at all, that out of a deep struggle preceding it, out of a struggle, the big question arose: How can mankind manage to, on the one hand, find a way to his soul-spiritual in the spiritual-supersensible where his own soul-spiritual nature originated from? On the other hand, how can mankind reach an understanding for how his soul is within the physical-bodily nature?

On the one hand the question could be answered by the Gnosis, and on the other hand it could be answered by an imagination towards the Pistis, which then came to Montanism in a visionary manner. The writer of the St John's Gospel was continuously placed in the middle, between these two, and we feel every word, every sentence only intimately if we do it in such a way as it flowed out of the course of the times, and in such a way that you feel the course of time during the Mystery of Golgotha as if it can be experienced forever in the human soul.

With an anthroposophic gaze we can look back at the turning point in time, to the most important turning point in the earth, when one wanted to have this experience of adoration of the St John's Gospel. The day before yesterday I said to you, one has, and must, have an experience when one reads the Gospels with an anthroposophical approach, by reading them time and time again. This admiration of the reader is always renewed with each reading by the conviction that one can never learn everything from the Gospels because they go into immeasurable depths. In Gnosis, my dear friends, you can learn everything because it adheres to outer nature and cosmic symbols. In Montanism one can learn all about it because everyone who is familiar with such things knows what a tremendous suggestive persuasiveness all this has, that can be experienced through microcosmic visions, stronger than any outer impression. You must first learn, my dear friends, in order to be able to talk someone out of a vision, you first need to learn how to do it. You could, if you want to convince a person religiously, rather talk him out of what he has experienced with his outer senses, than anything he has experienced as visions, as atavistic clairvoyance, because atavistic visions are far deeper in a person. By allowing atavistic visions into a person, he is far more connected to them than to his sense impressions. It is far easier to determine an error in sense impressions than an error related to visions. Visions are deeply imbedded in the microcosm. Out of such depths everything originated which the writer of John's Gospel saw from the other side, the side of the Montanists.

Montanism was the side of the Charybdis while the Gnosis was the side of the Scylla. He had to get past them both. I feel it at once, as our current tragedy, that our time has been forced —

really out of the very superficial honesty, which prevail in such areas — that the Gospel of St John has been completely eliminated and only the Synoptics accepted. If you experience the Gospels through ever greater wonderment at each renewed reading, and when you manage to delve ever deeper and deeper into the Gospels, then it gives you a harmony of the Gospels. You only reach the harmony of the Gospels when you have penetrated St John's Gospel because all together, they don't form a threefold but a fourfold harmony. You won't accomplish, my dear friends, what you have chosen to do in these meetings for the renewal of religion in present time, if you haven't managed to experience the entire depths, the immeasurable depths of the St John's Gospel. Out of the harmony of John's Gospel with the so-called synoptic Gospels something else must come about as had been established by theology. What can really be experienced inwardly as a harmony in the four Gospels must come about in a living way, as the living truth and therefore just life itself. Out of the experience, out of every experience which is deepened and warmed by the history of the origin of Christianity, out of this experience must flow the religious renewal. It can't be a result out of the intellect, nor theoretical exchanges about belief and knowledge, but only from the deepening of the felt, sensed, content which is able to be deepened in such a way as it was able to truly live in the souls of the first Christians.

Then, my dear friends, we see how Christianity was submerged by all that Christ experienced in Romanism — as I've presented to you — in the downfall of the world. Those who still understand Christ today will have to feel that the downfall is contained in all that is held by the powers of Romanism. By allowing the powers of Romanism to be preserved by the peoples who lived in this Romanism — the Roman written language, the Latin language had long been active — by our preservation of Roman Law, in our conservation of the outer forms of the Roman State, by our even uprooting the northern regions which contained the most elementary Germanic feelings experienced out of quite a different social community, in the Roman State outstripping all that is from the north, we live right up to our present days in a Roman world of decay because in Christendom, as it was considered in the vicinity of Christ Jesus himself, no other site could be found. This is because the Christianity of Constantine, which found such a meaningful symbol in the crowning of Constantine the Great in Rome, was a Christianity which expressed itself in outer worldliness, in Roman legalities. Augustinus already experienced, as I characterised yesterday and today, the feeling in his soul: Oh, what will it be then, if that gets a grip on the world, that which streams out of godless intellectualism, out of godless Romanism into the world? The principle of civil government will become something terrible; the Civitas of people will be opposed by the Civitas Dei, the God State. — So we notice the rise — earlier the indications had already been there, my dear friends — we see an interest emerging that was just seized in the following times in its fullest power in religious fields, that a light is cast on all later religious battles in the soul, which has just felt these religious battles most deeply.

Already with Augustinus this question emerged: How do we save the morality in the face of outward forces of law? How can we save morality, the divinely permeated morality? Into Romanism it can't spread. — This is the striving for internalization we find in the commitments and confessions of Augustinus, if we penetrate them correctly.

This occurs in the later striving in the most diverse forms. It appears in the tendency towards outer moral stateliness, which had to be developed according to Roman forms of the Roman Papal church, develop through the coronation of the kings becoming Roman emperors, in which the kings were accepted as instruments of the Roman Papal church, which itself was only fashioned out of ungodly Romanism. I speak in the Christian sense, in the sense of the first Christianity, which experienced Romanism as an enemy. How could one escape this which was being prepared? The first way one could get out was to not allow the internalised Christ to submit to the nationalization of morality, as it had evolved in the Roman Papal church. The nationalization, the outer national administration of morality was what Augustinus still accepted on the one hand, while, however, in the depths of his soul there were forces which he rebelled against.

We see in this rebellion, one could call it, the tendency of morality to withdraw within, at least to save the divinity within morality, according to what one had lost in outer worldliness. We see this morality being turned inward, being searched for as the "little spark" mentioned by Meister Eckhard, by Tauler, by Suso and so on, and how in particular it profoundly, intimately appears in the booklet "Theologia Deutch." This, my dear friends is the battle for the moral, which now came to the fore, not to be lost within the divine spirituality, when it has already been lost in outer world knowledge and administration of the world. However, for a long time one was not ready to use such force like

Suso regarding morality and seize the divine to penetrate the moral.

At first it was a question of arranging the whole in a kind of vague form, always envisioning the side of the outside world, for there had to be someone like a Carolus Magnus, who on the one hand was a worldly administrator, and who could transfer the state administration of morality to the crown of the emperor as an outward gesture, while the church worked in the background. It was imagined in such a way, I could say, that it became a kind of moral dilemma, a conscience that has become historical. This started in the 9th, 10th centuries and this inner conscience steered towards people looking at the world, and that man, because he stood in the middle of the search for the divine in the moral, didn't manage it in the world and searched for the enemies in the world which he felt within. Man looked in the world to find enemies. This resulted in the danger of Christians looking for enemies in the outer world, this led, my dear friends, to the mood of the crusades.

The crusade mood stands in the middle of the quests for internalization, yet people still didn't reach that place within themselves where the divine was grasped through the moral. The crusade mood lived in two forms; it lived above all in the moral impact of Godfrey of Bouillon and his comrades. From them the call went out against Rome: Jerusalem against Rome! To Jerusalem! We want to replace Rome with Jerusalem because in Rome we have become acquainted with outwardness, and in Jerusalem we will perhaps find inwardness, when we relive the Mystery of Golgotha in its holy places. — This is how the imagination came to Godfrey of Bouillon who we may think of as finding the enemy inwardly, even though he still looked for it outwardly, looking for it in the Turks. The striving to turn more inward and there find the ruler of the world, but at the same time to crown a king of Jerusalem, all this expressed itself in the historic mood of the 10th, 11th, and 12th centuries. All this lived in the people. For once try to place yourself, in both the worldly and the spiritual reasons of the crusades and you will discover this historical mood everywhere.

Rome saw this. Rome felt it indeed, something was happening in the north: Jerusalem against Rome. In Rome one felt the externalization, but Rome was careful. Rome already had its prophets; it was careful and looked into the future, seeing what people wanted: Jerusalem against Rome. So it did something which often happens in such cases, it introduced in its own way what the others first wanted, and the Pope allowed his creatures, Peter of Amiens and his supporters, to preach about the crusade in order to carry out from Rome what actually went against it. Study the history with understanding; take it as an impulse and you will see that already the first steps of the crusades took place in what Rome had anticipated and that which Godfrey of Bouillon and his supporters strived for.

So we see in the historic mood how outer actions were searching for what lay within. I could say we can understand this historic mood in a spiritual way when we see how the Order of the Temple has grown out of the crusades, orders which are already further in their turning within. As a result of the crusades it brought an inwardness with it. It only takes things in such a way that it knows that one does not actually internalize them if one does not penetrate the exterior at the same time, when one doesn't, in order to save the moral, see it as an enemy in an exterior way. As paradoxical as this might appear, my dear friends, what Godfrey of Bouillon saw outwardly in the realm of the Turks, this is like Luther's battle at Wartburg Castle with its devils as an inner power. The struggle is directed inward.

If you now look at all of this, what appears in programs about such people as Johannes Valentin Andrea, Comenius, what lives in the Bohemian brothers, then you will understand how in the later centuries of the crusades the pursuit of internalization has gone. I must at least mention the most symptomatic picture seemed to me always to be in a single place when I looked at this lonely thinker who lived in Bohemia, the contemporary of Leibniz, Franziskus Josephus von Hoditz und Wolframitz. For the first time, in all clarity — we don't only know this today — he stripped morality of legality. Everywhere in the early days of writing in the Roman spirit, the legal was bound to the moral. What lived in a religious way in most people, lived in a philosophic way in the contemporaries of Leibniz. He wanted the moral element to be purely philosophic. Just like Luther wanted to get the inner justification, because in his time it was no longer possible to get justification in the outer world, so Franziskus Josephus von Hoditz und Wolframitz as a lonely thinker, saw the task: How do I save, purely conceptually, morality from the encirclement and transformation of legality, with those poor philosophic concepts? How do I save the purely human-moral? — He didn't deepen the question religiously. The question was not one-sidedly, intellectually posed by Hoditz — Wolframitz. However, just because it is put philosophically, one notices how he struggles philosophically in the pure shaping of the substantial moral content living in the consciousness.

In order to understand these times which after all form the foundation of ours, in which the feelings of our contemporaries live — without knowing it — you should, my dear friends, always look back at the deep soul battles experienced in the past, also when a modern person feels that he has "brought it so delightfully far"; by looking back at this time of the most terrible human soul battles, only one period of superstition is seen.

So, I could say, the historic development of the struggle for morality came about. What was being experienced in this struggle shows up right into our present day, and it can be imposed on the spiritual search into religion, for religious behaviour, even into aberrations. Still, no balance has been found between Pistis and Sophia, between Pistis and Gnosis. This abyss is still gaping in contrast to the writer of the Gospel of St John who had infinite courage to stand above it and find the truth in between it all.

This summoning of strength in the search for the moral, in the will to save the divine, by applying it only to the moral, was felt in their simple, deep but imperfect way by those southern German religious people who are regarded as sectarians today, the Theosophists, who we find on the one hand in Bengel, and on the other, in Oetinger, but who are far more numerous than only in these two. They use all their might to strive, in complete earnestness, for attaining the divine in the moral, yet by trying to attain the divine in morality they realise: We need an eschatology, we need a prophecy, we need foresight into the course of the world's unfolding. This is still the unfulfilled striving of the Theosophists in the first half of the 19th century, started at the end of the 18th century when we must see the dawn of that which was completely buried at the end of the 19th and the beginning of the 20th century, and which must, from all those who experience the necessity for religious renewal, be seen.

For this reason, my answers to your wishes which are in pursuit of such religious renewal, can't turn out in any other way than they do. I would quite like to give you what I must believe you are actually looking for.

ORDINATION AND TRANSUBSTANTIATION

Lecture given in Dornach on 3 October 1921, afternoon.

My dear friends! I agree with licentiate Bock who suggested it would be best to take up yesterday's reflections plus those of the afternoon and orientate ourselves toward questions that had arisen.

Yesterday I tried to present a kind of overview of the seven sacraments. I tried to show how the sacraments either determine a kind of value of involution to an evolution value, or the reverse. In the questions which have been asked, there is a wish for something to be said about the sacrament of priest ordination. We have looked at how five sacraments essentially are arranged along the developmental line of each individual human being, how this line connects from birth up to death. We have seen how both the sacraments of priest ordination and marriage in the Christian sense fall away from the other (five) sacraments, and how the priest ordination ceremony points out the evolutionary element which is present in each human being as an involutionary process, namely the mysterious connection each individual human being has with the Divine.

Now let us first of all try to place the concept of this sacrament of ordination in front of us according to its development, how its

Christian content has gone over into Christian ceremonies and gradually crystallized life in Catholicism as the culmination of all ceremonies.

We must very clearly understand that the connection of human beings with the Divine in the sense of the epoch in which the Mystery of Golgotha took place, was such that it certainly existed way back, behind the consciousness of modern man today. If we go back far into the cultural development of humanity, we discover another kind of selection for the priesthood than what was later the case, and of the kind we actually want to talk about here. You must clearly understand that ceremonies, rituals and sacraments only become comprehensible within the entire relationship of human evolution, because the Christian sacraments are a kind of transformation of older sacraments. So, regarding priesthood, the relationship is different compared to olden times. In earlier times the one who was taken up into the mysteries by leaders of the mysteries was elected according to his soul characteristics; his entire human development was regarded as being worthy — if today we could select an apt term we would say: 'to be chosen.' This is a concept which has so much more meaning, the further we look back in human evolution. The point of view that people are equal is a modern-day opinion; it is actually essentially something that only emerged from the consciousness of the epoch around the Mystery of Golgotha. By contrast they believed that in fact, in olden times, one person was more worthy of being chosen than another, so that those who were worthy to be inducted into the Mysteries — or to be initiated, as one can clearly impress the imagination with other expressions — was to be discovered within the masses of people. When these individuals were in this or that way discovered, which was believed as predestination for a priestly calling, he had to go through with the initiation. This process of initiation meant that the person was brought into a situation where he had to manage another state of consciousness other than merely the one he experienced in the outer world. In olden times another state of consciousness prevailed, quite different from what it is today. Today quite a different state of consciousness is needed to be able to manage Imagination, Inspiration and Intuition. So when I take today's second kind of consciousness as a start, perhaps it can lead to greater understanding, in such a way that the usual daily consciousness still remains complete. A person should not for a moment — without falling sick — be somehow impaired by exercises or the like, as I have described in my book "Knowledge of the Higher Worlds"; a person should not be impaired in the management of his daily consciousness, it must be present. The other consciousness which lacks real freedom which consist in managing Imagination, Inspiration and Intuition must be there as something which can always change quickly, in an instant change to ordinary daily consciousness, like sleep can be changed into the waking state, only that this changing between seeing consciousness and ordinary day consciousness would be completely situated within human capriciousness. This is certainly something which can only be attained after practice and needs to be examined in all its being, in order to talk about this at all.

It is precisely this other consciousness which presents a completely different world compared with the world developed out of the senses and understood with the mind, aspects which feed back into the being of the human I, to stick to the human ego.

The human I is present in the other consciousness with great power, one doesn't have something which is merely permeated with a single imagination or feeling, but one has an image. One has the possibility of looking at it and knows, this I is something in which one not merely lives, but it is present as an objectivity. The other thing about this higher consciousness is that one doesn't gain any insight into the mineral kingdom — the mineral kingdom belongs only to ordinary human daily consciousness — by contrast it is fully aware towards anything plant-like, animal-like and the human self. One really lives in another world. What is between these two worlds is called the threshold; it must be crossed over but can only be crossed over after preparations have been achieved, after one has really faithfully practiced the exercises which I have presented in my book "Knowledge of the Higher Worlds and its Attainment." If one has not really prepared for this crossing, one could, through the acquisition of this new consciousness, slip down into physicality. *(During the following presentation a central drawing is made on the blackboard.)*

ORDINATION AND TRANSUBSTANTIATION

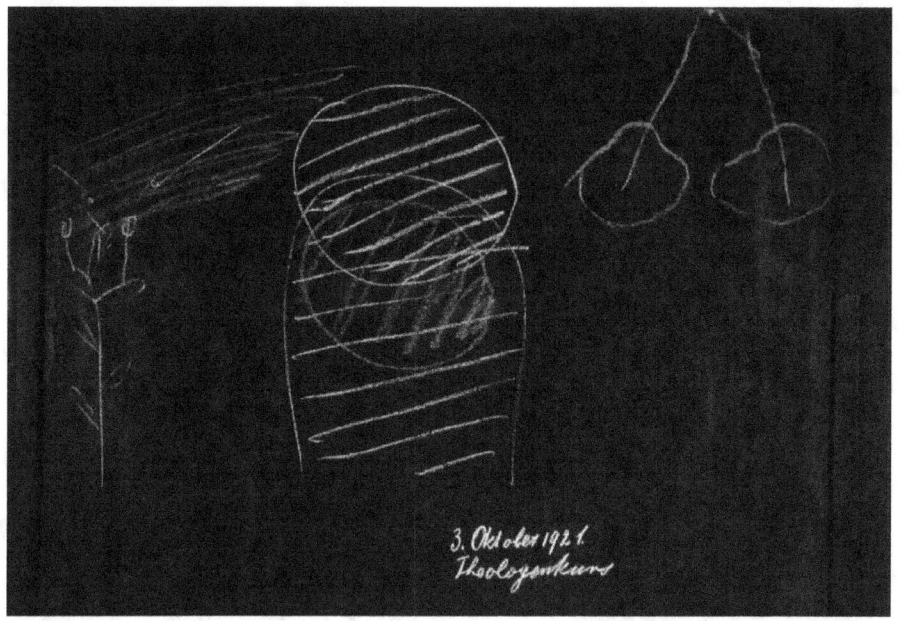

Plate 10   15th Lecture   3. October 1921, afternoon

I would like to sketch it in the following way. Let's accept that this daily consciousness is connected to human physicality. This higher consciousness is now lifted from it and one sees a completely new world. However, now one has to retain this higher consciousness; it must be purely soul-spiritual. It can't happen however, if one has not previously developed the strength through exercises — it can't happen if not accomplished in a lively way; what I'm implying is more of a hypothesis — so, when one has *not* acquired the strength through exercises, it can all collapse into physicality. This means one is not living in a free soul-spiritual consciousness but the processes in human organs will reveal what this consciousness observes; then one has to do with dreams, one does not really have actual objective imaginations full of content. The objective, content-filled

315

imagination exists as a result of, what one experiences, not being impregnated with bodily processes, but processes of the supersensible world. This must be achieved through exercises and by having achieved this, being able to step over the boundary between the sensual and supersensible which is designated as the threshold. This is the case today. Today our ordinary consciousness contains content known to everyone, but we have another content — which of course can be described as I have done now again from a certain point of view — which is certainly described as the content of a higher world as opposed to that of the ordinary world.

If we now go back to the times of human earthly development which I want to speak to you about here, in which the chosen ones were inaugurated, then we find they also sought another condition of consciousness but it was different to that of today in as far as the condition of consciousness which we regard as the normal human consciousness, was most extraordinary in each mystery pupil, and a certain image-rich imagination, observing the Divine in all the individual things, was the norm. So, what at that time in the old Mysteries was indicated as the threshold lay in quite a different place to where the threshold is situated for us today. We can even see this in outer things.

You see, today there is something which a child already learns at school, and that is the heliocentric world system. The heliocentric world system — you can find this actually historically handed down — has passed into literature through a kind of betrayal. The heliocentric world system already existed in Greek times, it was already clearly present earlier; it was taught in the Mysteries. What an ordinary child learns today at school, which forms their attitude towards the view of the world, this was taught in olden times only in the Mysteries. In outer normal consciousness people of that time had an image-rich consciousness. We can really say: in comparison to olden times, today every human being who has gone through school, has gone beyond the threshold. Those in the old Mysteries would regard it quite dangerous for people who have not gone through a regular initiation but through some or other elementary experience, to have gone over the threshold, for example by not adhering to the geocentric system — that the earth remains stationary and the sun and stars move — but believe in the immobility of the sun as the initiated students believed in olden times. People said you had to be prepared to tolerate what lies, for example, in the heliocentric world system or what lies, for example, in our current biology or psychology, and so on. This seems like a paradox to people today, yet it was so. One can say that historically human kind as such in the time of the Mystery of Golgotha crossed over the threshold which in earlier epochs in the Mysteries had to be artificially crossed in order to reach initiation. At that time those to be initiated learnt what every child learns today. Today we again learn to gain insight into Higher Worlds which later would be the norm. So it is with the evolution of humanity. It is not recognised through examples from olden writings that it was a given — for human consciousness was image-rich — in such a way that things were not seen outwardly but that all things were perceived for their inner spirituality. One must be aware that the words of these ancient writers are to be read in a different way to the way today's ancient language researchers or cultural historians or anthropologists and their equivalents read, because the consciousness at that time was image-rich. We could therefore say, in olden times the initiate was led towards the world we know today.

I would like to still add one more detail. When we go back to olden Greek times, we find people couldn't clearly perceive the colour blue as we can today. They had no sensual experience of the colour blue, they had much more of a sense developed towards the other side, towards vital colours, red and so on, so that for the Greeks blue appeared more green than it is for us today. From this point of view, one must understand everything as the ancients did. We must clearly understand that active thinking is connected to humankind's development towards an experience of blue. If blue is mentioned in ancient scriptures it is always in error, because those people didn't have the experience of blue as we have in today's active experience of understanding. Those people, upon looking at blue, didn't have the ability to be objective, for the out-flowing of the I as an objective, they had far more the experience of what stirred in red, which goes from the objective towards the subjective, which is outwardly active and touches and is sensed, where the awareness of the Divine lay in the objects.

So this initiation was already something quite definite, it involved the initiation being carried out in these olden times by the fact that man himself had to do things which he had to endure physically which to a certain extent formed a kind of inner sacrament. The sacraments in olden times were more inward. Take for instance some outer events which throw a person into a state of fear, caused by these external actions. For example, in Greece there existed Mysteries in which one of the most important processes consisted in a person being placed in total darkness, where he has to live into this darkness, and then suddenly the room was lit up completely — this is the perception he would have been given. What it meant at that time was the transformation of the state of consciousness from being in the darkness, in the blackness, to going into the light. Something happened in a person, fine processes took place inside. These fine processes which were happening in people, I can describe in the following manner.

When a human being, after he has for some time experienced this transformation out of the darkness into the light, salt is separated in him — depending on his individual nature — which is deposited. Salt deposits actually took place as a result of the transfer of going from a dark state to a light state, taking place during the change. These processes became something of which a person became completely aware as being accompanied by the feeling very similar to fear. These salt deposits were observed by a person; he was inwardly observing an interrelation taking place inside himself. At that moment when it happened in him through an external action, man had gone through an initiation process because in olden times initiation consisted in a person experiencing such processes out of himself. What is important now however, was what accompanied such a process of salt deposits within him. Such a salt depositing process within was accompanied by the person's consciousness being impregnated by the process of light perception, not merely of the light perception but from the inner light containing spirituality; he was thus taking in the light which contained spirituality. By the salt coagulating in his inner being, a person felt this coagulation of salts as a penetration of the Divine. To make these conditions conscious was the art of initiation in ancient times. A person could speak quite differently, in them the life of light was not a mere observation by the senses but it was a penetration of light, so that he could say: 'By me living in the light, matter coagulates in me.' With that which is contained in ordinary matter, in a certain sense he directly perceived the effect of that which lies above the substance of ordinary matter.

Now we will not understand these things, my dear friends, if we don't know that the entire constitution of people in older times was different to what it became later. Such a process, which I have sketched for you, you can observe today when waking up or going to sleep. When physical development reaches puberty, the conditions are such that you won't be able to do these things any longer. The influence on the human being is no longer possible in this intense way; people have hardened more in themselves. Today it doesn't happen for these fine spiritual processes which are taking place there, to be observed just like that. In this respect it will even change the human race. As a result, it has happened that what had taken place within, during earlier times, now is to be looked for outwardly. To a certain extent the opposite of the inner process is performed as a ceremony.

The old process of initiation, the process through which a person allows the spirit to reign, this process is now performed outwardly. The priest ordination was in olden times not at all the weakened process of today, but a process, despite it being performed outwardly, still making a deep impression on people. In later times, still in the time of the Mystery of Golgotha and afterwards, the act of baptism, for example, was at least performed as a deed which still accomplished something in people themselves. Those being baptised were immersed in water and thus brought in the same situation as someone being drowned, who sees the retrograde perspective of their life processes flash through them in a spiritual vision. This was part of baptism in earlier times; a person's past life was brought before his soul, so that he learned to see spiritually in a certain way. Later on the sacrament of baptism was temporarily postponed and so it could not be performed in this way, but only symbolically. It is the same with the priest ordination.

The priest ordination in itself is to a certain extent an outer process for that which earlier was evoked inwardly in those going through initiation, through the inversion of outer processes; it is what in fact places the human being in another world. A person is then made aware — I can depict this even more precisely — of certain interrelationships in the cosmos, which can't be studied in the outer world. A person is made aware that physical processes are taking place which do not coincide with the usual outer sensually perceptible processes and he becomes attentive to what is actually sacramental. He learns to see for instance, in dissolving salt in water, that something is happening which isn't created in a physical-chemical process of dissolution, but what happens in salt dissolving in water is actually something inward, I could call it, something radiant. He learns to recognise how processes happen which are only conceivable through the spirit in man. This becoming transported into the world of such revelations which can't be seen with the outer senses or understood with ordinary minds, essentially belongs to the priest consecration. Therefore, through the priest ordination the person will as much be penetrated by this world of the Divine, as the person in olden times was initiated through not merely sensing the penetration of his physicality with light, but that he feels permeated also with the soul-spiritual of the light.

So, I can put it like this: through priest ordination human consciousness is brought into such a condition that a person can with total inner conviction say: the world around us is actually only a fragment of the world; it is there to hide many things from us, namely hiding spiritual processes, from us. We see spiritually in the processes when we are prepared in the appropriate way to do so. Priest ordination involves such preparation which would allow for spiritual perception, to see, everywhere, the sense perceptible as well as the spiritual processes. Let's take a concrete example.

We can look at the development of leaves on a plant, the development of the flowers, the ovary, the stamens and see the ovary mature. *(He draws on the blackboard, left.)* We then observe how the pollen flies around, how it fertilises the flowers. If you only observe outwardly then you will evaluate according to the sense perceptible outer processes which you then combine in your mind. Someone who has become mature in spiritual seeing, must see a supersensible weaving which expands as a kind of wavering transmission over plant growth and all that is involved in plant fertilization. Through this however, the earth in which the plants have their roots, is brought into a reciprocal relationship with the spiritual environment of the earth.

A renewed way of looking must be introduced through priest ordination. Only then, when you have been introduced to this spiritual observing through the priest ordination, will you learn to recognise how the human word evolves in the world, how the human word is not a mere material movement of air but that the word carries spirit on physical air movement, how this spirit permeates certain substances which are fleeting, like for instance the smoke. So being a priest means: seeing how the expressed word grip the smoke, how the smoke weaves the matter, the words, and how through this, that it penetrates the words, how the words tinged with smoke envelops the matter in the words, changing the words themselves, just like in fact evolution continues, how a real, a spiritual reality is there in what happens in the outer world, in phenomena of the world. So being consecrated also means: to be able to perform actions which, besides their physical meaning, also have a spiritual meaning.

This is of course something — I always must stress this — which lies extraordinarily far from modern consciousness, but unbelievably close to that consciousness which was available at the time of the Mystery of Golgotha. During that time people stood in the middle, between the old and the new, they still knew about seeing the Divine-spiritual in everything natural, either through tradition or through atavistic vision, and they lived in fear of the conditions which would arrive when what is natural would no longer be regarded as natural and as a result the Divine-spiritual would be only be understood as a derived abstraction. At that time people still understood the weaving of the spiritual with the sense perceptible. The disciples of Christ Jesus simply knew that this being-in-his-presence meant something different than being in the presence of one another. They knew that he was the carrier of a supersensible being, they felt moved by this supersensible being, and this togetherness with him was for them without doubt the glow of supersensible consciousness.

Let's think about this. We see a number of people around Christ Jesus in a world, who say: When one is in his presence, one is brought into a world where one can see the Divine-spiritual. — Now, in connection with this, I want to call your attention to important concepts necessary for the understanding of the earliest Christian times. Those individuals who could still call themselves the apostles of the Lord, who, for the affirmation of their mission, did not only refer to the fact that they had heard his words. Having heard his words didn't really carry as much weight as we would experience today when we listen to some or other speech, or a teaching. The teaching of Christ Jesus was something that was felt to be completely charitable in his environment, but it wasn't the first thing you would consider as the most important. It was far more important for them to stress the results: we have lain our hands in his wounds, we have participated in looking at his Being. — The direct togetherness with Christ Jesus is something in particular which I ask you to please consider seriously.

You see, you will reach a conclusion of what actually is at a soul foundation when I say to you: you need to first sense the difference between what you experience when you place your one hand on an outer object, or on your own hand, or when you place it on some part of your body. You must come to the conclusion that you sense a difference, that there is a difference. You must also be able to feel something else; you must be able to feel you possess two eyes with two lines of vision which meet and cross. *(He draws on the blackboard, right.)* These two lines of sight which cross at what we are looking at — it is quite like when I hug myself with my two arms encircling myself. Just think about the difference between man and animal. An animal has, to a much reduced degree, the possibility to experience what we for instance experience when our one hand touches the other. Just look at the position of particular animal eyes; you can clearly distinguish how strong the egoism of an animal is, according to its eye positions. Animals which have eye positions with eye axes which can't cross are unable to develop egoism, because the experience, the sense of having an I, depends on a person being able to "grasp" his I, and that the right gaze of the eye can meet the left gaze by crossing. On this the sense of the I is dependant.

The disciples knew themselves to be so connected to the Christ that in a certain sense it was as similar as feeling their own hands, when they touched his wounds. So this direct connection with the Christ was something which gave them the awareness that they lived with him in a higher world. This was actually what the disciples felt, it was as if a spiritual island surrounded them and their Lord, and when they felt that their Lord had gone away and they had now become the teachers, they called themselves teachers, training for this how-to-be-together-with-him.

Then again, the disciples of the Apostles in turn depended on the imagery which they had experienced; you can even read this in individual letters. When some or other apostolic disciple, Polycarp of Smyrna for instance, could describe what some or other person who had taught him, looked like, the description was unbelievably more important than the communication of mere words. What is most essential here, was recalling the feeling of being-together-with everything in connection with the Christ, so that one can say the Apostles sensed the succession, but they could no longer inwardly experience every transformation which had been experienced in the old initiation mysteries. Don't misunderstand me, I don't suggest that the apostles or apostle disciples have made such deliberations, but their soul constitution was so that they could make such deliberations and it was characteristic of their soul constitution to formulate such deliberations. When they were asked to formulate their soul constitution, they would have said: Yes, we couldn't go through with it in the same way as was still possible in the earlier Mysteries, for instance experiencing the transformation of light to darkness; we can no longer experience how one is anointed with oil and so on, and we can no longer experience the inner pain through recalling; but here a God has incarnated in the form of Jesus who was here, and with whom we have relations and when we really in our consciousness take it up, not merely with intellectual grasping but when in all concreteness we live in it, then something lifts us up into the supersensible world.

With the apostles it was the direct living-in-community with the Christ, with the apostle disciples it was the community living-with-him, being carried over to them, who had laid their hands on those who had still been touched by the Lord, and transmitted to those in the third generation who had again laid their hands on someone who had had the Lord touch them. They would get a sense of apostolic succession when they would recall what I've just said, and they would also get a feeling for what it meant to stand inside a world which is spiritually, as it were, like standing in a physical line of ancestors. The physical line of ancestors flows through from birth. The spiritual ancestral line however, must go up to the spiritual father ancestor, the Christ Jesus, it flows through the ongoing, continuous fulfilment of consecrated ceremonies, which lead to the Christ, which certainly must always become more and more outward, because it must ever more make an intensive impression on people. As a result, besides the laying on of hands, other ceremonies were recorded in the next centuries, to make the outer impressions even stronger. A process of internalisation existed with those surrounding Christ Jesus: here Christ Jesus was performing a ritual himself. My dear friends, why was this necessary?

The life of Christ Jesus was the ritual for that which was around him, that which was accomplished in reality, that was the ritual/cult: the great offering of mass was fulfilled on Golgotha. Here we are led back to the first fulfilment of the ritual: at least this is what lives in Christian consciousness. This was followed by outward signs: it required the necessity for an outward imprint of activity, like remembrance, to show the eyes and to impress it on the soul in prayer, which could not be as alive as it had been with the apostles and the apostle disciples.

I know that many people who hear such things with today's consciousness say: Why don't you simply express it in a short and sweet answer, shaped in sharply outlined terms, this or that is apostolic succession? — If someone wants such sharply outlined concepts, his argument is inwardly untruthful. One only speaks truth when it introduces the view of something that has been experienced. Such a thing can't be understood in sharply outlined concepts.

Apostolic succession is something experienced first and then one knows that actually something is being experienced in a spiritual line of ancestors leading back to Christ, just like the ancestral line flowing through the blood links to the natural ancestral line, to any of the ancestors. This spiritual blood lies in the continuous fulfilment of the priestly ordination ceremony. It forms therefore the direct connection, for those who become priests, to the spiritual world. It is consecrated by someone who have themselves received such a consecration, and these, to those, and so on, up to the point where the supersensible descended into a human body and in this way for the first time brought a new, substantial fructification in the earth, which had become old.

We will want to develop the particular format of the priest ordination, into a ritual form. I would like, still today, to point out that you could eventually find something which remains incomprehensible in the priest ordination. Now, by me saying something like this you will understand, also in connection with the regular previous lectures up to this morning, that in fact a complete break had to take place regarding the understanding of such things, when the changed consciousness appeared from the middle of the 15th century. In me expressing these things, I'm using words, which actually for the general consciousness could only have been fully understood before the middle of the 15th century. Then people actually stopped having a real sense for the meaning of these words. It is basically only through the trust you have been able to put in me, that you can hear something here in the manner and way it happened in former times when the soul constitution experienced things in quite a different way. Then came the time when less importance was attached to a concrete connection, when people who still knew how to attach importance to this concrete connection, became rare. Now, the most importance was attributed to the comprehensible content of the Gospels, to the comprehensible content of religion as such. Thus, gradually it took on particular importance to discuss the content of the Gospels, to discuss the content of the sacraments and to a certain extent particularly look into the teaching material, at the teaching content. The teaching content gradually became the most important. Not actually the concrete, but the abstract, became the most important, that is the essential thing. While for the catholic consciousness — I don't mean merely the roman catholic, but the catholic Christian consciousness — the priest ordination placed the chosen one in a spiritual ancestry up to Christ, which actually for the modern person made everything quite comprehensible, from definitions to declarations which places nothing into a reality. However, we must be very clear about it, that we live again in a time where we need deepening again in *that* direction.

Well, the catholic consciousness has basically always acted quite consistently according to these prerequisites; quite consistently. In order not to be misunderstood regarding what follows, I would like to introduce it like this. When today we want to prepare someone — in fact, I mean for something which we see as a new ritual — when we, today, want to prepare someone to perform ceremonial actions, then we would for those who stand outside Catholicism in the world, no longer with full inner devotion be able to integrate a person into the apostolic succession. As I've mentioned to you, there have been remarkable Theosophists like Leadbeater and similar ones, who have likewise tried to place themselves in the apostolic succession, but that's going to resist any man who's honest with the world, if he is not imbued with Catholic consciousness.

We need to look for something else. We need to fully understand that a reality is not something which is spoken about, something abstract. We must also learn to understand the sacramental. We must learn to understand, throughout, that the content of the teaching does not contain the essential but that something must be added from real processes and in such a way that these actual processes are carried on the waves of reality as the weaving of the Divine. There have only been single individuals, like Novalis, who understood this — do read his Aphorisms, then you'll see. He spoke about magical idealism; he knew this wasn't alive in outer sensory worlds, but within people, there lived the soul-spiritual. Then there was Schelling — in his old age, that's why he was hardly understood — for whom it was quite absurd to believe that the essence of Christianity consisted in the acceptance of what Christ taught; rather, Schelling recognised the essential much more according to the account of Jesus going through the process of the entire Golgotha drama, in the description of actions which took place around Golgotha. However, there are individuals who tend towards the reality, who in turn want to enter into actual experiences connected to the spiritual. In totality one could say that the way Catholicism experiences it, is something quite antiquated which can't be introduced into modern consciousness any longer. For this reason we mustn't only search for a renewal of old rituals but we must search for a ritual which we can create out of ourselves, but created in such a way that it creates the Divine in us in the sense we have spoken about, so that the words of Paul become the truth — in Gospel interpretation, and in all religious activities: Not I, but Christ in me.

Catholicism, as Roman Catholicism, has actually always known how to act consistently. To a certain extent it has turned out, lifted out, from general humanity, all those who were descendants of Christ Jesus himself and so a sharp awareness has come about, separating the priestly spiritual generation, meaning those people connected to consecration, from all other people who had not attended consecration. Like a member of the nobility who for instance connects his bloodline back to the 18th ancestor and knows who carry this blood in their veins, their ancestral connection differs from that of the rest of humanity, in the same way there's a difference from those consecrated into the apostolic succession up to Christ himself, who have continuously and consistently received consecration, right down to those who had not received it. They felt themselves placed in this connection and felt others were different; that's why it was quite necessary during a certain time period that certain things were presented to people. A person gradually absorbed what had more or less consciously existed in his awareness and allowed this to be expressed in his actions. After this, because of the ever-increasing sharper awareness related to the Christ developed, came the necessity for greater withdrawal for the uninitiated: celibacy. The celibate already had his inner foundation and there where the celibate was dogmatised it was found throughout that the priest had to withdraw from connecting to all others, was a human personality who found it far more important to practice the priest consecration as a conscious inheritance of the father of his ancestors and because he was placed in this ancestral blood of a spiritual ancestry, he could not be in contact with that world from which he was taken out by the consecration ceremony. The moment a person strongly experienced this particular situation of priesthood in relation to the world, the necessity for celibacy was added, and of course there's no denying that one could also feel the political usefulness for Rome, and so on. However, you can be quite certain that during the time when celibacy was introduced — it was a time when the celibate person came from the monk priesthood — in the unconscious impulses was the urge for a certain honesty and truthfulness. It was certainly the case that the creation of celibacy was understood in the way I have presented it now. Just as in the 19th century, in a kind of natural way — as I said — the consequential process living in the Catholic consciousness resulted in the dogma of immaculate conception and how this resulted in the infallibility dogma, so at a certain time causes led to the consequences of celibacy.

Well, if you take all of this in then we already come to what is of particular importance today. Of particular importance today for us is to again return to the ritual, to ceremonies. You are experiencing, at least many of you have said you experience it like this: you are actually experiencing necessities based on what has come out of, and is given by, this time. Of course we can't undo events, we can't go back to untruths for instance, we can't reverse an untruth, such as taking something which no longer feels alive were to be changed externally, like being ordained by an olden-time Catholic priest. That would be contradictory to those who have already ignited the Protestant consciousness too strongly in themselves because for the Protestant consciousness this possibility doesn't exist; in their experience one can't oppose something which has been created out of quite other circumstances.

What you need to arrive at, if reality is at all part of your striving, is what can flow out of the spiritual world itself, which can be seen as flowing directly from Christ Jesus. We must strengthen ourselves in the words of Jesus: I am with you until the end of earthly days. —

These words out of the Gospels also announce such a process of the Christ impulse will be found on the earth for so long, that it will last until the end of the earth comes about. For this reason, one must firstly announce this as a postulate to a certain extent, that it must be possible — as a reality — to come to Christ, like with the Catholic consciousness, through the apostolic succession historically the spiritual family tree is searched for, reaching right to Christ. It must be able to find Him again, in a moment in the present; a connection to the Divine, a connection to the Christianized Divine as it was historically found by the Catholics in the apostolic succession right up to the Christian ancestors of this apostolic succession. That is why it must take place this way, that we find the spiritual again, not only in words about the Christian aspect, but so that we actually connect with what is real in the Christian aspect. Then we can create the ritual out of this, like the ritual was created within the apostolic succession.

However, we need to penetrate it with an understanding which goes far beyond the understanding of the time.

We must indeed move towards an understanding that can be expressed — I want to first formulate it as follows: In the world and in ordinary human thinking we experience the phenomenal: we however want to experience the nominal, we want to try and enter into the essential and out of this essence find the ritual. If you really want to find the ritual, then it must finally be so that this ritual is discovered as it had been during the second century, where gradually, what used to exist in simpler forms — only a few of which have been recorded — has now been transferred to the forms of later rituals.

How was the ritual experienced? A person was caught up in it, just like a person who smokes knows what he is doing by smoking; he knows he can express what he wants to, only by smoking. So you must again learn to feel that you, when you perform some or other ceremony, know for yourself: the ceremony must be performed in this way. A person knows what he has to say today when he turns to other people, he knows how to clothe his inner life with words. My dear friends, there is a moment in life, where one inwardly experiences that it is impossible to continue using words, where what you want to say no longer translates into words, where you have to stop with words or at most continue with words by carrying out the sacred act by starting to not merely letting the word sound out but where, for instance, the development of smoke must take place, where in particular one of the other actions must be carried out imaginatively. Where the words connect with a particular action, by coming into the original consciousness, where also, like your soul content, being enlivened by the Divine, pours into the words, now your soul content will no longer be merely a phenomenal one but a nominal one, then you will be lifted out of what the outer world comprises, there you will gradually enter into the sacramental.

Somewhat in this way, I've tried to clarify how one must enter into the sacramental. It actually makes no sense, let's say, in simply transforming holy water as is often done today by subordinate clerics. There is simply no point in performing the transubstantiation in this way, as is done by many subordinate clerics today, who are left in the dark in relation to the esoteric consecration of the Catholic Church. Regarding the old soul constitutions, it had made sense to be fully aware of one's actions when a certain word was spoken over the salt substance, and that they knew the salt substance had changed as a result.

Today experiments have already been done to make the gentle sensitivity of a flame visible, by placing a flame somewhere and a person speaking rhythmically at a distance from it, to see the flame copy the rhythm. Here a rhythm is being copied by something inorganic. If I know the right words in the right word correlation over the salt substance, then the salt substance will change. If I now allow this salt substance which has been permeated, to enter into water, then I have kindled a process, which, if I understand it, when I have performed it in spirit, is a sacramental act. We must be able, once again, to look at the nominal as such. This we will address tomorrow.

I think, in any case, my dear friends, that many questions could be conjured out of the soul by me speaking about these things, and I would love it if the questions, while you are all here, not in general, could also be formulated concretely so that no doubt remains. I completely understand that with earnestness your small circle has turned to me with the clear intention to really work toward a renewal of the religious life. It is not possible to do so by merely changing the teaching content; it is only possible when you enter with a changed soul constitution. We are now entering more deeply into things and, triggered through your questions we will become ever more acquainted with these things so that you're actually going to understand what I mean to convey.

(***Translator's Note:*** The lecture which follows this one, the sixteenth in the series, indicates that all participants in this lecture course were asked to sign an agreement that in the future, from that day onward, to only transmit the material presented to them from that point on, in a verbal form. These next lectures enter into all the details required of priests when performing the sacraments, with the wording, gestures and so on. For this reason, I will refrain from translating this material. It will remain available for those wanting to approach ordination into The Christian Community, in the oral tradition.)

OTHER BOOKS

translated by Hanna von Maltitz

All titles available at Amazon.com

THE IMPULSE OF RENEWAL FOR CULTURE AND SCIENCE
(by Rudolf Steiner, translated by Hanna von Maltitz):

This is a First Edition English translation of a series of seven lectures, entitled *The Impulse of Renewal for Culture and Science*, and published in German as, *Erneuerungs-Impuls für Kultur und Wissenschaft* (Bn/GA/CW Number 81 in the Bibliographical Survey, 1961). This course was organized by the Federation of Anthroposophical University Work and the Berlin Branch of the Anthroposophical Society. **ISBN: 978-1948302043**

THE SOCIAL QUESTION
(by Rudolf Steiner, translated by Hanna von Maltitz):

This book is a First Edition, never before translated into English, series of six lectures. Rudolf Steiner gave these lectures early in the year of 1919 at Zurich, Switzerland. Here Steiner proffers ideas to solve the social problems and necessities required by life, by studying the life sciences and social life, and the living conditions of the present-day humans. **ISBN: 978-1791660536**